T4-AKE-476

AMICUS DEI

KARL A. OLSSON

AMICUS DEI

Essays on Faith and Friendship

Presented to
KARL A. OLSSON
on his 75th birthday

EDITED BY PHILIP J. ANDERSON

Covenant Publications

3200 West Foster Avenue, Chicago, Illinois 60625

ISBN 910452-67-9 (book edition)
Copyright © 1988 by Covenant Publications
Design and layout: David Westerfield
Production assistants: Jane K. Swanson-Nystrom, Debra J. Almgren,
Gregory Sager, Jill Taylor
Cover design: David Westerfield, sketch by DW after a sculpture
titled "Die Meister" by Ernst Barlach, 1870-1938

Contents

Tabula Gratulatoria

Bonnie Agard, *Bethlehem, Pennsylvania*
Evelyn and Clarence Agard, *Spring Valley, California*
Paul and Barbara Aley, *Tiffin, Ohio*
Ray and Mary Almer, *Chicago, Illinois*
Annette and Jim Anderson, *Lynnfield, Massachusetts*
Chuck and Marilyn Anderson, *Omaha, Nebraska*
Chuck and Shirley Anderson, *Kalamazoo, Michigan*
Rev. and Mrs. Craig E. Anderson, *Chicago, Illinois*
Dr. Frances M. Anderson, *Chicago, Illinois*
Hazel and Carl Philip Anderson, *St. Paul, Minnesota*
Rev. James and Sally Anderson, *New Brighton, Minnesota*
Pastor and Mrs. Leonard O. Anderson, *Forest Lake,
  Minnesota*
Maynard and Virginia Anderson, *Buffalo, Minnesota*
Phil and Irene Anderson, *Chicago, Illinois*
Philip J. and Karna Anderson, *Chicago, Illinois*
Rev. and Mrs. C. Reuben Anderson, *Minneapolis,
  Minnesota*
Rev. Robert M. Anderson, *Boulder Junction, Wisconsin*
Sheldon and Anna Anderson, *Wauconda, Illinois*
Rev. and Mrs. O. W. Arell, *Holden, Massachusetts*
Rev. Frank Ashley, *Mason City, Iowa*
Robert and Marlene Bach, *Altaville, California*
Wayne and Dorothy Balch, *Seattle, Washington*
Charles G. and Marie J. Beckstrom, *Jamestown, New York*
Mrs. Bethel N. Bengtson, *Turlock, California*
Dr. and Mrs. Vern L. Bengtson, *South Pasadena,
  California*
Edla and Stanley Benson, *Cromwell, Connecticut*
Karen Benson, *Winthrop, Minnesota*
Rev. and Mrs. LeRoy A. Benson, *Plantation, Florida*
Conrad Bergendoff, *Rock Island, Illinois*

Carl and Stella Bergeron, *Holicong, Pennsylvania*
Dr. and Mrs. Richard Bevis, *Wayzata, Minnesota*
Dr. and Mrs. Stephen S. Bilynskyj, *Lincoln, Nebraska*
Robert and Eleanor Byrd, *Ontario*
Mr. and Mrs. Russell Camp, *Daly City, California*
Rev. Catherine L. Campobello, *Medellin, Colombia*
Bob Carlson, *Wheaton, Illinois*
Bruce Carlson, *Minneapolis, Minnesota*
David A. E. Carlson, *South Bend, Indiana*
Dr. and Mrs. Dwight M. Carlson, *Guilford, Connecticut*
Rev. and Mrs. Harold M. Carlson, *Plantation, Florida*
John and Betty Carlson, *South Bend, Indiana*
Rev. and Mrs. LeRoy L. Carlson, *Cottage Grove,
    Minnesota*
Phil and Pearl Carlson, *Jenkintown, Pennsylvania*
Douglas and Carolyn Cederleaf, *Minneapolis, Minnesota*
Russell and Virginia Cervin, *Vallejo, California*
Gordon Christensen, *Laurel Springs, New Jersey*
John and Adele Cole, *Minneapolis, Minnesota*
Rev. and Mrs. Norman Collins, *Chicago, Illinois*
Covenant Village of Florida Chapel, *Plantation, Florida*
Rev. and Mrs. David Dahlberg, *Hudson, Ohio*
Mr. and Mrs. Marshall Dahlstrom, *Arlington Heights,
    Illinois*
Kendall and Nancy Dahlstrom, *South Bend, Indiana*
Rosalie and Earl Dahlstrom, *Batavia, Illinois*
Albert and Gladys Damrose, *Woronoco, Massachusetts*
Joseph and Mildred Danielson, *Northbrook, Illinois*
Rev. and Mrs. Ralph Dirksen, *Webster, New York*
Lowell and Marilyn Drotts, *North Attleboro,
    Massachusetts*
Robert and Dorothy Dvorak, *Winnetka, Illinois*
Norman and Martha Dwight, *Taipei, Taiwan*
A. Royce Eckhardt, *Evanston, Illinois*
Jane and Hobart Edgren, *Chicago, Illinois*
Rev. and Mrs. Timothy C. Ek, *Chicago, Illinois*
Carol and Robert Elde, *Minneapolis, Minnesota*
Steven M. Elde, *Chicago, Illinois*
Rev. and Mrs. George Elia, *New Britain, Connecticut*
Dave and Marge Elowson, *Plymouth, Minnesota*
Dr. and Mrs. Milton B. Engebretson, *Northbrook, Illinois*

Olle and Margit Engström, *Lidingö, Sweden*
Rev. Dean R. Erickson, *San Gabriel, California*
Shirley A. Erickson, *Montgomery Village, Maryland*
Myrtle and Irving Erickson, *Chicago, Illinois*
Daniel and Anne Ericson, *Wheaton, Illinois*
Nancy (Lucas) Evans, *Malibu, California*
Joan H. and Don O. Franklin, *Pittsburgh, California*
Rev. and Mrs. Theodore E. Franklin, *Elk River, Minnesota*
Bill and Helen Fredrickson, *Chicago, Illinois*
Rev. and Mrs. David Fredrickson, *Sacramento, California*
Darrel and Priscilla Freeberg, *Apple Valley, Minnesota*
Rev. Tim and Marcia Fretheim, *Coquitlam, British
Columbia*
Donald C. Frisk, *Batavia, Illinois*
Rev. Mark and Karen Frykholm, *Duluth, Minnesota*
John and Grace Gilbert, *Livermore, California*
Evan and Elvera Goranson, *Oak Lawn, Illinois*
Wesley Granstrom & Dr. Sandra Granstrom, *Carmel,
California*
Virginia I. Groth, *Minneapolis, Minnesota*
Mr. and Mrs. Hiro J. Gulrajani, *Brookfield, Wisconsin*
Rev. Arthur Gustafson, *Merrill, Wisconsin*
Erick and Dagmar Gustafson, *Villa Park, Illinois*
Mrs. Evelyne Gustafson, *Chicago, Illinois*
Rev. Ross D. Gustafson-Peterson, *Mount Prospect, Illinois*
Jean and Ruth Hagstrum, *Evanston, Illinois*
Carol Hallgren, *Sumter, South Carolina*
Gunnar and Ann-Britt Hallingberg, *Jönköping, Sweden*
Rev. and Mrs. Glenn J. Hamilton, *Warren, Pennsylvania*
Mr. and Mrs. Gary Hanson, *Wheaton, Illinois*
Bill and Rose Hausman, *Wilmette, Illinois*
Carl E. Hawkinson, *Galesburg, Illinois*
James and Alyce Hawkinson, *Chicago, Illinois*
Zenos and Barbara Hawkinson, *Chicago, Illinois*
Herbert and Louise Hedstrom, *Glenview, Illinois*
Mary Helfrich, *Chicago, Illinois*
Willis and Laura Helfrich, *Chicago, Illinois*
Mr. and Mrs. Carl M. Helgerson, *Seekonk, Massachusetts*
Bev. Green Henkel, *Norfolk, Nebraska*
Mr. and Mrs. Stanley Herlin, *Sun City, Arizona*
Betty Jane Highfield, *Evanston, Illinois*

Robert and Lois Hirsch, *Lake Worth, Florida*
Bob and Marilyn Hjelm, *Chicago, Illinois*
Worth and Genevie Hodgin, *Mount Vernon, Washington*
Gordon and Lorraine Holmen, *Bradenton, Florida*
Robert and Ruth Honnette, *Modesto, California*
Sue and David Horner, *Evanston, Illinois*
Rev. and Mrs. Everett Jackson, *Skokie, Illinois*
Steve and Bobbi Jackson, *Palatine, Illinois*
Rev. Carl and Doris Janson, *Grand Rapids, Michigan*
Marvin W. Jensen, *Carol Stream, Illinois*
Alayne and Clifford Johnson, *Rockford, Illinois*
Rev. and Mrs. Arnold H. Johnson, *Chicago, Illinois*
Alden S. Johnson, *Waltham, Massachusetts*
Rev. and Mrs. Carl H. Johnson, *San Andreas, California*
Rev. and Mrs. Cecil Johnson, *Scottsdale, Arizona*
Craig and Christine Johnson, *Omaha, Nebraska*
Doug and Mary Johnson, *Princeton, Illinois*
Rev. and Mrs. Dwight L. Johnson, *Chicago, Illinois*
Harriet and Eldon D. Johnson, *Houston, Texas*
Howard and Arleen Johnson, *Portland, Oregon*
Jeremy T. Johnson, *Galesburg, Illinois*
Jerome K. Johnson, *Seattle, Washington*
Jerry and Letica Johnson, *Minnetonka, Minnesota*
Kathy and Greg Johnson, *Palo Alto, California*
Kenneth and Patricia Johnson, *St. Petersburg, Florida*
LeRoy and Carole Johnson, *Chicago, Illinois*
Marianne A. Johnson, *Hinsdale, Illinois*
Norbert and Elaine Johnson, *Chicago, Illinois*
Paul and Agnes Johnson, *Modesto, California*
Phil and Sandy Johnson, *Minneapolis, Minnesota*
Randy and Judy Johnson, *Des Plaines, Illinois*
Rev. Raymond L. Johnson, *Batavia, Illinois*
Mr. and Mrs. Rodney K. Johnson, *Glenview, Illinois*
Roger and Linnea Johnson, *Clarendon Hills, Illinois*
Rosemary and Eldon Johnson, *Jamestown, New York*
Rev. Thomas W. and Patricia L. Johnson, *Des Moines,
  Iowa*
Dr. and Mrs. Timothy Johnson, *Topsfield, Massachusetts*
Timothy J. and Beth E. Johnson, *Chicago, Illinois*
Timothy L. Johnson, *East Hampton, Connecticut*
Drs. Walter and Martha Johnson, *McLean, Virginia*

Rev. and Mrs. Walter W. Johnson, *Plantation, Florida*
Robert K. and Anne Johnston, *Wilmette, Illinois*
Rev. and Mrs. Warren M. Jones, *Chanute, Kansas*
Albert and Anna Josephson, *White Rock, British Columbia*
Herb and Carla Kamphausen, *Harbor City, California*
Calvin and Johanna Katter, *Chicago, Illinois*
Ted and Carolyn Kelly, *Quito, Ecuador*
Tom and Janice Kelly, *Mexico City, Mexico*
Carl and Frances King, *Federal Way, Washington*
Beverly B. Kiss, *Deerfield, Illinois*
Rev. Jack and Mrs. Catherine Kraaz, *South Easton, Massachusetts*
Bruce and Dorothy Lake, *Joliet, Illinois*
Rev. Jean C. Lambert, Ph.D., *New York, New York*
Herbert Lamm, *Crown Point, Indiana*
Irma Langford, *Chicago, Illinois*
Paul E. and Elizabeth Larsen, *Northfield, Illinois*
Dusty and Jinny Larson, *Stambaugh, Michigan*
John and Dorothy Larson, *Collinsville, Connecticut*
Paul and Gladys Larson, *Chicago, Illinois*
Werner and Sandy Lemke, *Rochester, New York*
Elinoi and Tour Lenehen, *Los Angeles, California*
Glenn L. Lindell, *Overland Park, Kansas*
Evelyn V. Lindgren, *Chicago, Illinois*
Pastor and Mrs. L. W. Lindholm, *Warroad, Minnesota*
Roy and Jean Lindquist, *Bellevue, Washington*
Rev. P. Richard Lindstrom, *Stanton, Iowa*
Rev. and Mrs. John Lovgren, *Tucson, Arizona*
Jerry and Vicky Love, *Mexico City, Mexico*
Vernon and Elaine Lund, *Minneapolis, Minnesota*
Eugene V. Lundberg, *West Palm Beach, Florida*
Rev. and Mrs. Arthur Lundblad, *Batavia, Illinois*
Janet R. Lundblad, *Donaldson, Indiana*
Dr. and Mrs. Dean A. Lundgren, *West Hartford, Connecticut*
Rev. and Mrs. Donald R. Lundquist, *Minnetonka, Minnesota*
Bruce and Carole Magnuson, *Hinsdale, Illinois*
Marilyn Magnuson, *New Orleans, Louisiana*
Ron and Marlene Magnuson, *Three Oaks, Michigan*
Julia and Sandy Marks, *Westboro, Massachusetts*

Aaron and Margaret Markuson, *Vashon, Washington*
John and Diane Martz, *Lafayette, Indiana*
Rev. Alvin Mattox, *Bellewood, Nebraska*
Rev. and Mrs. David A. McDowell, *Albert Lea, Minnesota*
Bob and Carol McNaughton, *Cromwell, Connecticut*
Mel and June Metcalf, *Gresham, Oregon*
Carol Christesen Meyer, *Iron Mountain, Michigan*
Mary C. Miller, *Flossmoor, Illinois*
Sandy and Bonnie Mohlman, *Montpelier, Vermont*
Helen M. Nagel, *Chicago, Illinois*
Arthur and Laurel Nelson, *Wilmette, Illinois*
Betty J. Nelson, *Chicago, Illinois*
Chaplain and Mrs. Harold R. Nelson, *Tucson, Arizona*
Rev. Gordon and Helen Nelson, *Plantation, Florida*
LeRoy and Eloise Nelson, *Chicago, Illinois*
Margaret and Wesley Nelson, *Chicago, Illinois*
Quentin and Ruth Nelson, *Northbrook, Illinois*
Rev. and Mrs. Thomas Nelson, *Dennis, Massachusetts*
Fredrick Neth, *Milwaukie, Oregon*
Ron and Ingrid "Inky" Newlin, *North Canton,*
    Connecticut
Charles Neywick, Ph.D., *Boston, Massachusetts*
Donald and Terri Njaa, *Chicago, Illinois*
Revs. Craig and Carol Nordstrom, *Portage, Indiana*
David and Marilyn Noreen, *Chicago, Illinois*
Jeffrey and Kathie Norman, *Rockford, Illinois*
William and Sandra Notehelfer, *Scottsdale, Arizona*
Douglas Nystrom and Jane Swanson-Nystrom, *Chicago,*
    Illinois
Glenn W. Olsen, *Salt Lake City, Utah*
Al and Kathy Olson, *Mason, Michigan*
Don Paul and Geri Olson, *Chicago, Illinois*
K. Wesley and Harriet Olson, *Omaha, Nebraska*
Mark and Doreen Olson, *Aurora, Nebraska*
Myron Olson and Annette Widman Olson, *Cedarburg,*
    Wisconsin
Roy E. and Helen M. Olson, *Skokie, Illinois*
Christopher Olsson, *Minneapolis, Minnesota*
Nils William and Dagmar Olsson, *Winter Park, Florida*
Elmer and Ruth Ost, *Greshem, Oregon*
Cecil and Dorothy Osterberg, *Minneapolis, Minnesota*

Everett and Eleanor Ostrom, *Kent, Washington*
Gilbert W. Otteson, *Mercer Island, Washington*
Doug Palm and Nancy Small Palm, *Beaver Dam, Wisconsin*
Glenn and Sharon Palmberg, *Olathe, Kansas*
Robert and Diane Pearsall, *Bethlehem, Pennsylvania*
Don and Dorothy Pearson, *San Diego, California*
Rev. and Mrs. Lyle R. Pearson, *Helena, Montana*
Luke and Barbara Pederson, *Williams Bay, Wisconsin*
Mr. and Mrs. Wayne R. Penn, *Riverside, Illinois*
Jim and Arlys Persson, *Littleton, Colorado*
Mr. and Mrs. Scott Peters, *Brockton, Massachusetts*
Rev. Richard H. Petersen, *Portland, Maine*
Alton and Christie Peterson, *Rochester, New York*
Carl H. and Elsie E. Peterson, *Mercer Island, Washington*
Carol A. Peterson ("C. P."), *St. Paul, Minnesota*
Rev. and Mrs. David A. Peterson, *Plainville, Connecticut*
Eric and Enid Peterson, *Turlock, California*
Gary and Marilyn Peterson, *Seattle, Washington*
Helen Peterson, *Jamestown, New York*
Judy and Carleton Peterson, *Eagan, Minnesota*
Leonard M. Peterson, *Kanagawa Ken, Japan*
Margaret Peterson, *Batavia, Illinois*
Mr. and Mrs. William Peterson, Jr., *St. Paul, Minnesota*
Chaplain and Mrs. John C. Philipp, *Waukegan, Illinois*
Deborah J. Power, *Tacoma, Washington*
Edward R. Rabe, Jr., *Evanston, Illinois*
K. Ejnar and June Rask, *Cromwell, Connecticut*
Paul and Edith Rees, *Boca Raton, Florida*
Jeanette L. Reid, *Chicago, Illinois*
Russell and Carol Robinson, *West Hartford, Connecticut*
C. Rodney and Beatrice Rosengren, *Lowry, Minnesota*
Cpt. Jimmy L. Rucker, *APO New York*
Dolan and Barbara Rundquist, *Loomis, Nebraska*
Rev. and Mrs. William V. Salo, *Glendale, Arizona*
Rev. Reynold and Betty Samundsen, *Chetek, Wisconsin*
David W. Sandquist, *Foster City, Michigan*
Dick and Isabelle Sandquist, *Bellevue, Washington*
Carol and Dewey Sands, *Moline, Illinois*
John and Lois Satterberg, *Lexington, Massachusetts*

Ramsey and Lenore (Strandine) Schaffnit, *Glen Ellyn, Illinois*
George and Marie Schermer, *Bettendorf, Iowa*
Jean Kellgren Seltzer, *New York, New York*
Dr. and Mrs. Lars Silverness, *Floral Park, New York*
Rev. and Mrs. David Smith, *Salem, Oregon*
Mr. and Mrs. Melvin Soderstrom, *Chicago, Illinois*
Bill and Judy Solie, *Richfield, Minnesota*
Paul and Gunnie Sparrman, *Shrewsbury, Massachusetts*
Paul and Joan Spjut, *Ceresco, Nebraska*
Mr. and Mrs. Lars-Birger Sponberg, *Deerfield, Illinois*
Stoneridge Covenant Church, *Allison Park, Pennsylvania*
David and Beth Stordahl, *Bellevue, Washington*
Les and Eleanor Strand, *Cromwell, Connecticut*
Paul and Linda Stromberg, *Moraga, California*
Bill and Lynn Stromdahl, *Yountville, California*
Cassius and Irene Sturdy, *Camano Island, Washington*
David and Bonnie Summers, *Hinsdale, Illinois*
Jim and Carol Sundholm, *Minneapolis, Minnesota*
Rev. and Mrs. Orville Sustad, *San Jose, California*
Berner and Harriet Swanson, *Turlock, California*
Chip Swanson, *Mountain Village, Alaska*
Dave and Linda Swanson, *Washington, D.C.*
Rev. James A. and Beverly Swanson, *Springfield, Virginia*
Loren E. and Arlene M. Swanson, *St. Paul, Minnesota*
Rev. and Mrs. Milton Swanson, *Des Moines, Iowa*
Richard and Helen Swanson, *East Dennis, Massachusetts*
Roger and Silvia Swanson, *Princeton, Illinois*
Rev. and Mrs. Gerold A. Swenson, *Yorktown Heights, New York*
Daniel and Candi Tepke, *LaGrange, Illinois*
The Genoa Club
Paul and Viola Theorell, *Mercer Island, Washington*
Rev. Leyden Thorpe, *Chicago, Illinois*
Peter and Helen Three Stars, *Lake Stevens, Washington*
Eldon and Jerrine Toll, *Kirkland, Washington*
Edmund and Dorothy Train, *Schaumburg, Illinois*
Mary L. Train, *Chicago, Illinois*
Rev. Alfred Ulner, *Desert Hot Springs, California*
Reynold and Dorothy Vann, *Chicago, Illinois*
David and Grace Vennberg, *Sugar Grove, Pennsylvania*

John and Lois Weborg, *Chicago, Illinois*
Fern M. Weiss, *Marysville, Pennsylvania*
Harry E. Westberg, *Chicago, Illinois*
Mark and Alice Westlind, *Medellin, Colombia*
Drs. Bruce and Marilyn Whisler, *Winter Park, Florida*
Marden Wickman, *Deerwood, Minnesota*
Rev. and Mrs. James C. Widboom, *Naugatuck,*
   Connecticut
Ken and Marie Wiebe, *Camarillo, California*
John and Alice Wiens, *Hinsdale, Illinois*
Mr. and Mrs. Kenneth R. Wilson, *Mexico City, Mexico*
Velma Bane Wheeler and Dr. Darlene Wilke, *Evanston,*
   Illinois
Bernie and Esther Windmiller, *Fort Hood, Texas*
DuWayne and Eunice Winters, *Silverhill, Alabama*
Ivar and Harriet Wistrom, *La Porte, Indiana*
Chaplain Douglas R. Wootten, *Garlstadt, West Germany*
Dale and Sally Young, *Turlock, California*
Dr. Joan E. Zetterlund, *Chicago, Illinois*

Foreword

Every family of faith in the larger body of Christ has a story to tell, and every story thus told, while incomplete in itself, becomes a window on the glory yet to be revealed in the fullness of time.

The individuals God calls and gathers to be part of such families—and to lead them in special ways—have stories that further illumine our way. The wider the circle is drawn around those individuals by friends who have shared in their specific pilgrimage, the richer the tapestry becomes.

The Evangelical Covenant Church, still close to its historic Reformation and Pietist heritage, is rich in both faith and story. Because many do not know much about that, Covenanters are especially grateful to those who in spirit, witness, and life have committed themselves to studying its faith and sharing its spirit.

Time has now come, on Karl A. Olsson's seventy-fifth birthday, to give tangible expression to that thanks by publishing this *Festschrift* in his honor.

We express our gratitude first to those who honored us in honoring him by drafting and editing the essays here included. We also thank those, listed in the *Tabula Gratulatoria,* whose contributions testify to their love and respect for the honored and their willingness to support this project.

Finally, our thanks to Karl Olsson himself, for demonstrated scholarship, churchmanship, piety, imagination, loyalty, and faithful witness within and on behalf of his primary church family. We could say it no better to him than he once said in our hearing to one of his sons, who on receiving a personal word of "Thanks" one wistful spring evening many years ago asked, with awakened curiosity, "For what?" and was told straightforwardly, "For being you!"

JAMES R. HAWKINSON
Executive Secretary of Covenant Publications

Friendship

"Those friends thou hast, grapple them to thy soul"
Ah friends—they are our sleep and our awaking
And meat and drink—they are the things we are.
A white rose blooming and an argent star
Alone upon the heavens—things we feel
Sharply as pain, keenly as scorn or steel.

KARL A. OLSSON
May 1934

Preface

A long life may be passed without finding a friend
in whose understanding and virtue we can equally
confide, and whose opinion we can value at once
for its justness and sincerity.

Samuel Johnson

Blessed whoso loveth Thee, and his friends in Thee,
and his enemy for Thee. For he alone loses none
dear to him, to whom all are dear in Him who cannot be lost. And who is this but our God, the God
that made heaven and earth, and filleth them,
because by filling them He created them?

St. Augustine

The theme of friendship has been expressed by all the great
writers, from Plato and Aristotle, to Coleridge and Byron, to
Emerson and Thoreau. It represents one of the most profound
forms of human affections and relationships, and encompasses
the full range of one's life experience. The person who has
real friends is fortunate indeed. The theme of faith relates naturally to friendship, and the Christian tradition contains a rich
and varied treasury of expression of the friendship of God
towards his creation and the community of friendship established in Christ—who said to his followers: "No longer do I
call you servants, for the servant does not know what his
master is doing; but I have called you friends, for all I have
heard from my Father I have made known to you" (John
15:15).

It is also natural to think of Karl Olsson in terms of faith
and friendship, and in many ways his person and vocation have
combined these rare qualities. He has deep friendships with
people of all ages and walks of life; he has been a stimulating
friend and servant of Christian higher education; he has chron-

icled and interpreted the Mission Friend tradition with tender
yet critical affection; and as a minister of the gospel he has
illumined and embodied the biblical and experiential wonder
of God's friendship to us and our friendship to each other.
This volume of essays seeks to be a tribute to one of the most
distinguished and respected leaders of The Evangelical Covenant Church, whose life has modeled consistently the privilege of being *amicus Dei*—friend of God.

The essays in the book have been contributed by a group
of Karl Olsson's friends and colleagues, and though the topics
vary, they pursue the themes of faith and friendship from perspectives of personal and family reflections, Covenant history
and identity in Sweden and North America, theologies of
friendship in mission and worship, ecumenical relationships
and peacemaking, among others. Carl Philip Anderson reviews
Dr. Olsson's life and work; Nils William Olsson delineates
aspects of a remarkable family genealogy; and Jean Hagstrum
and Herbert Lamm write about the meaning of friendship that
extends over many years. A constructive theology of friendship is developed by Jean C. Lambert, offering it as a helpful
way of seeing the missionary task of befriending others in the
name of him who befriends all that he has made.

Another set of essays focuses on issues related to the life
of the Covenant Church. Gunnar Hallingberg looks at the role
of popular subcultures in the free church movements of Sweden and immigrant America and their effect on Mission Friends,
with implications for today; J. Irving Erickson reviews Sweden's new hymnals and the friendly cooperation of the state
and free churches; the pioneering role of education, particularly from a Pietist perspective, is the subject of the essay by
Zenos E. Hawkinson; the editor reflects upon the complex
topic of identity and pluralism among those united in the
friendship of faith as a denominational expression; and C. John
Weborg examines the liturgy as story and a place for stories,
and suggests some creative ways to worship. Olle Engström
and Milton B. Engebretson explore ecumenical themes from
both sides of the Atlantic, giving attention to what has uniquely
been a twentieth-century form of institutional friendship and
desire to confess the oneness of the faith. The quest for world
peace and the turning of enemies into friends is the subject
of Conrad Bergendoff's contribution. And Robert K. Johnston

assesses current evangelical understandings of the atonement, God's greatest gesture of friendship in redeeming his creation.

Karl Olsson's prolific pen is well known, and Timothy J. Johnson has probed in every direction to compile the extensive bibliography included in the book. The full citations of Dr. Olsson's columns over many years should serve to make this wealth of instructive and edifying writing more readily accessible.

As a young intern pastor in St. Paul during the summer of 1933, Karl Olsson, wrestling with his future and vocation, wrote to his beloved mentor David Nyvall: "The summer should determine for me whether or not I can be of service in the kingdom. If not, I hope that the mind that was in Christ will prevail upon me to do the thing that should be done." Nyvall responded a few days later simply encouraging him to trust God and inclination and choose with confidence. "To be a preacher of Christ," wrote Nyvall, "one must be a friend of Christ able to experience his friendship." Thus began more than a half-century of committed service in the kingdom of God.

Only a few months earlier, Karl Olsson (then nineteen years of age) wrote a poem of tribute that he had opportunity to read on the occasion of David Nyvall's seventieth birthday. Its concluding lines apply equally well to its author at this important point of passage and celebration:

> That which we owe our fathers cannot be
>   Wisdom for wisdom or an honor earned,
> But Truth's cause furthered in humility,
>   This, and the splendor of a lesson learned.
> Such is the man it would be vain to praise.
>   The good disciple needs no victor's wreath.
> Service has crowned him long before our days
>   With Beauty and a song that has no death.

Dr. Olsson's many friends join the contributors of these essays and those named in the *Tabula Gratulatoria* in hoping that this tribute will give him pleasure and assure him of their gratitude for his friendship in the faith.

PHILIP J. ANDERSON
North Park College and Theological Seminary

Karl A. Olsson: A Sketch of His Life

Carl Philip Anderson

For me, the Karl Arthur Olsson story began with his coming to St. Paul in 1933 to begin a brief ministry as assistant to A. E. Palmquist, pastor of First Covenant Church. He was young—only twenty—but I was younger by four years, and I related to him with the same degree of trust and respect I would have shown a much older person. Many years have passed since then, and I have followed Karl's life and ministry from the perspective of one who knew him first as youth pastor and counselor, later as partner in ministry, and through more than a half-century as valued friend.

While I can review the facts of his life and career quite objectively, I do so with the appreciation of one on whom Karl had a strong influence while I was still a teenager in the process of making major decisions about life after high school. My commitment to Christ and the church was firm, but what about college and career? Because of Karl's counsel and guidance I enrolled at North Park College rather than the University of Minnesota, and instead of pursuing studies leading to a career in architecture or engineering I registered at North Park as a pre-seminary student.

The Karl Olsson story, however, began not in St. Paul but in Renton, Washington, where he was born to Nils Albin and Mathilda Olsson on June 10, 1913. He was not yet two years old when the family moved to Sweden early in 1915, a move necessitated by his father's transfer to Russia by the Pacific Car and Foundry Company of Renton, by which he was employed. Karl's mother had died shortly after his birth, and the motherless family of four children went to live with their paternal grandparents in Killeberg, Loshult Parish, in the province of Skåne.

The move to Sweden and separation from their father was a difficult and traumatic one, and Karl speaks with affection about his Aunt Karna, who cared for him and his brother and sisters. In a reference to her in a *Covenant Companion* article in September 1968, he wrote about her as "my father's sister, a nurse by profession, and for a few months during my infancy a substitute mother. Some of my earliest memories are associated with her pretty laughing face, her crown of auburn hair, and the mystery of her uniform. She provided a merry shade under which my childhood could now and then forget the sorrows of war and the dolors of hunger and sickness."

Shortly after his arrival in Russia, Karl's father met Elsa Viktoria (Tora) Larsson, a missionary with the Swedish Covenant who was working with a Swedish colony in St. Petersburg (now Leningrad). Following their marriage, the children joined their father and stepmother in Russia in the fall of 1916. The reunion of the family was short-lived, however, for conditions in Russia were deteriorating, and the children and their new mother returned to Sweden a few months later. Nils Albin Olsson remained in Russia until 1918 when Pacific Car and Foundry's contract with the Russian government was terminated following the withdrawal of American financing.

On their return to Sweden the family settled in Örebro. There they became involved with the local Covenant congregation and had many contacts with missionaries and evangelists, friends and associates of Karl's stepmother, until the family moved back to Nils Albin's home parish. They remained there until 1922 when the family moved to the United States to join their father, who had preceded them to the States in December of 1920.

After arriving in America and settling in Sharon, Pennsylvania, where Nils Albin had found employment, the family affiliated with the Covenant church in Youngstown, Ohio, and they remained in Sharon for three years. The next move was to Pittsburgh, where they affiliated with the Swedish Congregational Church; this church, like many Swedish-American churches in the East, had ties with the Congregational denomination as well as with the Covenant. From this point on the family's contacts with the Covenant increased sharply, and in 1927 the Olssons attended the summer conferences of Covenant churches at Lake Chautauqua for the first time. There

they became acquainted with a wider circle of Covenant people and, more importantly, learned about North Park College.
As a result, and with the encouragement of Isak Skoog, pastor
of the Pittsburgh church, Karl's older brother Nils William
enrolled at North Park in 1929. Karl followed him two years
later, and in time their two sisters, Agnes and Lillie, also found
their way to the North Park campus.

When Karl came to North Park in 1931, he came with a
scholarship from Allegheny County and an interest in writing,
an interest that had been strongly encouraged by an English
teacher, Mary Lou Ogden, whom Karl speaks of with great
appreciation for her guidance and influence. He had been
editor of his high-school newspaper and quickly became
involved with publications at North Park, first with the college paper and in his second year as editor of the yearbook.

It was at this point that Karl was directed to First Covenant Church in St. Paul in response to a request to Dean Nils
W. Lund of North Park Theological Seminary for a young man
who could work with youth, who needed someone who was
fluent in English, and with older folk, who needed someone
who could speak Swedish! Here was an assignment for which
Karl was admirably suited, and he met the needs and expectations of young and old. To the scores of young people who
were active in the church at that time Karl brought the kind
of leadership and stimulation to which they responded with
enthusiasm and which made a lasting impression on many lives.

While in St. Paul, Karl also continued his education, enrol-
ing first at Macalester College and, in the fall of 1934, when
he completed his brief but important ministry in St. Paul, at
the University of Minnesota. His pastoral service continued
during this time with a one-year ministry at the Bethany Covenant Church of Stillwater. The following year he became pastor of the Tabernacle Church of Chicago and a student at North
Park Theological Seminary, completing his seminary work in
1936. Studies at the University of Chicago followed, and in
1938 he received his master's degree in English. In the fall of
that year he began teaching at North Park and except for some
years of graduate studies and military service he was associated
with the Covenant's primary educational institution until 1970.

During the 1930s, the Great Books movement had sur-
faced at the University of Chicago, and Karl found it to be an

exciting place in which to study and, later, in which to teach, serving on the faculty 1940-1942 and again 1945-1948, following service with the United States Army. Of his many experiences and contacts at the University of Chicago, Karl speaks with particular appreciation about the Jewish philosopher Herbert Lamm, who gave him valuable guidance in his philosophical and analytical reading. While teaching at the university, Karl completed his work for his doctorate and was awarded a Ph.D. in literature by the University of Chicago in 1948.

Regarding his military service, it should be noted that Karl saw it as his duty and did it. He never chided others who did not volunteer and never boasted of his service to his country. Always afraid of heights—and uneasy about air travel—he did not fear the battlefield and was awarded a Bronze Star and a Silver Star for "gallantry in action" as a U. S. Army chaplain between 1942 and 1945.

It was while serving as pastor of the Tabernacle in Chicago that Karl began reading Karl Barth and Reinhold Niebuhr and pursued his interest in psychological and analytical literature. It was at this time that he also developed a strong interest in Augustine's *Confessions* and somewhat later in the writings of C. S. Lewis. Regarding the writings of Lewis, he describes *The Screwtape Letters* as a bombshell in his intellectual life.

Karl's full-time involvement with North Park began in 1948 and continued until 1970 except for two years (1950-1952) when he was called back to military service. This was a difficult but valuable period and gave him a good background for the administrative responsibilities he was to carry during his years as president of North Park College and Theological Seminary.

When he returned to North Park in 1948, his duties included teaching in both the college and the seminary. He devoted half of his teaching time to each department, teaching English in the college and a variety of subjects in the seminary, with church history his primary responsibility. In 1952 he began teaching denominational history as well as church history and found himself drawn increasingly to these areas of interest, study, and research.

While I had been in touch with Karl during my years at North Park and done some work for him as a student assistant, it was not until 1955 that our work brought us into fre-

quent contact. As I prepared to assume my responsibilities with
the Department of Covenant Publications, I decided that our
denominational periodical would be enriched by the addition
of columnists with specific assignments whose writings would
appear in each issue. One was asked to write on matters related
to Covenant life and thought. Another was asked to provide
a column dealing with the Scriptures, and the third, Karl
Olsson, was asked to write about anything that interested him.
Delighted to have the world as his oyster, as he described it,
his first column appeared in the July 15, 1955 issue of *The
Covenant Weekly,* as it was then called, and his writing for
the denominational periodical continued for more than thirty
years. This was no small achievement, for we had a weekly
publication schedule for many years, and in addition Karl's
work took him away from Chicago frequently. In time we were
able to interest other publications in carrying Karl's column,
and he developed a following in other denominations as well
as in the Covenant.

In 1959 Karl was elected to the presidency of North Park
College and Theological Seminary and led the school through
an exciting period of development—expansion of the campus,
new buildings, new programs and services, the transition from
a junior college to a four-year liberal arts college, and a growing enrollment. These were difficult years, however, as well
as exciting years, for our country was to experience campus
unrest to a degree unknown prior to that time. The trauma
of the 1960s was felt at North Park as well as on other campuses, and Karl was uniquely prepared to cope with it—intellectually, emotionally, and spiritually. Karl, fortunately, was
blessed with a supportive family—his wife, Sally, whom he
describes in one of his books as "my good companion, advi-
sor, and faith exemplar," and his children, Alan, Kurt, Karl,
and Sarah—and a remarkable ability to relax under stress. An
example of this was my coming to the Olsson home one afternoon for a meeting with Karl and finding him propped up in
bed totally absorbed in dictating his translation of Olov Hartman's *Helig Maskerad,* which was published in an English edition entitled *Holy Masquerade* by Wm. B. Eerdmans in 1963.

It was during these years that Karl not only gave strong,
creative leadership to North Park but began a writing career
that has established him as the Covenant's pre-eminent

researcher, recorder, and interpreter of Covenant history, and has given him wide recognition as a columnist, author, and translator. Reference has just been made to his translation of the Olov Hartman volume, but of even greater significance to Covenanters are his many translations of Swedish hymns, all of which have been enriched in the process by Karl's poetic gifts.

Mention must also be made of Karl's public service during his North Park years. Early in his tenure as president he developed rapport with Chicago's political leadership, a valuable asset for any institution but particularly for a school removed from the center of the city not only physically but culturally as well. As a result of the recognition Karl achieved as an educator and administrator (and North Park gained as an educational institution), his talents and interests opened new doors of service to him. Of particular significance was his being singled out to head the citizens' commission appointed to make a study of Cook County Hospital and for which he was named Citizen Fellow by the Institute of Medicine of Chicago in 1965 for exemplary service to the Chicago medical community. Also in the area of public health he gave much time and effort to integrating Swedish Covenant Hospital's School of Nursing with North Park and establishing an accredited four-year nursing program. As one of the founders of the North River Commission, Karl helped deepen and structure the school's involvement in its Chicago community.

Karl's production as a writer is documented elsewhere in this volume, but mention must be made here of his major accomplishments as an author. First and foremost is his monumental volume entitled *By One Spirit,* published in 1962 shortly after the Covenant's seventy-fifth anniversary. Described on the dust jacket of the hardcover edition as "the definitive history of the Covenant Church for which the descendants of the Mission Friends have long been waiting," it was followed in 1975 by *A Family of Faith,* a smaller volume that sought to present the denomination's history in terms of its feeling and will, rather than external events. Then in 1985 the first of two volumes entitled *Into One Body* appeared as the denomination celebrated the centennial of its founding; in these two volumes Karl has provided a comprehensive, scholarly, and fascinating review of the Covenant's first hundred years.

The production of *By One Spirit,* it should be noted, was begun in 1955 with a year of research in Sweden and completed when Karl was in his first years as North Park's president.

Other titles produced during his years as president were *Seven Sins and Seven Virtues* (Harper and Row, 1959); *Things Common and Preferred* (Augsburg, 1959), a collection of some of the nearly 200 columns he had produced since 1955; *Passion,* another Harper volume which appeared in 1963; and *The God Game,* a novel published in 1968 by World Publishing Company.

Following his resignation from the presidency of North Park, Karl became associated with Faith at Work and shortly thereafter produced a volume quite different from anything he had written previously. Titled *Come to the Party,* it appeared in 1972 and was an invitation (partially autobiographical) to a freer lifestyle. This was followed in 1974 by *Find Yourself in the Bible* and *Meet Me on the Patio* in 1977. The latter volume is an excellent presentation of the relational theology of which Karl is recognized as a foremost exponent. *When the Road Bends,* his last volume before returning to the writing of Covenant history, was published in 1979.

Karl's decision to join Bruce Larson and Ralph Osborne in Faith at Work was not an abrupt one but the culmination of changes in his own thinking and concerns in the 1960s and his involvement in a number of conferences for clergy and lay people across the country. He remained with Faith at Work until 1977 and at that time founded his own organization, Relational Ministries, which continues to bring him into churches of many denominations for a productive and satisfying ministry.

Frequently controversial and occasionally misunderstood, Karl has been respected through the years for his courage in dealing with critical issues, his ability to come to the heart of problems quickly and objectively, and his total commitment to the gospel. Now, in his retirement years, he is increasingly perceived as a counselor with a remarkable understanding of human nature and a genuine compassion for people in all walks of life.

To conclude this brief review of Karl's life and ministry, I quote from James Hawkinson's foreword to *A Family of Faith:*

The Covenant Church is proud of Karl A. Olsson. It is proud of his talents and gifts, his consistent love for the Church, and, perhaps most of all, his continuing rediscovery of the fount to which we all came so many years ago, and still keep coming— God's grace to us in Jesus.

Karl Olsson's *Ahnentafel*

Nils William Olsson

Asked to contribute to this *Festschrift* in honor of my brother's seventy-fifth birthday, I thought it might be appropriate to look at Karl's genetic background as well as his environment to find some clues to his considerable gifts as historian, speaker, and author. In attempting this analysis I will comment briefly on his formative years and then refer to his *Ahnentafel* so that we may study his forebears and perhaps find hints that may explain his personality and life work. In choosing the word *Ahnentafel* to map his hereditary strains I am using the German word meaning ancestral lines or, in other words, his pedigree. The German word is used more frequently nowadays as a more precise definition of what we have in mind. The Swedes use the word *antavla* which is, of course, a direct translation of the German.

There is little doubt in my mind that some of Karl's gifts were imparted to him in his early years, when after the death of our mother in 1913 our father married Elsa (Tora) Larsson. She came to us in the summer of 1915, when Karl had just turned two. Since I was four years older, her entrance upon the scene affected me less. Our stepmother had no children of her own and she immediately and affectionately accepted Karl as her "baby." Reinforcing this relationship was the fact that Elsa, a former nurse, gave everything of herself to restore Karl to health after he had suffered a nearly fatal bout with double pneumonia at the age of two and a half. During the recuperative period, most of our stepmother's attention was devoted to Karl's well-being. She provided not only excellent nursing care but also emotional and spiritual support which was bound to influence him deeply.

Elsa drew upon her experiences as a Covenant missionary among Swedish sailors in the Russian port of St. Petersburg (today known as Leningrad), where she regularly visited Swedish merchant vessels to hand out religious tracts and invite the sailors to divine services in the Swedish missionary chapel in the capital city.

Elsa was also musical, had a remarkable voice, and had sung in solo appearances as well as in choral groups. Her repertory was endless, including not only religious songs but also ballads, folk songs, and some of the more sentimental ditties popular in Sweden at the turn of the century. I can recall how my stepmother's singing penetrated the walls that separated Karl's sickroom from the rest of the house.

Elsa always dreamed of Karl's becoming a minister or doctor. She nurtured an unbelievably strong affection for doctors, clergy, and missionaries. As a result, our home was always wide open to preachers, religious leaders, and missionaries. One of our earliest memories is the several days' visit of the venerable Wilhelm Sarwe, Swedish Covenant missionary to the interior of Russia, and J. A. Hultman, a gospel singer beloved both in Sweden and the United States. There is little doubt in my mind that Karl's later career began in our drawing rooms, where we children would sit for hours hearing about the mission fields in Russia, China, and Africa.

If Elsa was the spiritual mentor to Karl, Nils Albin, our father, was the stern patriarch who kept our feet solidly on the "straight and narrow." He had become an evangelical Christian as a boy of seven. Once wandering in the woods of his native Skåne, he suddenly felt a terrible burden of guilt and beneath a tall pine tree he gave himself to the Lord. His religiosity, however, was grounded in old-fashioned, austere Lutheran orthodoxy. Like others of his kin, Dad had a comic bent and was a superb storyteller. When inspired, he could tell anecdotes and stories, which kept us in stitches. But Dad's conscience was often pricked by this outburst of levity, which he felt was not quite Christian. He once told us a story of how as a young convert he traveled from Malmö to Copenhagen by ferry with a number of young people to attend a young peoples' conference in the Danish capital. On the ride back to Malmö late in the evening, Dad's funny bone began tickling and he regaled the crowd for an hour and a half with stories and anecdotes that had the entire group convulsed with

laughter. Dad then told us of how on the following morning
he became deeply contrite that he had wasted his energies on
storytelling rather than on more serious topics.

Dad took his Christianity very seriously. He was a person who began and ended his day with Bible reading and
prayer. Though he had little sympathy for the priesthood, he
felt himself called to witness at every opportunity. Wasting
time was a heinous sin to Dad and he would use any spare
moment to meditate on the Christian life. Among his papers,
which we have had an opportunity to examine, we have found
hundreds, if not thousands, of pieces of paper upon which
Dad had expressed opinions on all aspects of human existence.
We both feel that Dad was born to preach and was always looking for an audience, even though it might only consist of his
four children and his wife.

Thus Karl's childhood and youth were spent in an environment where the Christian philosophy was paramount, where
father and stepmother provided not only examples of Christian exhortation but also provided the nourishment for Karl
to exploit these drives. On the secular side we children were
early exposed to literary influences. While the books in our
library were not numerous, they represented the very best in
world literature, history, and the fine arts. Early in life we were
exposed to the offerings of the village library in Killeberg in
northern Skåne, open two hours a week on Saturday evenings.
Our weekly visits to this gold mine of literature and information kept us going through many a dark and wintry night. Writers such as Tegnér, Geijer, Lagerlöf, von Heidenstam, Rune-
berg, and Topelius were household names. After our return
to America, we became frequent visitors to the city libraries
wherever we lived.

What about Karl's heredity? I believe that his genetic
makeup played a major role in his development. Since Elsa,
our stepmother, obviously had no function here, we shall leave
her out of this discussion and instead concentrate on his blood-
lines. We know very little about our mother, Mathilda Lejkell
Lindström. She died three months after Karl's birth, when I
was four years old. Her early life was clouded in misery and
poverty. Her mother, Olivia Laurentia Lejkell Brown (7), was
divorced by her husband, Anders Gustaf Brown (6), six months
before the birth of Mathilda. He took Olivia to Copenhagen

for divorce proceedings. There before the Swedish consul she swore an oath that she was deserting her husband. In Sweden a hundred years ago this was a mandatory procedure for a husband desiring to rid himself of an unwanted wife. Because of her mother's poverty, Mathilda was born to unknown parents according to Brännkyrka parish records. Because she had no parents of record, she became the ward of the city and was farmed out to the lowest bidder. When Mathilda was four years old, her mother, Olivia, appeared at the parish office and announced that she was the mother of the child. Subsequent research has shown that Anders Gustaf Brown was actually the father of Mathilda.

At about the same time that Olivia acknowledged to the authorities that she was the mother of Mathilda, the daughter was placed in the General Orphanage in Stockholm from which institution she was adopted by Swedish railway official Wilhelm Lindström and his wife. Mathilda adopted the Lindström name and thus came to America as Mathilda Lindström in 1907.

By examining the lives of Karl's four grandparents we shall try to see if they possessed traits that might have had a bearing on Karl's development. Our paternal grandfather, Nils Olsson (4), a farmer in Skåne, was a tall, strapping man, handsome and very convivial. He was less interested in farming than in carousing with neighbors and friends. Until his conversion as a grown man, he had been a gallant dancer, an enthusiastic partygoer and heavy drinker, and sometimes quite oblivious of his duties to his family. He loved to visit county fairs and had a passion for trading horses but was so-so at business and usually came out on the wrong end of a horse-swapping deal. His wife, Cecilia Hansdotter Olsson (5), came from a well-to-do farming family in southern Skåne. The only daughter, she stood to gain much by marrying within her social circle. Instead, she encountered our grandfather, Nils Olsson, in a country store in her home parish, was struck by his handsomeness, and fell for him on the spot. Our grandfather at that time was a salesman for a lumber company and swept Cecilia off her feet by his smooth sales pitch. Despite murmurings in the clan at her marrying beneath her station, the marriage was solemnized. She was already carrying Nils's child.

If we are to pinpoint anyone of the four grandparents as having passed on important genes to Karl, I would have to nominate our paternal grandmother. Cecilia was an unusually able person, who was yoked to someone not her intellectual equal. She possessed very little formal education, but yearned her whole life to know more. She had a store of information on her family history, of her local history, and of things in general much superior to others in her community. She was the mother of eight children and carried much of the burden of running a farm. Her penchant for reading and studying was so intense, and not having opportunity to fulfill her desires, she took the night hours to accomplish what she could not do in daylight. Our father recounts that occasionally he would wake up at two or three in the morning to see Cecilia sitting by the kerosene lamp, reading anything that was available. Truly here was a woman who, provided with the educational opportunities of today, would have gone far as a medical doctor or writer. Her many letters to her son Nils, our father, show her grasp of politics, literature, and current events. There is little doubt in my mind that some of her genes were passed on to Karl.

I have already mentioned Anders Gustaf Brown (6), our maternal grandfather, who settled down in Stockholm after having made his fortune in the 1870s in the diamond mines in South Africa. He was a restless youth and impatient with the status quo, who departed for South Africa and worked in the rough and tumble atmosphere of the diamond field. He drank heavily and partook in tough fights with other miners, always carrying his knuckle iron (still in the family) to guard himself against mayhem and death.

Anders Gustaf bought himself a fine apartment house on Stockholm's south side, married Olivia Laurentia Lejkell (7), and settled down as an agent for an emigration company. He fathered five daughters, of whom Mathilda was the youngest. He divorced his wife for the alleged reason that she had not produced any sons.

Olivia Laurentia was a softspoken person, musically talented, who after her divorce earned her living by playing the piano at Novilla, a *fin de siècle* restaurant on Djurgården in Stockholm.

As we move backward in time the picture becomes more diffuse, but it is still possible to identify traits of character that might help us understand Karl's personality. We begin with our great-grandfather, Ola Persson (8), a maker of clogs in the city of Lund. Ola was a very pious person and in the 1870s he had been one of the founders of the Covenant chapel (*missionshus*) in Lund. He was understandably very critical of his son Nils's worldly ways. Despite the difference in temperaments, our grandfather respected his father and when Nils Olsson (4), returning from a party on a snowy night, ran off the road with his sleigh and a team of runaway horses and as a result suffered a fractured collarbone, the first thing he asked for was that his father be called. When Ola arrived he found a penitent son who wished to renounce his dissolute behavior and become a Christian believer. Ola was only too happy to oblige and from that moment alcoholic beverages disappeared from grandfather's table and the old farmhouse resounded with the singing of Christian tunes and psalms. We know nothing about Ola's wife, Elna Persdotter (9), except that she seems not to have shared her husband's religious fervor. As an aside, it should be noted that Ola Persson's brother, Nils Persson, converted to Mormonism with his entire family and emigrated to Utah in the early 1870s.

Our paternal grandmother's father, Hans Andersson (10), was also a farmer in southern Skåne. We know very little about him. His wife, Karna Nilsdotter (11), however, came from a well-established Skåne family. Her brother, Pehr Nilsson, also a farmer in the parish of Espö, became a member of the Swedish Parliament (*Riksdag*), and created a formidable library, concentrated heavily on Swedish ancient history. Anders Gustaf Brown's father, Anders Svensson (12), was a gardener on the estate of Mem in Östergötland, owned by Baron von Saltza. His wife, Christina Källström, came from the ancient city of Skänninge. Olivia Lejkell's father, Johan Petter Lejkell (14), was a baker in the city of Söderköping. The mother was Ingrid Ådahl.

Going back one more generation we are unable to spot likely sources for genetic influences. While it is a fact that one ancestor on our mother's side, Sebastian Ådahl (60), had been a minister in Stockholm, his career had ended abruptly in 1807, when after a trial before the Stockholm Consistory he was found guilty of having committed double adultery. He was defrocked and forced into banishment from the capital. His father, Fredrik Ådahl (120), had been a successful minister in the parish of Undenäs in Västergötland.

In conclusion and summing up the evidence at hand, it seems that while genetic influences may have had a share in Karl's development as a preacher and author, it appears to me that his early tutelage under a devoted stepmother and a devoutly Christian father probably weighed more in shaping his philosophy and abilities, and in ushering him into the field of Christian communications.

Karl Olsson's *Ahnentafel*

I   1. OLSSON, Karl Arthur, b. in Renton, WA 10 June 1913; m. in Iron Mountain, MI 14 September 1935 Dorothy Sally Carlson, b. in Iron Mountain, MI 5 September 1914, dau. Charles (Charlie) Blixt Carlson and Selma Fredrikson. Res. in Columbia, MD. Children:
    a. Alan Charles, b. in Chicago, IL 6 December 1936.
    b. Kurt Oliver, b. in Chicago, IL 16 September 1941.
    c. Karl Frederick, b. in Chicago, IL 3 March 1945.
    d. Sarah Ann, b. in Chicago, IL 7 November 1950.

II   2. OLSSON, Nils Albin, b. in Össjö, Södra Ljunga Parish (Kron.) 1 October 1878; emigr. to the U.S. 11 February 1902; m. (1) in Seattle, WA 17 September 1908; m. (2) in St. Petersburg, Russia 22 April 1915; d. in Miami, FL 5 August 1972.
    3. LINDSTRÖM, Mathilda Lejkell, b. in Brännkyrka Parish (Stock.) 29 June 1884; emigr. to the U.S. 1907; d. in Renton, WA 7 October 1913.

III   4. OLSSON, Nils, b. in Hagstad, Södra Rörum Parish (Malm.) 15 June 1851; m. in St. Petri Parish, Malmö 16 December 1876; d. in Killeberg, Loushult Parish (Krist.) 25 February 1935. Farmer.
    5. HANSDOTTER, Sissa (Cecilia), b. in Anderslöv Parish (Malm.) 16 March 1851; d. in Killeberg 25 December 1930.
    6. BROWN, Anders Gustaf Svensson, b. in Å Parish

(Ög.) 6 May 1848; m. in Söderköping 22 October 1876; div. 8 January 1884; d. in Maria Parish, Stockholm 2 June 1926. Emigration agent.

7. LEJKELL, Olivia Augusta Laurentia, b. in Söderköping 15 April 1852; d. in Solna Parish (Stock.) 26 July 1909.

IV 8. PERSSON, Ola, b. in Kristinetorp, Hammarlunda Parish (Malm.) 28 October 1820; m. in Södra Rörum 30 August 1845; d. in Kävlinge Parish (Malm.) in May 1911. Maker of wooden shoes and clogs.

9. PERSDOTTER, Elna, b. in Röslöv, Södra Rörum 29 October 1819; d. in Södra Rörum in December 1891.

10. ANDERSSON, Hans, b. in Anderslöv 11 August 1812; m. in Anderslöv 1844; d. in Anderslöv 22 June 1870. Farmer.

11. NILSDOTTER, Karna, b. in Grönby Parish (Malm.) 2 January 1814; d. in Anderslöv 8 June 1884.

12. SVENSSON, Anders Peter, b. in Mem, Tåby Parish (Ög.) 8 February 1819; m. 21 April 1844. Gardener.

13. KÄLLSTRÖM, Christina Maria Olofsdotter, b. in Kättilstad Parish (Ög.) 26 June 1816.

14. LEJKELL, Johan Petter, b. in Caroli Parish, Malmö 24 January 1824; moved to Söderköping; m. in Stockholm 5 October 1851; d. in Söderköping 22 December 1895. Baker.

15. ÅDAHL, Ingrid Augusta Josephina, b. in Maria Parish, Stockholm 28 June 1828; d. in Söderköping 9 March 1880.

V 16. SVENSSON, Per, b. in Gumlösa Parish (Krist.) 16 December 1780, m. in Sireköpinge Parish (Malm.) 18 August 1811; d. in Broby Parish (Krist.) 18 July 1865 by accidental drowning in Helge River. Crofter.

17. OLSDOTTER, Botilda, b. in Sireköpinge 7 August 1781; d. in Färlöv Parish (Krist.) 6 August 1839.

18. ESKELSSON, Per, b. in Södra Rörum 10 September 1780; m. in Södra Rörum 30 January 1813; d. in Funderset, Södra Rörum 18 March 1846. Crofter.

19. PERSDOTTER, Elna, b. in 1784; d. in Södra Rörum
    24 March 1846.
20. MAGNUSSON, Anders, b. in Anderslöv 30 January
    1783. Farmer.
21. ANDREASDOTTER, Sissa, b. in Virestad, Bösarp
    Parish (Malm.) 6 November 1773; d. in Anderslöv
    8 February 1840.
22. JÖNSSON, Nils, b. in Grönby 28 September 1765;
    d. in Grönby 28 July 1820. Farmer.
23. PERSDOTTER, Kersti, b. in Lilla Beddinge Parish
    (Malm.) 7 April 1779.
24. SVENSSON, Sven, b. in Skönberga Parish (Ög.)
    13 March 1788. Crofter.
25. ANDERSDOTTER, Anna Christina, b. in Tingstad
    Parish (Ög.) 8 August 1785.
26. KÄLLSTRÖM, Olof Månsson, b. in Kättilstad in
    1782.
27. ERIKSDOTTER, Anna Maria, b. in Skärkind Parish
    (Ög.) 8 November 1783.
28. LEJKELL (LEICHEL, LEUCHEL), Johann Friedrich,
    b. in Nassau-Weilburg (present-day West Germany)
    16 September 1779; joined the Swedish Army in
    Germany in 1806 and fought in the Napoleonic
    Wars; settled in Sweden; m. in the Garrison
    Parish, Malmö 26 December 1810; d. in Caroli
    Parish, Malmö 21 September 1842. Carpenter.
29. OLSDOTTER, Margareta, b. in Skabersjö Parish
    (Malm.) 27 February 1786; d. in Caroli Parish,
    Malmö 19 March 1833.
30. ÅDAHL, Ulrik August, b. in Nikolai Parish, Stock-
    holm 24 September 1801; m. in Maria Parish,
    Stockholm 8 October 1826; d. in Maria Parish
    28 May 1851. Journeyman bookbinder.
31. KLERCK, Ingeborg (Inga) Juliana, b. in Stockholm
    12 April 1806; d. in Maria Parish 16 August 1886.
VI 32. BENGTSSON, Sven, b. in Stoby Parish (Krist.)
    1755; m. 14 December 1777; d. in Gumlösa
    11 June 1790. Farmer.
33. PERSDOTTER, Ingeborg, b. in Önnestad Parish
    (Krist.) 23 May 1742; d. in Gumlösa 1 March
    1816.

36. TRULSSON, Eskel, b. in Södra Rörum ca. 1743; d. in Södra Rörum the night between 1 and 2 May 1810. Farmer.
37. MÅRTENSDOTTER, Hanna, b. in Södra Rörum ca. 1745; d. in Södra Rörum 12 February 1809.
40. CARLSSON, Magnus, b. in Lemmeströ Parish (Malm.) 13 September 1734; m. in Anderslöv 17 May 1776; d. in Anderslöv 20 April 1786. Farmer.
41. SVENSDOTTER, Hanna, b. in Anderslöv 6 December 1751; d. in Anderslöv 29 January 1825.
42. RASMUSSON, Andreas, b. in Lilla Beddinge 1743; m. in Simlinge Parish (Malm.) 1768; d. 1776.
43. ANDERSDOTTER, Elsa, b. in Virestad, Bösarp 1751; d. 1786.
44. HANSSON, Jöns, b. in Grönby 1720; m. in Espö Parish (Malm.) 1756. Farmer.
45. SVENSDOTTER, Kerstin, b. in Espö 1733; d. in Grönby 24 May 1808.
46. NILSSON, Per.
47. HANSDOTTER, Kerstin.
48. SVENSSON, Sven.
49. JÖNSDOTTER, Catharina.
58. MÅNSSON, Ola, b. in Skabersjö 17 January 1753. Farmer.
59. LARSDOTTER, Sissa, b. in Skabersjö 12 March 1760; d. 2 November 1820.
60. ÅDAHL, Sebastian, b. in Undenäs Parish (Skar.) 12 April 1769; ordained minister but defrocked for conduct unbecoming a cleric; d. in Örebro 28 December 1832. Itinerant schoolteacher.
61. BERGMAN, Catharina Elisabeth, b. in Kristinehamn 25 July 1769; d. in St. Jakob Parish, Stockholm; 13 May 1828.
62. KLERCK, Lars Johan, b. in Benestad Parish (Krist.) 22 August 1767; m. in Katarina Parish in Stockholm 27 May 1802; d. in Stockholm 27 October 1838. Innkeeper.
63. NÄSBOM, Christina Margareta, b. in Katarina Parish, Stockholm 26 November 1770; d. in Stockholm 4 May 1837.

This *Ahnentafel* covers six generations with some *lacunae* because of missing information, most of it as a result of the destruction of some parish records by fire.

It is not the purpose of this brief study to go beyond six generations, but it is interesting to note that as we go back and seek to chart earlier generations, we find that they contain a multitude of clergy, active in Stockholm, and the dioceses of Lund, Skara, and Karlstad. One of them, Gabriel Erici Florén, who served the church in Nyed in Värmland from 1685 to 1705, became widely known for his sermons which he edited and published. One of these volumes entitled *Sömnlösa nätter,* or *Sleepless Nights,* remained popular reading for 150 years after his death, and was characterized by Peter Wieselgren in 1866 as a book which the "common people still held dear."

Whether we can trace Karl's skill in homiletics and authorship back to his ancestor, Gabriel Florén, is difficult to say, but the similarity in their success in reaching a large audience by means of the written word is startling. At any rate, I have tried in this short essay to provide some clues as to the origins of Karl's outstanding skills.

Friendship—and Diverging Ways

Jean H. Hagstrum

On a winter day in 1943 Karl Olsson referred to our meeting some ten years earlier—on "that breathless and blistering day on the road snaking north." The metaphor is expectedly a just one—since Karl (it would be unnatural for me to refer to him in any other way despite his many achievements and the usual formalities of a *Festschrift*) is a poet and a novelist with a great sensitivity to language. The road we drove on that summer day in 1933 was not the present multilaned superhighway (90 and 94) that leads from Chicago to St. Paul but the old winding number 12 (or possibly the equally sinuous number 14, though I think not). We have both said several times that on that day in 1933 we sensed an immediate and deep coincidence of spirit and mind. But though we were both young and idealistic Christians with the ministry in our immediate futures, we were not above one-upmanship. I recall a considerable amount of learned swordplay and sparring for position, and I am sure that Karl took the high ground. Even now I have vivid recollections of his considerable knowledge of geology (I had and have none) as we passed the beautifully or oddly shaped rock formations near the Wisconsin Dells. I was certain at the time—and still am—that his two years at North Park College had taught him more than my three years at the University of Minnesota. The friendship that began then has lasted some fifty-five years, and I wish to say something about it and also about friendship in general.

From Aristotle at least through Emerson some of the best minds of Western culture have written on this subject, and most agree that its bedrock lies in similitude of character, mind, and manners. Beside such deep consonances Karl and I hold in common many early images, memories, and experiences, and I believe I can apply to our friendship the wonderful lines of John Milton from *Lycidas:*

> For we were nurst upon the self-same hill,
> Fed the same flock; by fountain, shade, and rill.
>   Together both, ere the high Lawns appear'd
> Under the opening eye-lids of the morn,
> We drove afield.

The imagery of shepherd and sheep is fully apposite, partly because it is biblical and partly because we both studied at the same seminary and both became Covenant pastors during our early and middle twenties. Other mutualities existed and exist, and they animate the many long letters Karl wrote to me from August 14, 1937, to the present—in the earlier years as frequently as once a month. These letters (now in the collection of my papers in the Archives of the Northwestern University Library) are informal, witty, exuberant, poetic, quirkish, frank. They constitute an enduring tribute to the sturdiness and steadiness of Karl's faith and his loyalty to its denominational embodiment. On the personal level they express a healthy, hearty, even salty humanity, an unsentimental realism, an unblushing concern with the body, the gift for language I referred to earlier, and acute powers of rich and precise observation.

What I should like to concentrate on here is the breathtaking range and depth of learning revealed in the letters, a scholarship achieved early, never abandoned, and continuously expanded and freshened with new thought. Karl used to write to me at length on Thomas Mann (especially *Joseph and His Brothers*), on the light imagery in Dante and Milton, on Sophocles' *Antigone* (a six-page letter), on the eighteenth century in France and England (an early and abiding interest of mine), and on religion, humanism, rationalism, love, the flesh, death, Dewey, Aristotle, Reinhold Niebuhr. And I do not mention experiences we shared outside the groves and grooves of academe in discussions of the army, the war, the Covenant, our religious backgrounds, the American Midwest versus the East.

While agreeing about the need for compatibility, writers on friendship have likewise stressed the importance of dissimilarity—of the need for spicy difference to keep things lively and interesting. Our relationship had plenty of that! We were, in fact, often engaged in what William Blake approvingly called intellectual battle in urging the importance of contrarieties in life and thought, without which there can be no progression. When I seemed to be drifting toward the kind of humanism (that of Irving Babbitt or Paul Elmer More) then fashionable at Yale, he pulled me up sharply by invoking the harsh realities he was finding in Marx, Freud, and the Bible. And he was always an intellectually abrasive and stimulating enemy of easy vocabulary. He once challenged me to define romanticism and literary classicism, and he himself tossed off six possible meanings of rationalism in Enlightened France and four possible meanings in eighteenth-century England. I feel certain that I was influenced by his brilliant taxonomy when I came some years later to write my article on "The Nature of Dr. Johnson's Rationalism."

I have said enough to show that Karl and I were far from being clones of one another and that we expressed ourselves and our differences freely and without fear of compromising essential respect and fundamental love. I do not now have access to my own letters (I hope that some day they will join his), but it is apparent from what Karl says that I was equally frank and open—he once referred to a letter of mine as "rich and angry." But difference is not divergence, and the day came when divergence and not difference is the proper term to describe one development in the relationship. I came to the point "when the road bends," to use the title of one of Karl's books, a time in which I felt what Karl in a later and public context called "the pains of passage." In our personal world these were pains for me and pains for him. For in my own pilgrimage, journey, "walk" (I am not after some forty-five years of saturation in a secular academic milieu completely comfortable with these words, though I honor their use in the Bible and by Dante and Bunyan) I decided to change denominations, to desert the path that would have led to ordination, and to choose a large secular university over a small Christian school and seminary. In announcing my decision I had apparently been harsh in assessing my religious past, and Karl reacted honestly, firmly, uncompromisingly. He may well have been right in what he then said or implied about the fruitlessness of denominational change, and I confess to feeling then—

and even now on renewed contact with the documents of our
past—the solemnity and the sorrow of his response. Our
friendship survived, and the letters continued abundant and
exuberant, though later geographical separation, vocational
divergence, and the demands of that world that is too much
with us late and soon have inevitably taken their toll.

Thus the Covenant is for me a road not taken, and we
know today, as we have never known so clearly before in our
history, that such roads partly traveled but not followed all
the way continue to wind through our psychic landscapes.
The only reason for writing about such matters here is that
it is not inconceivable that those who have remained faithful
to their first callings might wish to contemplate what motivates
desertion, apostasy, or change of this kind. Two of my words
are emotionally charged, and I use them only because I have
used them of myself and felt something of their force. The
dark emotionality of such terms arises from the fact that Christianity, for understandable reasons, has imbued separation
from its fellowship with fatal consequences, when indeed it
has not denied even the possibility. (The eternal security of
believers, or the persistence of the saints, was an idea much
debated in the religious culture of my youth.) In any event
a change for better or for worse in this realm leaves a permanent mark, even change within the family of faith, and certainly it excites curiosity, within the individual involved if
nowhere else, about why it should have taken place at all. I
have said that I am now without documents relevant to my
own change of course, and I must confess, in the language of
Wordsworth's *Tintern Abbey,* that "I cannot paint/What then
I was."

There is thus limited usefulness in trying too hard to reconstruct a past through the mist of years and the distortions that
time and self-interest work in the memory and the mind. But
perhaps a few considerations are valid and of interest. I have
had some contact in my childhood and youth with what Karl
has called the Covenant mystique, and I read the two volumes
of his latest work with unflagging attention and often with
deep self-involvement. The heritage he so carefully delineates
and transmits came to me mostly from my mother and her
mother, from their contact with the St. Paul Tabernacle, as
we then called the church that was the scene of Karl's first

full-time and very youthful ministry. Its longtime pastor, A. E. Palmquist, I knew and respected, and he was for me the very epitome of the Covenant heritage. But opportunities to hear him or receive his ministrations and sense his spiritual presence were rare. Theodore W. Anderson was a more constant source of light and warmth during my high-school years, and through him and some of his colleagues I came to feel on my pulses the combination of faith and learning that has been so central in the Covenant gift. That ideal has remained fresh and strong in Karl, as even my very brief discussion of his letters to me must have shown. As late as 1978, in a long and fascinating letter that is an intellectual autobiography *in parvo,* he says: "I believe in the discipline, the solemnity, and the joys of learning," adding, "I am avidly interested in academics and deeply appreciative of those who give themselves to scholarship."

Had the presentation of the faith come to me with that emphasis and had it hinted at such opportunities, I might have stayed the denominational course on which I had come to manhood. But Karl's intensity, his own fire from off the altar, was not the kind that burned itself into my youthful soul. It was the tabernacle in Minneapolis, not St. Paul, that early seized and seared my spirit. And what alternately burned and froze my mind were anti-intellectual diatribes, sermons reeking with suspicion of learning and scholarship, a gospel of rigid dispensationalism that denied the applicability to our lives of the Sermon on the Mount. Versions of apocalyptic terror thundered and lightened as people were frightened into often unseemly kinds of rapture that were intended to prepare them for the Rapture. Karl, with admirable objectivity and learning, has in his latest history established the context for the dispensationalism, premillenarianism, and antidenominationalism that invaded Covenant thought and practice. But that perspective came much too late to mitigate the effects on tender teenage and preteen sensibilities of highly charged emotions. Personal and even familial divisions (though not within my own nuclear family) may have arisen directly from the fevers of anti-intellectual dogmatisms untempered by Christian charity. For fanaticism breeds schism and war and sometimes tears down the temple of faith as well as learning, eating its own children. I can personally testify to the importance of main-

taining the synthesis between faith and intellectual works (even
of scholarship on the Bible and on the history of the Church)
that Karl has so long and so cogently tried to hold together
and help institutionalize. And my reading of the current scene
in our country and worldwide is that the task has not become
easier but much more difficult than in the days of our youth.

I cannot now be absolutely sure that the analysis of my
divergence from Covenant commitment is fully accurate or
complete. Passages in the Olsson-to-Hagstrum correspondence
suggest that I may have found sub-ethical or extra-ethical social
and personal habits or mores (the equivalent of eating meat
offered to idols) to be restrictive or irrelevant or obfuscatory.
And I must suggest—though I do not wish to be self-depre-
catory, only honest—that, like many secular academicians of
immigrant stock, I may have been personally ambitious in ways
that pushed aside a church with foreign origins and traditions.
Along with many others I may well have been a thirties' and
forties' version of the later Yuppies, though one with the smell
of the lamp about him. We were young and wanted to be
upwardly mobile to the full professorship and to high administration. And we did not want emotional or intellectual fet-
ters to impede our rise. Karl always seemed to me an example of the reverse of this kind of climbing, for he said no to
the flesh-potty temptations that beckoned to academic and
administrative advancement in the great secular agglomera-
tions.

Finally, having ventured an analysis that treats economic
and other worldly considerations as motivating forces and thus
has more than a Marxist tinge to it, I may as well round out
the picture by being slightly Freudian, though I do not want
to end up in the morass of depth psychology. Unconsciously
siblings bounce off one another, and their careers roll in different spheres not simply because of different tastes or apti-
tudes. So one brother turns to science because an elder has
already moved into the humanities. It is so too with friends,
and strikingly diverse traits and needs can arise out of—indeed,
can be stirred up by—a highly cherished mutuality and can
then mysteriously pull one east and the other west. It would
be too solemn—and carry too many unwanted parallels—to
say that I played Horatio to Karl's Hamlet in the Olsson-
Hagstrum drama. But he was always more imaginative, more

creative, more fiery and intense than I—and in the earlier years more tempestuous. My more equable and rationalistic temperament was attracted to secular scholarship, his required a greater continuity with his past, with his own legacy.

All this is of course oversimplified and could be illusory. But of one thing I am certain—and now I fancy I am back in the daylight realm of observed fact: Karl kept alive and healthy in the world of his spiritual inheritance a phenomenally retentive memory, a keen natural intelligence, a trained mind, and fine taste in literature and the arts. And as for myself I am conscious that even outside the walls, as it were, I was attracted, because of my heritage, both to the sturdily and traditionally Christian Samuel Johnson and also to that charismatic, dissenting, and personally turbulent Christian, the poet-painter William Blake, to both of whom I have devoted so many years of my scholarly life. It is a measure of my respect and affection for Karl and of my intellectual debt to him that I could talk to him about these geniuses—and about virtually everything else as well.

Ad Amicum Verum:
Karl A. Olsson

Herbert Lamm

The moment of time in which we celebrate someone's date of birth involves different bases on which we respond to the occasion—from what is due to mere acquaintance, to what is appropriate to a friend. The birth day is a temporal event, and even in relation to one's friends it is to be presumed that we were not present at the time of their birth, though our interest in them might lead us to inquire into their childhood and youth. At the time of our first meeting we judge them primarily in terms of our becoming interested in them at their maturity. But even then, there is a kind of aggregate contiguity. We might at first get to observe them seated somewhere in a room. But this may move to another level—e.g., they say something and our interest is attracted in such a way that at the moment we consider them friend. That is not a local motion or a quantitative change through increase or decrease in size, but a generative change that is sudden, and not like falling asleep from having been awake. For that entails a continuum, a growing point of experience; our relation might amount to horizontal exchange of mutual monologues, a monologue like that of Stephen Daedalus and Bloom in Joyce's *Ulysses*. But as time goes on the focus of attention should be on what we could participate in, the ground determining the participation.

We have two levels, just as there are two kinds of numbers: 1) numbering; and 2) numbered numbers. These two are like the modern distinction of cardinal and ordinal numbers (e.g., when a farmer has put out cows to graze and at the end of the day returns them to the barn and counts them to see if any are missing). The numbers numbered are part of a series that is variable, whereas that which numbers them is invariant and eternal in structure. Is a team of horses many or one? We can talk of unity and duality independently of the members of the class. A team of horses is one, not many, though the horses are two in number. The things that are created are in a reciprocal relation to the knowledge of the things born, in which the intelligible, creative activity of the creator and the structure is eternal.

There is a reorientation in Augustine concerning the nature of science. It is no longer temporal nor mutable as a subject matter but has a changeless basis. It is not a product of the laboratory. There is an eternal structure above our finite minds that is present from the very beginning. When attracted and then we act, particulars are modified. But if we turn upward and contemplate, we rise above particular things and see clearly in relation to an eternal structure intimately present but transcendent as a mode of being.

We turn to ethics whose immediate principle is the Holy Spirit, which is the *ordo vivendi,* whereas physics is the *ordo essendi,* and logic (*logos*) is the *ordo intelligibilis.* Ethics is analogous with both physics and logic, so that knowledge pursues a desirable end. Therefore, knowledge pursues a desirable end only as we know it, and so knowledge of the good is implied by pursuit of the good. A mistake in ethics is analogous to a mistake in knowledge. In ethics the error is sin which is most of all to be avoided. Sin is mistaking a partial good for a complete good; e.g. covetousness maintains that money is the only good, because of the failure to recognize the proper place of money, which is merely a part of the good—it is an exchangeable good. In logic we mistake a partial explanation for the whole as a sufficient one.

Ethics has analogies with both physics and knowledge (logic), so that the intelligible is discoverable in things, not just in the mind. In knowing we pursue a desirable end, so that in the pursuit of a desirable end knowledge of the good is implied. But we err, such as in covetousness, when we presume that money is the only good. On each level we fall into an opacity, calling for transparence. The motion of the soul in pursuing the good, however, is in some respects like bodily motion, yet with a difference. Without a will, the motion of a body can proceed in only one direction, whereas with a free will the soul does not will uniquely.

In ethics the question is, "How can I desire or will the

good at all?'' For example, there is the problem of memory
(as a thesaurus), both for conscious activity and for a kind of
Jungian unconscious. Suppose that we have forgotten or lost
something. We try then to recall words that are associated with
it. Having lost an object we hunt around in those places where
we last had the object. But such a phenomenal state of affairs
is not adequate to or commensurate with an ideal pursuit as
the object of the free will. If we are to pursue the good, we
must tend in some direction. To be is to strive to continue
to be—but on what level are we? There is the tendency to conserve life, but there is beyond that the tendency to conserve
the good life. Between both there is a tension for which there
ought to be a resolution.

On each level we have a symbolic situation. Now a symbol may be looked at or seen through. Looking at it involves
an opacity, since a symbol refers to something that may have
its mode of being on various levels. We have primarily a mode
of being, and in referring to that ontological mode there is
a mode of conceiving it and signifying it by appropriate parts
of speech. We have here something approximating the division of the liberal arts, namely the *trivium* and the *quadriv-
ium*. Let us first take the *trivium* which consists of grammar,
rhetoric, and logic or dialectics. In order to apprehend their
respective functions, I compare grammar to the process of cal-
ibrating an instrument—it should be cleansed of impurities
prior to applying it. Rhetoric puts the instrument to use, applying it, for example, to conditions of temperature and pressure
as dynamic conditions, so that rhetoric can move an audience
for the purpose of persuasion, its "soul" being, as in Aristo-
telian rhetoric, the enthymeme or rhetorical syllogism.

The third act of the *trivium* is logic or dialectic which
I interpret by an analogy to be the art of taking a reading of
the significance of the two former arts. Now Augustine makes
rhetoric the basic discipline. If I pursue the good concretely
as aimed at attaining the art of speaking well, I find a paradox
here, in that there must be a sense whereby in order to study
it as a student, I know what it is that I desire. Yet being a student, I do not know it. At the beginning of the process I do
not know how to speak well—so I may be said to love it (which
is what is meant by "student") but in terms of what I do not
know I pursue it, following the hint of those things I do know.

Having fulfilled its function, rhetoric may have two different vectors: it may be pointed downward and even implicate
the sophists using it for victory, and may even be used to
deceive; or it may be pointed by an upper vector. To move
an audience by a sermon may point us upward to the *sum-
mum bonum* which is God. Now then, there is an eternal structure, as was indicated by the distinction of numbers numbered
and numbers numbering. This structure is above, transcending
our finite minds, but present to them *ab initio.* On the phenomenal level, action consists in the possibility of modifying
particular things. In contemplation, we rise above particular
things—all in relation to the eternal structure, which is ultimately to be discovered in the mind of God. In morality, to
pursue good is to pursue the eternal basis in which there is
a proper subordination to the final end: love of God. This
brings us to Augustine's distinction of using and enjoying what
we ought to enjoy, and where there is a proper subordination to the final end. Short of it, body and soul are to be used
for a further end in opposition to what stands in the way of
a proper love that is the eternal basis. Particular formations
and patterns control bodies but may be used for a further end.

There is, therefore, a series of intermediate steps prepar-
atory to the ultimate end, which is an immediate perception.
Knowledge is not a series of propositions. Theology is not a
theoretic science, as in Aristotle, but an affective science, full
of love and unction. What is called by St. Anselm a demonstration, is in Augustine manuductive. We cannot prove anything directly, but there is a leading of the mind by the hand,
by means of an analogy in which knowledge in itself is a perception. The supposition underlying knowledge is what today we call presupposition, which is preparation for the immediate perception. In all this there is a proportion, an ordering
of terms. Here, though, it is generally true that in analogy all
the terms are heterogeneous, but the relation is one of identity. This illustrates the question of how finite creatures can
know God, who is infinite. Mediately, it is a problem of the
known by a series of analogical steps. This is where Augustine goes to the known object—the triune God—a trinity of
appropriated quality: first, shadows; then, traces or footprints
(vestiges). At first, there are vague indications; then on the level
of any animal, we get specification by three causes and can

differentiate the traces of the trinity, where causal efficacy is manifested. Finally, we have the image (as in "God created man in his image"), namely, the image in which God is the object and the human soul is not merely an impression on the soul, but a return upon God, where the faculty is the unifying principle, unifying knowledge and its object, in which we have the soul's awareness of its identity. A person's image can then reflect on the trace, and by seeing this trace become self-active. In this self-activity we have a mark of a higher step in the hierarchy.

Shadows are those things that are seen under circumstances that recall God, but in the animal kingdom we have a unity of organization and animation. In the animal kingdom the highest image is that which is proper to humans. So for shadows we have inanimate things: e.g., a stone which does not live and thus has no sense perception. For the animal we have traces, but for humans we have image.

The soul is primarily active located in a world of sensible objects, and looks out on material objects. At the beginning of the process there is no knowledge, but the soul knows itself partially where there is recognition of the mind because of contact with and activity upon the external world. Then it gradually knows itself, and the more it knows itself it loves itself and better discovers the existence of unchanging things. Then the mind emerges into a series of relations when it begins to know itself, and this process points to an interior teacher in which the previous external sensible world becomes internalized and can be subjected to the internal master as its judge and moderator.

If imitation is the broader term and more specifically is the image of God made in God's likeness, then what is imitated is something eternal and changeless and therefore has perfection—then God both is and is perfect. But does God exist? That is not the prior question. Rather, what does existence mean? Then we have at least the order of mere subsistence; stones and animals have that mode of being and the physical human has at least that existence. Since the person also lives, one has the power of sensing and understanding; and the higher level presupposes the lower, and the person exists as well as has sensibility and understanding. Thus we have imitation of the top by something down below. Or to look at it another way, imitation of the creator by creatures is a product of God's creative activity. Next follows a methodological question. What kinds of things are imitations? Human actions are imitations of the good and bad. The relevant method is one of platonic dialectics that entail not a myopic or cyclopean way of looking at things, but one of plurisignificance—being able to look at the same thing from different standpoints.

The principle is what God *did,* just as in imitation we have something like that relation of a child to a parent, a reflection in a mirror. But there are likenesses that are not images; footprints are such likenesses. Only the human being is an image, but being an image does not make one co-equal to God in perfection, else we would have heresy. The person can only approximate God and gain a greater degree of perfection as one's mind is elevated and ennobled by actions that are *honesta* rather than utile. But even these by themselves are not to be enjoyed but are to be used in that elevation. An example of such elevation is common sense as distinguished from the proper senses. External sense is oriented to particular objects that have private validity. Take the sense of vision—it is externally related only to color as its object. For example, if I put down a piece of chalk on a table, I look at and I know I can see it. But if I look at a direction away from the table I do not see it, and in looking in the direction away from it I see that I do not see it. This is a reflective act, above the material sensibility which has only a private validity.

Augustine's dialogue on music is in five books. The first four books discuss the nature of music. In book five, the question is "How can we know music at all?" Take a bar of music or a line of verse—*"deus creator omnium."* How does it exist? It exists on several levels, each of which has been treated as its basic concern. 1) It exists in air as a kind of motion. 2) It exists on my lips as I pronounce it. 3) It exists in my ears as I hear it. 4) It exists in my memory as I recall it. 5) It exists in my judgment as I estimate it. At a concert, as I apprehend the tones they disappear, yet I can apprehend them in the context of the whole pattern of tonality. I have moved upward.

Now common sense is such an example. It finds its place above what is an exclusively consumable process, as in the digestion and assimilation of food as subject to the operation of enzymes. Once eaten, the food is mine and is not reversible and not available to other consumers. We talk of productivity and consumption today in economics. The "goods" are limited to that sphere. Yet economic knowledge is on a higher level. But when it comes to judging we must presuppose a region in which we can think of "goods" as Plato talks about the Good which is the measure of different modes of satisfaction, of which the above is merely one (e.g., how to solve a mathematical equation or a moral or artistic problem). In looking at a beautiful church steeple, two responses are possible to it as an object. If I want to take a look I may jostle others to get the best position and push others out of the way; I put myself thereby into an acquisitive society. Or else, I may avoid jostling by waiting to move into another position and hope to get a universal perspective.

This is in the region of common sense as a communal sense so that what at first was a conversation, which horizontally was a dual monologue (as in Leibnitz's windowless monads), transports us into a nonphenomenal level in which we participate and thereby can move down and bring about a universal communicability. It is such a participation which I believe has taken place in me and my friend Karl Olsson, whose birthday I join in celebrating, in virtue not of something that happened to us, but of what we are—participants in the supreme good which is God.

Befriending in God's Name
Preface to a Missionary Theology of
God as Friend

Jean C. Lambert

Members of The Evangelical Covenant Church share an historic
"name" with a handful of other Christians for whom "friend"
has been a primary self-description. With the name, they also
share a silence. Their theologies, like those of the wider church,
include scant reflection on the implications of calling the
Divine "Friend," or of describing themselves, in the words
of the Covenant confirmation textbook, as "God's friends."
Yet this way of describing the divine-human relation has a wide
use in the church, as reflected not only in many biblical texts
but also in hymns.[1]

What may it mean to name as "Friend" the Holy, whom
the heavens cannot hold nor earth contain? What may it mean
for human beings to call ourselves God's friends? Particularly
important since we call ourselves an evangelical people, a people committed to Christ's mission in the world: does our sense
of the friendship of God influence our interpretation of evangelism, and of mission? This essay is a preliminary sketch of
"a theology" of the friendship of God. In the first part I
identify some of the "extended family" who—like Mission
Friends—might have developed such a comprehensive theological perspective, but did not. In the second section I present one contemporary theologian's experiment with "friend"
as a model for language about God. And in the third I propose a few key affirmations around which to develop a more
thorough account of God's friendship, and of the missionary
invitation and challenge it extends to Jesus' disciples.

I. Family Connections

By the name "friends" Covenanters are linked at least super-

ficially with "The Religious Society of Friends" who began
in seventeenth-century England and have more commonly
been called Quakers. It also links Covenanters to "The Friends
of God," a late medieval lay movement in the area around
Strasbourg in Alsace.[2]

A. *Characteristics*

A brief glance at some shared characteristics of the three
groups indicates that the links are not entirely superficial, and
offer starting points for theology.

Source of Knowledge of God. Some continuities pertain
to valuing personal experience of the Divine. Covenant forebears in the nineteenth century called themselves "Mission
Friends" and meant that they were people who had experienced the friendship of Jesus Christ and were committed to
sharing the news of this possibility with others through both
word and deed. A Mission Friend was one who recognized
that he or she had been befriended by Jesus, and who in turn
both celebrated this common status and sought to extend it
by "befriending" Christ's mission: inviting someone to come
to new life through repentance of sin and personally experienced faith in Jesus, and joining to share that new life with
other friends in the fellowship.[3]

Among Quakers and the Alsatian Friends—no less than
among the Mission Friends—the term "friends" had a directly
personal content. Quakers were friends to each other because
of the inner light they believed all human beings shared, awareness of which God had granted them. Believing that there is
something of God in every person, that this light warrants the
deepest respect despite any evil that might be obscuring it,
the Friends felt particularly connected to each other; "this is
that cement whereby we are joined as to the Lord, so to one
another," wrote Robert Barclay in *An Apology for the True
Christian Divinity* early in the movement.[4]

The literature of the Friends of God expresses the movement's passionate affiliation with Christ "The Friend." Rufus
Jones describes them not as a sect but as a "type of Christianity" that came to articulation in a "prophet class" of the four-
teenth century.[5] This movement appears to have been less communal and corporate than either the Mission Friends or the
Religious Society of Friends, and to have pursued a spiritual-

ity of individual, though practical and world-touching, mysticism. Alsatian Friends sought direct, experiential knowledge of God, spoke with God "face to face" in ecstasy, and cultivated a hidden life of humility and renunciation of worldly pleasures and temptations, rejoicing in anonymity and in being "captives" of the Lord.[6]

Validity of Knowledge of God. Besides their emphasis on a personal experience of God, fruit of an inner capacity for relationship true of both God and humanity, the three historical expressions are linked also by their confidence that the spiritual presentness of God in Christ is a certain guide to truth, and must be experienced by the believer for salvation really to have come to him or her.

It is true that the Mission Friends came to faith—corporately and historically—through personal, communal, and devotional study of the Scriptures. In their twentieth-century offspring, The Evangelical Covenant Church, these Friends have continued to give fairly consistent programming emphasis to corporate Bible study, and officially describe the Bible as "the only perfect rule for faith, doctrine, and conduct."[7] At the same time they value the Bible, however, Friends/Covenanters seem to have agreed to work in confidence that rests beyond the text of the Word, in God who dwells spiritually in the believer by faith. Delight in experience, even surpassing their profound respect for the written word, is richly expressed in some of the hymns emerging from the early days of the Mission Friends, where a primary title or descriptor of God is "Friend." Nils Frykman wrote two of these that are translated in *The Covenant Hymnal* of 1973. In number 283, his hymn about the power of the Word in Scripture, he begins: "The highest joy that can be known, By those who heav'nward wend—It is the Word of Life to *own,* And God to have as friend . . . " (emphasis mine).[8] The highest joy is not knowledge of Scripture, or even assurance of salvation from sin and death, but rather "owning"—presumably, making the Word part of oneself—and personally knowing God as friend.

Similarly, in hymn 416, praise that traces Jesus' atoning action on behalf of humankind, Frykman writes: "I have a friend who loveth me, He gave his life on Calvary; Upon the cross my sins he bore, And I am saved forevermore. O hallelujah, he's my friend! . . . "[9] Of course, the friend one meets

is the friend introduced through Scripture as having died for
one's sins. But the joy lies not merely in that scriptural deliverance (as in Anna B. Warner's text, hymn 612, "Jesus loves
me! This I know, for the Bible tells me so") but in the experienced, present reality of walking with the friend, an experience in principle available to everyone. The Friends of the four-
teenth century and the Religious Society of Friends likewise
held in tension inner and external authority.

The Friends of God adopted an expression that had been
used 200 years before by Bernard of Clairvaux—*ausgewählter
Gottesfreund,* "chosen friend of God" or "special friend of
God"—and made it descriptive of the soul "elevated through
Christ out of slavery into the friendship and sonship (*kindschaft*) of God."[10] Interpreter Rufus Jones holds, however, that
their sense of this friendship was mystical, and related closely
to the teachings of Henry Suso, whose dates overlap those of
the Friends' major writer, Rulman Merswin (fl. 1367). Jones
quotes Suso to illustrate this dimension of the Friends' experience:

> God and man should be wholly united, so that it
> can be said of a truth that God and man are one.
> This cometh to pass on this wise: where the truth
> always reigneth, so that true perfect God and true
> perfect man are at one, and man so giveth place to
> God, that God Himself is there, and this same unity
> worketh continually, and doeth or leaveth undone,
> without any I or me or mine—behold there is Christ
> and nowhere else.[11]

Yet, while embracing religious experience as delivering
true knowledge of God, the Friends of God remained loyal
to the Roman church and accepted its disciplines and definitions, while at the same time seeking a larger role for and recognition of lay Christians who had experienced the spiritual
friendship of God and knew themselves and each other, therefore, in fresh and freer ways. One might argue that whereas
among Mission Friends the Scriptures functioned both as vehi-
cle for meeting the risen Christ and as guide to discernment
of the Spirit, among the Friends of God it was the rites and
definitions of the Roman church that filled these functions.
Neither were willing to settle for subjective feelings as guides

to life. Yet, the present reality of God as "Friend" was for both the source of confidence, life, and joy.

A comparable situation exists among Quakers, as records of their meetings show. When the Religious Society of Friends refers to the Bible it is clear that for them it is a faithful articulator of God's truth. They appear to rely both on Scripture and on a corporate spiritual discernment to qualify possible errors or excesses of an enthusiastic individual. But Friends historian Howard Brinton quotes a remarkable statement to describe the Friends' reliance on experience in preference to Scripture: "To the illumined one who hath known the Indweller all the Sacred books are as useless as a reservoir in time of flood."[12]

The words Brinton quotes probably overshoot the mark for most Covenanters, who would be unlikely to say the word "useless" about the Bible in any spiritual context. But they are related in that Covenanters have typically wanted to listen for the word of Christ speaking *through* (not *as*) the biblical text. Without usually experiencing the Holy Spirit in a pentecostal way, Covenanters have been eager to discern and welcome the Spirit's guidance; specific biblical texts have not always been wrestled into service as though discernment needed justification. Indeed, there have been diverging opinions at Annual Meetings in recent years concerning the role "Biblical Position Papers" ought to play in the taking of particular policy positions.[13]

If one were to draw any implications from these similarities in name and ways of being faithful about actual historical connections among the groups, more substantial demonstration would be required. There are resonances, however, and an heir of the Mission Friends may recognize spiritual cousins, no matter how distant.[14]

B. *Absent Reflections*

Perhaps it is significant then that the three movements that share the use of "friend" to describe their affiliation with God and with each other, and that share a respect for the freedom of God's truth-bearing Spirit to "blow where it will," also have in common a silence. Typically they do not articulate reflection or analysis of the theology implicit in their language: not the Friends of God, not the Religious Society of Friends, not the Mission Friends/Covenanters. Those who might have been expected to do so have not.

Other Christians have generated some "theologies of friendship," usually pertaining to human relations, and explorations—particularly in sermons—of God as friend. The ideas have been "in the air" for millennia.[15]

Possible explanations for not developing them further may serve to caution us. We would respect the humility of the spiritual person before the mystery of God; or the intellectual diffidence of the unschooled people who initially constituted the majorities in these movements; or a believer's reluctance to make formal or verbal anything about the most intimate aspect of one's life. Nor would we wish to overlook the growing emphasis on empirical science and on correcting oppressive social structures that have preoccupied theologians in the nineteenth and twentieth centuries. The rational strictness of Kant and the empowering reason of Hegel led Christian theology in directions foreign to an interpretation of God as friend.

In addition, the language in which newly found personal faith expresses itself is often passionate and ecstatic, casting up profuse images as the soul struggles to find words for the experience. When the first heat of encounter has cooled, this language—far from recalling the beauty and power of the original impulse—may seem sentimental, awkward, at least inadequate. For example, Jones, commenting on the climate of the times in which the fourteenth-century "Friends" emerged, noted the political and economic troubles and the apocalypticism that characterized religious perspectives. At that time Jones said, "Every sensitive person was overwrought and strained."[16] How much more, if that were the case, might not the inheritors of their traditions find their language at best unclear.

Similarly, in a 1953 article about the beginnings of the Mission Friends/Covenanters, Karl A. Olsson alludes to such a phenomenon, speaking about the contrasting influences on Covenant hymns: formal Lutheran hymnals and the "sentimental mood of songbooks influenced by Moravian and Wesleyan piety." After illustrating from a couple of explicitly bloody hymn texts, he speaks of a later "process of sobering up the hymnody."[17]

Any theologian who does try to speak both authentically

and responsibly about powerful personal religious experience and its influences in forming new groups of Christians, might understandably reach for language more pre-refined, weather-beaten, and tamed. A theologian who writes of God as Friend needs to use care to avoid language that trivializes or distorts through emotional excess. Whatever the reasons, the intimate and assuring relational possibilities of "friend" language have remained unarticulated in a comprehensive doctrine of God. Likewise, such a theology's implications for mission have remained tacit.

II. A Contemporary Model

A. *Shifting Power: Without to Within*

Theologian Sallie McFague recently published a genuinely fresh approach to language about the Holy. In *Models of God* (Philadelphia: Fortress Press, 1987) she seeks to offer an appropriate theological approach for "an Ecological, Nuclear Age." Our age needs a saving God no less than any other, she says, but she is convinced that a message of salvation for us must deal with our concrete enemies: threats of ecological and nuclear disaster.

As context for her own suggestions, she criticizes the standard Christian theological model of God the Monarch: God as King. In so doing, she recognizes that her own concerns are part of a larger chorus of voices dissenting from hierarchical and power-preoccupied models of God—among them those of feminists and Third World liberationists—as well as from the theologies developed to warrant them.

In the first part of her book McFague probes the conceptual root of the problem, kingship, the guiding metaphor that gives direction to standard theologies and on which they are founded, though often implicitly. Specifically she finds that constructing theology around a primary image of God as King, as Monarch, undergirds an enculturated bias in people toward seeing God as "other" and as "power over" the world, the world from which God is disconnected. In an ecological and nuclear age—a time when human interference with the basic natural systems of the earth threatens to destroy them, thereby making the entire human race homeless or extinct—she finds these biases dangerous. They have encouraged humanity to see the world as ultimately alien from God, as unrelated to God, and therefore available for human exploitation. They have led us to interpret Genesis 1 as a warrant for exploitation rather than a challenge to stewardship. They have primed generations of theologians to understand God as able to affect the world only from without. God the king is not here, she notes, and any salvation he offers is one that reconciles humanity to his alien ways, ultimately in another world, not this one. Moreover, the model of God as king undermines humans' self-esteem and motivation to take responsibility for our own ecological and nuclear interventions.

> It is a powerful imaginative picture and . . . has resulted in what Gordon Kaufman calls a pattern of "asymmetrical dualism" between God and the world, in which God and the world are only distantly related and all power, either as domination or benevolence, is on God's side. It evokes feelings of awe and . . . supports the "godness" of God, but these feelings are balanced by others of abject fear and humiliation: in this picture, God can be God only if we are nothing.[18]

As an alternative to the alienated and alienating monarchical model she proposes taking a different root metaphor, picturing the world as God's body. We can understand images of "internal relatedness" like this one, she says, from our own experience of being at once bodied and yet capable of self-transcendence. Through this metaphor too we may then more clearly see how God's commitment to the earth proposes a salvation large enough for all creatures—including but not restricted to the human ones. Or, putting it more apocalyptically, the model of "God as embodied in the world" encourages human beings to regard ecological and nuclear disaster as enemies not only of ourselves but also of God, and as part of the evil addressed by God's salvation.

McFague's goal is not an attempt to make a new idol of God in an image suitable to the needs of twentieth-century persons so that we may find new, escapist pseudo-solutions to our human problems. As a Christian she is faithful in reminding the reader of the metaphorical character of theologizing. Rather, according to my restatement of her purpose, she hopes that by finding and assembling lost bones of the gospel's message about God and the divine matrix in which human life is lived, and by clothing these bones in the flesh of a fresh vision, she may introduce contemporary believers to the divine Companion who can motivate and empower human beings to take their share of responsibility for the earth, that is, to participate fully in God's salvation.

McFague's methodological section is careful and persuasive, though surprisingly compact. In it she explains how a model of the world as God's body need not be a "pantheism" and why she believes personal, agential language about God is still strongest and most appropriate for a discussion of the Holy and the way God offers salvation. It concludes with a proposal of three personal and agential metaphors for use in her alternative model of God: God as mother, as lover, and as friend. Their implications she sketches in the second part of her book where each of the three is shown to model "different aspects of God's one love, the destabilizing, non-hierarchical, inclusive love of all."[19]

B. *God as Friend*

As McFague muses on the ambiguous term "friend" as applicable to human relations, she also suggests its applicability to relations of human beings with God. Despite its positive human associations, in Christian circles *philia* has often been seen as inferior to *agape.* "God has no favorites," the saying runs, so God's love cannot be compared to "mere" *philia.* She draws tacitly on a vast and mostly premodern literature concerning friendship, concluding that today it is "a primary (though perhaps, for many, dormant) human relationship" and asks what understanding of friendship is most relevant as a model of God.[20]

She notes that the Scriptures "on Jesus as friend" have a definite character and are "mutually egalitarian."[21] She cites Matthew 11:19 ("friend of tax collectors and sinners") and John 15:12-15 ("I call you no longer servants but friends."). These are significant, especially as we apply them to God-human relations. Yet, friendship has particular complexity and mystery, she believes, that are lacking in the more clearly definable relations of mother-child and lover-beloved. She asks: what sort of divine love does the model suggest? What does it say about existence in the world? "Brief answers," she replies, "are *philia,* or sustaining, and companionship."[22] She notes that most basically friendship is the bonding of two people "by free choice in a reciprocal relationship."[23] Though we may give the name "friendship" to certain relations that are useful or one-sided, we recognize friendship's fundamental meaning as "affection and trust," as Immanuel Kant says.[24]

Paradoxes emerge from this primary definition.[25] First, in a free relationship a bonding occurs. By virtue of free choice, a chosen loss of freedom results, with affection and loyalty giving the freedom of mutual responsibility to the relationship a priority of value, replacing the absolute freedom of the individual. Loyalty is so fundamental in friendship that friends refuse to "open the door, even a crack, to the enemy."[26]

Second, in a relation of two individuals, an inclusive element is implied. Friends' "posture"—unlike lovers'—is not primarily face to face but side by side, absorbed in a common interest, either external or internal. She speaks of the "common vision" uniting Yahweh and Israel, the covenant that held promise for them both. While friendship is the result of choice (I choose you/we choose each other), it is the nature of side-by-side bonding not to be exclusive. It admits of including others, as hands clasp hands and form additional relationships. "The friends who join together in common vision . . . can be not only numerous, but also different."[27] Thus, according to McFague's understanding, friendship bonds are not exclusive to "equals" any more than to "like minds." Neither equality nor gender-identity (which were criteria for friendship according to classical definitions) pertain, nor do the elitist results.

> Friendship is, then, potentially the most inclusive of our loves, for though in its purest form it is highly particular (involving a unit of two), its other can be anyone. Moreover, if all life, including both subhuman and divine life, is basically relational, then in some extended sense, we can be friends across ontological barriers as well. We can be friends with other forms of life in our world—and we can be friends with God. In sum, from its base in the bonding of two by free choice, friendship, rather than being necessarily an exclusive, individualistic, and

elitist relationship, is potentially inclusive in a number of ways. In fact, because it is the freest of all our primary relationships, it has the capacity to be the most inclusive: we can choose to be friends with any other.[28]

Third, in a relationship supposedly "for" children insofar as it need not be complicated by sexual passion, adult characteristics are required. Responsibility must be taken on both sides: "a strong case can be made that of the three primary relationships [mother-child, lover-beloved, and friend-friend] it is the most adult."[29] She understands "adult" not in the sense of independence but in the sense of responsible relatedness, working for mutual fulfillment.

In summary, she says that the first character of God's love as friendship, *philia,* is sustenance—the joy of all forms of life as companions (from *compania,* the sharing of bread with another) who are united with one another and with the source of life. From this issues the community formed by God as friend, where meals are shared.

> It suggests that communities identified with God as friend are not just marginally or occasionally concerned with economics but centrally and continually. The partners in the *koinonia* are *oikonomoi,* economists, involved in the just administration and distribution of goods and services. Moreover, if the *koinonia* is understood to include not just like-minded human beings but all human beings, and not just human beings but all life, the serious ecological dimensions of such communities become evident.[30]

A second character of God's love as friendship is companionship, out of which, McFague says, emerges a community of care and an ethical approach relevant both to human and non-human creatures. She articulates her idea here by offering reflections on prayer.

> We ask God, as one would a friend, to be present in the joy of our shared meals and in the sufferings of the strangers; to give us courage and stamina for the work we do together; to forgive us for lack of fidelity to the common vision and lack of trust in

divine trustfulness. Finally, we ask God to support, forgive, and comfort us as we struggle together to save our beleagured planet, our beautiful earth, our blue and green marble in a universe of silent rock and fire.[31]

McFague does not offer a systematic theology based on her models and cautions throughout the book that readers remember they are dealing with metaphors, albeit with appropriate ones, for disorienting and reorienting thought about and relation with God.

C. *McFague's "Salvation" and a Call to Mission*

The salvation of God is offered the world through Jesus, McFague says, who shows us God as friend, and invites us to become part of a fellowship of friends who are called to befriend the world as God has befriended us. While salvation includes people, it is not restricted to the human realm. She invites us to meditate also on

> plants, animals, objects, places . . . cherished aspects of our world—and dwell upon the specialness . . . until the pain of contemplating their permanent loss . . . to all, for all time, becomes unbearable. This is a form of prayer for the world as the body of God. . . . This prayer, though not the only one in an ecological, nuclear age, is a necessary and permanent one. The prayer we wish to pray . . . of thanksgiving for the joyful feast in the presence of God, depends upon accepting responsibility for our beautiful, fragile earth, without which there will be no bread and no wine.[32]

Thinking of God's salvation in Jesus Christ being offered "to all" comes easily to Covenanters. That is the clear purpose of evangelism, missions, church planting, Christian education, pastoral care, the clear reason for establishing colonies of missionaries throughout the world—indeed, of being the Church. But "all" has not often meant "all creatures"; it is hard enough for any of us to include all people. McFague's critique of Christian insensitivity to "the non-human world" as an arena for ethical activity certainly can be applied to Covenanters, and thereby suggests a direction for dramatic expansion of our Covenant sense of mission. Covenant hymnody reflects our forebears' heart-intuition of the friendship of God, and with it a synchrony of appreciation with McFague's discussion. Many of us have tasted God's friendship for ourselves and have been careful to let God's friendship inform our personal relationships within the family and among our friends and fellow Christians in the church, and even in one-to-one relationships with those outside this circle. We have only infrequently allowed our confidence in it to guide our ways of forming policy and of doing business, in either the church or in the world; to inform our use of the world's natural resources; to inform our corporate "positions" about national or global political and economic issues. Remarkably, as I have said, we have not even much used it to guide our thinking and speaking about God, our theologizing.

In the third part of this essay I articulate some theological affirmations that grow for me from this intuition and experience of God as friend, and suggest how they might guide our theological reflection. Particularly I focus on broad topics in theology that pertain directly to the Church's call to be in mission: *faith,* particularly the process of coming to faith; *the gospel* itself, particularly communicating the gospel as faith seeks to reach out; and *doctrine,* what it is faith wants new friends to understand about God, themselves, and the world.

I would formulate the overall question for the next section, then, in this way. Given that "a missionary theology" is faith's word about extending (technically, about sending) the salvation of God into the world to any who may be able to respond, what has God's friendly call to be friends to do with the sending of salvation? How does our self-understanding as those who have been befriended by God the Friend guide our efforts to bring new persons into that relationship?

III. A Proposal

A. *Jesus and One Whose Name Was Legion: Faith*
"No one is fearless when it comes to being alone." The story of our human situation could begin that way and continue with a phenomenology of fear and solitude. Or, it could begin: "Nothing in the universe got to be itself all by itself."

Such a beginning might lead to cosmological speculation.

Instead of either, I begin autobiographically with a woman alone on a rock, in the dark. No, better, a woman on a rock who imagines herself to be alone. The rock feels or does not: the woman does not care. She is filled with fears; they send her thoughts racing in random motion, and the thoughts gather data—possibilities, facts, memories, feelings—that fuel the fears, which grow stronger.

She knows of no one who cares what she may experience, so she does not dare to experience it herself. She keeps it all from touching her at her core; she uses most of her energy reciting mentally: "They said. It's not my fault. I can't help it. It isn't my responsibility. Don't blame me. They do what they want to. They never ask me." Sometimes a surge of anger or pain or sadness rises momentarily. She fears giving in. If she isn't strong who will take care of her? She pushes the surge aside, growing cold and tired.

In the dark a stranger approaches. "May I sit there with you on the rock?" The woman is not sure the apparition is even there. She ignores it. It stands there and later asks again. It seems to care about her opinion at least in this respect. She notices that. Later she nods, almost imperceptibly.

Now there are two on the rock, in the dark. The woman is tense. She doesn't speak. The stranger sits with her in the long darkness. She begins to think about the one on the other side of the rock, and wonders whether or not fears preoccupy over there as well. She wonders what the person is doing there. She doesn't ask.

"I'll be going," the stranger says. "Thanks for letting me sit with you. I'll look for you again."

In some way such as this the Christ found this lost creature of God, and kept finding and building a conversation until a relationship of mutual recognition was woven, like a rope-bridge slung across a chasm. It was not until other conversations with other strangers had developed, and one of them expressed doubt or criticism of the Stranger-Christ, that I found myself defending him, and in the process valuing myself. Then I began to suspect the truth. In my nascent awareness of loyalty to him, I discovered he had made me his friend.

Friendship, as it turns out, entails more than predawn silences in rocky places. There is continual conversation in

which attitudes and actions inimical to the friendship are identified and grief-marked for future reference. These lead gradually to a revision of life. There are moments of delighted discovery, in which the Christ allows one to know him, as well
as carefully accepting what one hesitantly discloses. There are
moments of gasping terror, as the reality of who he is opens
a previously unknown vacuum in one's being. Most signifi-
cantly, perhaps, friendship with Jesus Christ gradually leads
to "dawn," to light shed on the whole world—first pale, then
more brightly—until discernment becomes possible. The neighbors on other rocks, so to speak, become visible, along with
sky and land, and one begins to feel connections with them
and to accept them as related to oneself.

Withdrawing is replaced by reaching out, fear by curiosity,
self-defense by acceptance of responsibility, and of affection
and forgiveness. A phrase philosopher Alfred North Whitehead
used to describe the process of creativity in the world describes
the unifying and self-transcending events that have taken place:
"The many become one, and are increased by one."

When Jesus confronted the man whose name was Legion,
in Mark 5, he chose to deal with the troops of occupying alien
forces within him by "driving them out" into a herd of swine.
In my experience he introduced them to each other and they
began to work together as cooperative parts of myself. Perhaps
that is why the metaphor of "befriending" appeals to me as
descriptive of how God works in the soul. For some such
reasons, it seems appropriate to me to describe Christian life
as friendship with God in Jesus Christ which brings unity and
harmony to the disoriented self, thereby enabling relations
with other people and the world. Fruits of the relationship
are freedom to love and to take responsibility in the world
as fellow-creature and friend of any who will likewise take
the risks friendship requires.

A range of experiences such as I report is the actual base
for any Christian's theologizing, I believe. The particulars of
each person's isolation are different, and the Stranger—precisely because the action is one of befriending—approaches each
in a way responsive to that particular person. The pattern is
illustrated in the New Testament, which can help a twentieth-
century person recognize it. Jesus meets a woman at the well
(John 4:7ff) or fishers beside a lake (Matthew 4:18ff). He en-

counters a skeptic under a fig tree, or an untouchable in a crowd (John 1:45ff, Mark 5:25ff). He goes to visit a social pariah in his home (Matthew 9:9, Luke 19:2ff). Whether the encounter is objectively one to one, or a matter of converse with a host of observers, Jesus calls forth persons' loyalty to himself in the process of embodying his own loyalty to them—to their questions, fears, hesitations, enthusiasms, high spirits, futures.

The conviction grows in those who meet Jesus that in encountering him they are meeting someone who is more to them than just another son of Adam. "What sort of man is this?" (Matthew 8:27). "When the disciples saw it they marveled . . . " (Matthew 21:20). "He told me all that I ever did . . . " (John 4:29). "I will follow you . . . " (Matthew 8:19). Their reflection eventually leads them to see in him the fulfillment of ancient promises come to them from the Holy One, by means of prophets. Their reflected experience leads them to assent to the astonishing words uttered of him by a few of the poets and preachers among them: Son of David; Son of God; the Lord; the Anointed One; God (Mark 10:48, Matthew 4:33, Matthew 8:21, Matthew 16:16, John 20:28). They do not use language like "Source of life" but they have heard of an ancient being who rejoiced with God in the creation of the world, and call Jesus, "The Word who was with God . . . through whom all things were made" (John 1:3). They do not speak of "meaning giver" but they believe that they have moved from blindness to sight, from being lost to being found (1 Peter 2:25). They remember his own words, and make sure they will continue to be remembered. Thus we are able to read (John 15:12-15 and Mark 15:19):

> This is my commandment, that you love one another as I have loved you. Greater love has no man than this, that a man lay down his life for his friends. You are my friends if you do what I command you. No longer do I call you servants, for the servant does not know what his master is doing; but I have called you friends, for all that I have heard from my Father I have made known to you.

> Go home to your friends and tell them how much the Lord has done for you, and how he has had mercy on you.

When I read these texts I sense between the friend who met me in my isolation and these Galileans a harmony, a resonance. I believe we have come to trust the same friend.

When a person has this kind of fundamental encounter that leads to a sense (however inchoate) of the friendship of God, all models or doctrines of God must, I think, be "felt" as qualified by the power of this experience. It might be a positive influence or a negative one. One might say, "Yes! That is how God in Christ is!" Or one might object, as Paul did when writing to the Ephesians: "You did not so learn Christ!" (4:20). Missional theology begins with reflection on the friendship God has established with the one doing the theology.

B. *Good News: the Gospel*

The gospel comes to awareness only, so far as we know, in human beings. For us it is news of the friendship extended to us by the Source of life in all the astonishing fullness of that divine self-disclosure in Jesus. It is the news that God's friendship is meant not only for us but for all creation.

The focus of the prophetic word on human beings, even in an expression of hope for all creation, such as Isaiah 11, should not beguile us into thinking humanity any better loved by God than any other creature. When the "shoot from the stump of Jesse" is imagined there, deciding with equity for the meek of the earth, and when the wolf and lamb dwell together, and the leopard with the goat, and the young of cow and bear lie down together, and "they shall not hurt nor destroy in all my holy mountain" because "the earth shall be full of the knowledge of the Lord," all of this is good news not just for humanity but for all the creatures.

McFague has done us a good service by noting the inclusive character of friendship, though it may add complexity. Potentially no one need be left out. The fact that we humans cannot now imagine nourishing ourselves without preying on some other life, or living at all without "destroying" water and air and soil in some respects, does not change the prophecy. At least we can read it as hope that earth's life may—through the fulfillment of God's salvation—reflect wholeness, harmony, the lively interplay of beings in which all are challenged and excited and fulfilled without the destruction of any.

This vision is what biblical writers called *shalom,* and the

vision of this possibility inclines this theologian to wish song-
writer Joel Blomqvist had thought a bit differently when he
wrote the wonderful hymn which is number 81 in *The Covenant Hymnal,* "Praise the Lord, All Praise and Blessing." After
expressing praise for stars, earth, seas, microbes ("smallest
creature"), angels ("highest being"), he writes: "Yet of all that
God created Man to him most precious is: O what wonderful
devotion, How it fills my heart with bliss! With a childlike
joy I sing Praises to my God and King!" In light of the inclusive
friendship of God about which McFague reminds us, it may
be questionable whether human beings are, indeed, "most precious" to God of all creatures. The question, at least, can dis-
suade us from carelessness as we manage/use/manipulate/
deplete the rest of earth's creatures. The gospel is good news
for the world, which—after all—John 3:16 has always taught
us God loved so much that he gave his only begotten Son to
redeem it.

All of this leads us away from theological perspectives that
begin with the concept of God as sovereign Monarch, and proceed to variations on the theme of Jesus Christ as King. Three
"movements" may be seen to mark such a theological shift
as it might apply to a theology of our mission among fellow
human beings. Much could be said about each. Here I will only
sketch the direction of each "move."

1) *Instead of gearing all energies to getting a message
told, a missionary's primary call is to establish relationships.*

Relationship is the *substance* of the gospel, not merely
the context for its communication. The goal for mission is not
that a person be able to say the right words, or that one's thinking be changed so as to give mental assent to the right ideas,
or even that one align oneself with "fellow believers," however valuable and important all these things turn out to be.
The primary purpose for Christian mission is to introduce
others to the Friend and help them experience God's friendship calling them into loyalty, as the missioner has first been
called.

A Christian does not make friends in order to buy a hearing for a verbal message. Rather, a Christian makes friends
because God has made friends, and he or she understands that
"friendly" is the mysterious secret of the love of God in the
world. Friendship among people is, at best, the mirror into

which we can look to see God reflected—just there, in front of the glare of our own faces. A Christian does not feed the hungry in order to make it possible for the fed to listen to a sermon. He or she feeds the hungry because they are hungry, and because God has fed us, and because the Christian, valuing the new life nurtured by God-given food, wants to share it.

I would not deny for a moment that people do come to friendship toward Christ through the work of the Salvation Army, for example, which typically "serves" a sermon as one course of each soup kitchen meal. Christ's love can reach us through anything, even the rock door of a tomb. But it is not a disservice to Jesus the Friend to serve the meal in his name and to let the love come wordlessly from the servers to the served.

In a missionary theology of God as Friend the categories of God's availability, trustworthiness, and responsiveness are important and relate to categories of human response including relationship, trust, and taking responsibility. These all supersede in importance categories of God's transcendence, credibility, and omnipotence calling forth awe, belief, and dependence.

As I understand it, this means that truth, for example, is no less a concern for a theology arising from a loyalty to God-the-Friend than it is for a theology propelled by commitment to God-the-Sovereign. However, in this perspective "truth" can never be mistaken for one or more propositions, and revelation can neither be identified with nor confined to a book. "Truth" is authenticity in relationship.

This understanding can inform scholarship, for example, by granting concern not only for accuracy in observation, integrity in reporting, and creativity in suggesting possible application, but also by granting a posture of openness, humility, and respect toward whatever is a subject for study. In fact, "the studied" must, in this view, always be "subject"; in a world where the Source of all is primarily known as "Friend" nothing can be merely object. Other applications may be drawn out in related ways.

Would such a theology change Covenant missionary practice? I think relatively little of present practice would be likely to change. As I understand what has been the practice in Covenant world missions during my lifetime, at least, the primacy of relationship-building over message-delivering has already been established. It is reflected not only in such bureaucratic terminology as "indiginization," and such economically "befriending" projects as those that characterize the Covenant mission in Thailand, but also in the warmly personal style of missionaries who escort groups of national Christians to North American Covenant gatherings where they may preach, testify, or simply "be with" the persons of the sending church. The theological approach I am advocating here adds a different interpretative perspective, however. It would put the statistical emphasis on what sometimes is known by pastors as "the prospect list" rather than on "members." Or better, it would find new ways to speak of the continuum of relationship in which persons are nurtured from acquaintance through friendliness to reliable loyalty which is also open to becoming a cultivator of friends on God's behalf.

   2) *Conversion ceases to be an accurate label for the still essential process of having one's life "turned around." Instead it might be better to think of "finding and being found."*

   Instead of seeking conversion expressible in assent to standard verbal formulae, the Christian in mission seeks, through becoming a friend, to elicit a response of affection and loyalty. This means loyalty not only to her- or himself, but also to the Friend in whose name she or he attends to the other, listening intently for the other to begin to let the true soul show. When the soul of the other becomes interested in the would-be friend, he or she may entrust such of his or her own "soul stuff" as their growing trust seems to warrant. There will be talk about the Friend, of course, according to ordinary human patterns in which one makes a friend aware of the existence of another and may introduce them. There will be loving mentions: "I wish you could meet"; memories of past interactions: "Once when I was in trouble. . . . " There will be study of Scripture and of subsequent Christian literature. There will be enthusiastic claims about how great this Friend is. We do it in ordinary conversation, though not always in the process of "witnessing." When the outsider resists, expresses skepticism, or reports bad previous experience with the One we know as Friend, the missioner informed by such an understanding will respond not with proofs or arguments but with personal protestations: "I haven't found it that way." "It is hard for me to respond because I want to respect your experience, but it is so different from mine."

It will be apparent to both friends when the Friend has become an experience they share. As their lifestyle and behavior come into conflict with each other and with each other's growing appreciation for the friendship of God, friends can learn from each other. They can learn to trust the Friend to lead each in the way appropriate to that person and to trust their friend's loyalty to their relationship to bring to light any troublesome aspects for mutual correction. "Conversion of life" can happen, in other words, leading to genuine discipleship, without bringing an alienating "external standard" to bear.

3) *Instead of responding to a commandment to "go and do unto," the missionary responds to, and offers, an invitation to come along and be with.*

There is probably no more frequently cited Scripture for motivating and setting the guidelines for the church's mission than Jesus' great commission in Matthew 28: "Go and make disciples of all nations, baptizing them in the name of the Father and of the Son and of the Holy Spirit, teaching them to observe all that I have commanded you." As I will be stating when I conclude this study, so I will insert here: I do not believe a theology of God as friend supercedes or invalidates all prior theologies. Thus, I am not asking Christians to pretend Jesus' words lack relevance for us, nor do I suggest that my words seeking to express Jesus' intent for his friends are better than his own. In offering an alternative to the words of Jesus' great commission I am, rather, calling attention to the mode of his presence and ministry among people, which sometimes appears to contrast with these words he said.

There is something lordly, masterful, commanding about the verbs in the great commission. Go! Make disciples! Baptize! Teach! Strongly motivating Jesus' disciples and the earliest centuries of Christians, the commands have acquired a shadow side, however, in the context of our highly patriarchal culture, developed as it has been in hierarchical, technological, and bureaucratic directions. To my ears, at least, the great commission has an "atmosphere," so to speak, that suggests power being applied "from the top down" and the "superior" doing

something to the "inferior." Are persons who know and love
the God they have met through Jesus Christ superior to those
who have not shared the experience? Are our neighbors—
whether in New York or New Guinea—inferior if they hold
different views and value different relationships? No matter
how foreign it is to the evangelistic style of many actual bearers of the gospel, it is no accident that disrespectful jokes about
masculine dominance in sexual intercourse refer to "the missionary position."

I do not propose that Jesus did not speak the words in
Matthew 28:19. But I would suggest that he did not himself
approach persons coercively, dominatingly, or dogmatically.
His authority did not take those forms. It could not, Jesus being
in the position he was as a wandering teacher whose views
were usually slightly out of synch with the orthodoxy of his
time. He lacked institutional backing to give his words coercive credibility. He was not rich, so he could not buy a hearing for his opinions. But all this was part, I believe, of the "theological point" of the way God chose to come among us in
Jesus, as well as of the way Jesus himself chose to be in his
presence and ministry. His authority to speak, his power, his
right to be recognized as Teacher, Master, and even Lord
emerged gradually in the awareness of the hearers and even-
tual disciples who were surprised to discover it.

They had responded to a simple invitation: "Come, follow
me." Only afterwards did they begin to grasp whom it was
they had followed, and whom they had come to love, trust,
and grant their loyalty. Covenanters will not need reminders
of these events: Jesus' invitation to the fishing brothers; his
invitation to all his disciples, in fact; his gentle and open-ended
conversations with the Samaritan woman at the well, the
woman taken in adultery, the sisters in Bethany; his humble
response to the centurion who himself used precisely the
"command" language when he besought Jesus for a cure for
his child, and Jesus (without either acquiescing in the Roman's
order-giving model or acting the "true teacher" by correcting
the Roman's understanding) accepted his expression as "faith"
and told him he could return home to find the child well.

Upon rising from death, Jesus gave clear examples of his
"style" of mission. He did not first show up where he knew
his inner circle would be gathered and instruct them to rally

the rest so he could announce the Truth to them all at once. Nor did he establish a school to make sure all of them "got it right" and could "teach it right." Rather, person by person, small group by small group, congregation by congregation, he "appeared." Sometimes, apparently, he said something and sometimes not. The remarkable incident recorded in Luke 24 is paradigmatic. He simply walks along with two who are already "on the way" (in both senses), and gradually restores them to awareness of his living, present friendship through the process of being with them, listening to their pain and grief, talking with them about the concern most heavy on their hearts, "applying Scripture to the wound," and eventually playing his familiar role with them at table.

No wonder they were moved to announce and proclaim, "He lives!" It is also not surprising, as I think of it, if some of Jesus' friends easily translated "It's too good to keep to ourselves" to "You must tell it and persuade." But this "must" business was not Jesus' demonstrated way, however commandingly he taught. For introducing people to God the Friend, invitation seems a method more harmonious with the desired end than an argument or any of the various forms of coercion.

C. *Glossing the Catechism:*
Notes Toward Development of Doctrine

Whether a systematic theology of God as Friend is a valuable possibility, a wrong road, or a contradiction in terms remains to be discovered through the shared work by many people over a period of years. Some indications may be given, however, as we begin to think together about directions in which doctrine may develop. I offer here thirteen short "glosses" on what I take to be our common memory of a shared theological tradition, which may serve as a kind of provisional dictionary of terms with which to develop a different kind of theological thinking.

1) GOD. God is knowable to human beings insofar as God gives godself to us to be known. Through experience of something real, generous, and strong, that defies adequate definition—experience mediated severally through the person of the human Jesus, through the Scriptures of the Hebrew and Christian Bibles, through fellowship with people, through our inner spiritual being, through the processes of nature and of human

society, ultimately through personal experience, however mediated—we come to know God as relation-maker, as free respecter of the freedom of creatures, as loyal to those with whom a mutually loving relationship has been forged, and as able at once to save, to give meaning to, and to knit into a fabric with others the lives of those who become "God's friends."

2) JESUS/CHURCH. Jesus was a human, a member of the centuries-old extended family of "friends of God" who were known as "Jews" by the time he was born. He accepted God's offer of friendship and was so formed in that relation that his life and ministry both embodied and made active among human beings God's character as Friend. His friendship to humankind was manifested in spending time with a small group of men and women whom he came to know intimately and whom he invited into his intimacy, such that they shared their bread, lives, and days. Through this association they learned a way of life guided by generosity, mutual service, mutual forgiveness; a way of response to God characterized by trust, love, and faithfulness; a way of response to others that respected their potential inclusion in the circle of God's friendship and sought to make clear and appealing to them their having been invited to join. They came to understand that Jesus had been chosen, anointed by God to make possible this relation and this fellowship of the friends, and therefore recognized Jesus as "the Anointed," "the Messiah," "the Christ" who had been promised. As their loyalty to him grew, it became effective in enabling others' friendly relation and loyalty to God, so that it became true—if somewhat peculiar—to say of them that they were "the body of Christ," a corporate continuation of Jesus' personal being on earth. This corporate continuation, the Church, "stands in for Jesus" after Jesus himself has ceased to be physically present.

3) HOLY SPIRIT. Holy Spirit is the personal presence of God on earth, in all times and places, guiding to fulfillment of God's purposes the creatures God has called to exist in freedom. Spirit's activity is sometimes maternal, sometimes paternal, by human standards; sometimes it is encouraging and sometimes preventive. Its mode of effecting change is not coercive, but invitational, and to all creatures—from subatomic particles through human beings to complex social- and eco-

systems—Spirit presents a possible course or possible courses of becoming and action that will, if followed, lead the creature toward the fulfillment God has purposed for it. This is the primary mode of "befriending" that characterizes God's action toward the world.

4) HUMANITY. Humanity is one among many of the classes of God's creatures, one in terms of which human beings cannot help but interpret everything else, from the simplest forms of creaturely existence to the uncreated simplicity of God's own self. In terms of ourselves we construct the metaphors by which we inevitably interpret everything else.

a) We feel ourselves to be "between" creatures, aware that we are very much "of the same stuff as our fellow earthlings" and yet having reasons that seem adequate to us to believe we can "transcend" them (and even ourselves) and view each and all from a position in some strange way "apart."

b) Taught by our immediate experience as well as our historical experience, which includes the Scriptures we hold sacred as well as those we do not, we know ourselves to be capable variously of both generosity and selfishness, of both actions we regard as "good" and those we regard as "evil." We also know that deciding to be faithful to the generous and the good—to be loyally "friendly" to our fellow creatures— is not sufficient to prevent our treating them at other times in the manner of an enemy.

c) We find our situation fundamentally frightening. We feel as though we should know who we are, and yet find ourselves continually oscillating between the soil and the stars, so to speak, between the roles of cherisher and destroyer. Most frightening, we cannot seem to help it. Though much of life comes to us as a blessing, enough comes as threat that we can never completely escape the fear that gnaws within.

5) SIN. Sin is at once a) an inner posture possible for human beings; b) a quality of action, perhaps for all creatures; and c) a condition into which creatures can "fall" and from which they can be rescued. Fundamentally, sin means being ruled by the fear described in paragraph 4(c) above, and thereby means disloyalty to God the Friend, whose friendship can replace fear with fundamental trust. Inwardly, sin means incapacity to trust God, and consequent flailing about seeking for somewhere else to place one's bedrock "existential" trust.

Actively, it means pretending by attitude and behavior that
one is not afraid, or straightforwardly failing to act because
of fear, following the two modes of action Reinhold Niebuhr
called "arrogance" and "sloth," often both at once. The one
pretends it is in control and fears nothing; the other pretends
it has no power or freedom and resists responsible action
entirely. As a condition, sin means much the same thing for
a human being as having the handbrake on does for an auto-
mobile: it is possible to move in that condition but it wears
on the engine and ultimately erodes the capacity to stop when
one decides to do so. Therefore, uncorrected sin becomes
self-perpetuating and stopping and starting over fresh eventually become impossible, short of a crash.

    6) GRACE. Grace is God's unbreakable loyalty to all crea-
tures, regardless of our own infidelities. It is shown by the
continuity in which God maintains the world, finding new
ways to maintain ecosystems despite creaturely interventions
that threaten them. It is shown by the forbearance of punishment that is characteristic of the world process, in which most
assaults by creatures on each other and on the fabric of life
that supports us result not in destruction of the assailant but
in opportunities to act the friend at a later time. It is shown
in the resources made available to individual and collective
victims of oppression, analogous to the stamina of the natural
order itself when under attack. Rape victims, for example, may
survive through their anger to turn to neighbors in love and
care rather than bitterness and hostility. Whole populations
who are ill-treated because of others' racism or economic
greed, sexism or political ambition survive through their time
of deprivation to offer new life to their fellow victims, and
even sometimes to former oppressors. Christians see grace
most clearly in God's restoration to life among his friends and
his former persecutors of Jesus the Christ, who—though he
had reason to abandon them all as inconstant or hopelessly
closed to offers of friendship—returned with loving presence
and with the invitation to widen the circle to include any who
would accept it.

    7) SALVATION. Salvation is the name human beings give
to what we believe is God's great hope for creation, given that
it is now ruled to such a large extent by the fears of human
beings. It is the hope of fulfillment for all beings despite this

fear, through a process of accepting the friendship of God as offered through Jesus the Christ, and of extending that "befriending" to fellow human beings and to other creatures until all the world is in harmony, in such manner perhaps as that imagined by the prophet Isaiah in chapter 11. It comes through "repentance of sin and acceptance of forgiveness" no less than it did in the "monarchical model of God's relation to the world." Here, though, salvation extends to those creatures who cannot, so far as we know, make a conscious "decision for Christ," and means the active befriending of all creatures by all creatures, in mutual respect and care according to their varying capacities and needs. Put simply, salvation is the process by which all creatures in their various ways know God and each other as friend, and are so known.

8) SANCTIFICATION. Sanctification is the intermediate stage between beginning to live by one's loyalty to God as Friend and the final salvation of all creatures. It is a stage characterized by growth in loyalty and faithfulness to God and to the world, and by being ever-more-open to include all God's "called friends" as one's own actual friends.

9) SACRAMENTS. Sacraments are deliberate actions that celebrate God's friendship toward the world. Chief among them are those that Jesus "consecrated" by performing them: the washing of each other's bodies; the sharing of food in his name; healing touch; and the forgiveness of sins. The first both symbolizes and actually conveys God's grace as cleansing from the sins of arrogance (none is superior to the other) and sloth (none need say there is nothing of value she or he needs to do for the other). The second both symbolizes and actually conveys God's grace as continually offering life and fellowship regardless of human disloyalty to the Friend of friends. The third both symbolizes and actually conveys God's grace as removing barriers to health in the body and spirit, and uniting the broken fragments into wholeness once more. The fourth both symbolizes and conveys God's grace as restoring broken relationships and openness to their continuity, without distortion by past infidelities. Receiving less emphasis are the "life-stage-marking" sacraments of the ancient church, whether they be stages in "ordinary" life or in the life of faith: baptism, confirmation, marriage, ordination, final unction. These may well hold respected places in the community of

friends but receive less emphasis primarily because they mark *moments* in an individual's friendship with God and the human community, and distract from the *continual process character* of the ongoing friendship. In addition, attempts to clarify their precise meanings have occasioned as yet unremedied disruption of friendship among God's friends throughout the history of the Church.

10) WORSHIP. Worship is the affirmative response of creatures to the invitation from God to say "yes" to God's offer of friendship as they live their lives. Its most statistically frequent mode is probably unconsciously motivated actions of obedience, which are guided by habits. Those who would argue with this might first recall that I am speaking of the worship by all creatures of their befriending God, and that "all creatures" includes the simplest parts of our bodily and spiritual selves, as well as the simpler organic and inorganic creatures of earth. Its simplest humanly-aware or semi-aware mode is prayer. Corporate worship in all its forms, plain to liturgically complex, builds on this base of the turning toward God in response to God's invitation of friendship.

11) EDUCATION. Education is the process by which human friends of God transmit to each other the awareness that friendship with God is possible, and enable the positive response of individuals to God's invitation. Communication of information is part of the task, but the fundamental dimension is relationship-building and, again, "befriending" in the name of God. Attending to the persons whom one wishes to teach, therefore, is prior—usually in time—to the task of conveying data. The old byword of evangelism that Christianity cannot be taught but must be caught applies here. Valid also is the proviso that inasmuch as human beings are cognitive as well as relational beings, information about what it is that has been "caught" is a valid part of the catching. Nevertheless, in teaching doctrine it should be remembered—no less than in the initial stages of friendship formation—that the person of the learner is of value and to be respected, including her or his questions, doubts, resistances, celebrations, growing pains, aging pains, and all the rest. In teaching one is befriending no less than in any other activity as a Christian.

12) EVANGELISM. Evangelism is the whole life of the Christian once she or he has become aware of being in a rela-

tion of mutual loyalty with God and God's other friends. This does not mean that one "subordinates" all one's feelings, activities, and dreams to an overarching one of making friends for God. At least I cannot see from observing Jesus' life that this is what he did, not in any conscious way. That would be a too-calculated description of the model we have in him. Rather, it appears that once one has made a kind of fundamental commitment to being in a friendly relation with God, God's own "conversation" with the self can be relied on (if one pays attention) to guide both unconsciously and consciously toward the "evangelizing" end. I understand "evangelizing" according to the rather barbaric translation of "gospelizing" insofar as "evangel" and "gospel" mean the same thing. That is to say, to evangelize is to embody the good news of God's friendship in one's ordinary life, either tacitly or explicitly, depending on the circumstances. What detergent I buy is an evangelical matter; it concerns the effects of chemical effluents on all creatures. What I do with the catalytic converter on my car's exhaust system is an evangelical matter; it concerns the effects of poisonous ions in the air on the world's ecosystem. How I assemble a wardrobe is an evangelical matter; do I use the skins of my fellow creatures, usually (in my personal case) cattle, with respect and restraint? One cannot think of any aspect of life that is "out of range" of the gospel insofar as it can be reviewed in the light of one's friendship with God. In this sense Christian ethics and evangelism are two sides of the same concern.

13) HOPE. Hope means standing with God's creation as a friend in expectation of healed relations among all creatures, in which enmity shall pass away and mutual service as parts of God's body give to each part (that is, to each creature) its fulfilled harmony of being.

D. *Forward: An Invitation in Conclusion*

Unanswered questions—indeed, unasked questions—tease from all the crevices in this essay. A Covenanter must ask: what about the Bible? What about other strains of the biblical witness that appear to be dismissed by this "friend" discussion as though no longer valid? A professional theologian must ask: what about the roles of reason and tradition? Is not the former overused here and the latter undervalued? And what about the preservation of orthodoxy? Does memory have no role to play in the service of present friendship? And other academicians must be bothered by the lack of methodological precision.

This is not a manifesto any more than it is a systematic theology. I hope it is part of a theological conversation "in the narthex" before church, friend to friends. If it elicits further exploration it will have served its purpose. It does not seek to replace all prior conversation on the subject nor does it intend—despite its length—to keep anyone out of the sanctuary.

Endnotes

[1] *The Covenant Hymnal* (1973) includes thirteen hymn texts explicitly naming God as "friend," including only six from the Mission Friend tradition. Notable among the others is hymn 166, "My Song Is Love Unknown" in praise of the Savior, which concludes "This is my Friend, in whose sweet praise/ I all my days could gaily spend." The text by Samuel Crossman dates from the seventeenth century. Most "friend" hymns, in fact, speak of the friendship of Jesus. One of the best known hymns in the Lutheran tradition, celebrated not only by Bach but also by Pietists because of its twelfth-century mystical text adapted by Paul Gerhardt in 1653, is number 197, "O Sacred Head, Now Wounded," with its final stanza which opens, "What language shall I borrow to thank thee, dearest friend." Perhaps it is significant that only two in *The Covenant Hymnal* speak of God in more "absolute" terms as friend, and these are both from the Swedish tradition: hymn 283, Nils Frykman's "The Highest Joy That Can Be Known" (" . . . and God to have as friend"); and hymn 488, C. O. Rosenius's "With God and His Friendship."

As for biblical sources, most Hebrew references to "friends" concern human-human relations, with 2 Chronicles 20:7, Isaiah 41:8, and Exodus 33:11 notable exceptions. Jesus refers to people both intimately and ironically as friends (see John 15:12ff and Matthew 20:13). The explicit construction "friend of God" occurs in James 2:23, where it refers to Abraham.

[2] According to Covenant historian Philip J. Anderson, a comprehensive study of this tendency in Christian thought might also include groups who called themselves "brethren," from the medieval period to the present time (letter, November 1987).

[3] Among references in Karl A. Olsson's *By One Spirit* (Chicago: Covenant Press, 1962) that lead to this interpretation are p. 221, paragraph 2 (a quotation from *Missions Vännen,* February 1875, p. 138); p. 223, paragraph 3; and p. 224, paragraph 3.

[4] Cited in Howard Brinton, *Friends for 300 Years* (New York: Scrib-

ners Sons, 1952), p. 44.

⁵ Rufus Jones, "The Friends of God," in *Studies in Mystical Religion* (New York: Russell and Russell, 1909 [1970]), pp. 281ff.

⁶ Cf. *ibid.,* p. 271.

⁷ Cf. however, Klyne Snodgrass's article in the December 1987 issue of *The Covenant Companion,* which questions the depth and extent of modern Covenanters' commitment to the Bible as God's word as demonstrated by the actual reading of it, in contrast with verbalized pieties about it.

⁸ *Sions Basun* (Chicago: Svenska Evangeliska Missionsförbundet i Amerika, 1909). The text of "Lifvets ord" reads at this point: "Den högsta lycka på vår jord/ För Sions vandringsmän,/ Det är att äga lifvets ord/ Och hafva Gud till vän."

⁹ The text here, also from *Sions Basun,* has been altered more than the translation of "Lifvets ord," but the crucial matter is not distorted: "Jag har en vän, som älskar mig/ Så högt, att han lät offra sig/ I korsets död på Golgata./ Mitt hjärta, sjung: Halleluja!/ Halleluja! Jag har en vän. . . . "

¹⁰ Fred J. Powicke, "Friends of God," in *Hastings Encyclopedia of Religious Knowledge* (New York: Scribners Sons, 1908), vol. 6. It will be of interest to feminist readers that his translation of *kindschaft* is no more accurate as "sonship" than translating *atham* in Genesis 1 as "man."

¹¹ H. Suso, a spiritual forerunner of the Friends of God, quoted in Rufus Jones, "The Friends of God," p. 295.

¹² Brinton, *Friends for 300 Years,* p. 33. Here he is quoting an unidentified author who originally used the phrase to describe the Hindu religious text *Bhagavad-Gita.* I understand Brinton to mean that the thirsty follower of Christ who seeks his guidance "drinks" from Scripture and is thus kept alive, but when the Spirit is quickened and speaks livingly in the person, it sets aside the immediate need to read.

¹³ Cf. *Covenant Yearbook,* 1976, p. 178, where the issue of "scriptural basis" was raised concerning the ordination of women, and subsequent years' discussions.

¹⁴ There may be historical links between the writings of both the Friends of God and their precursors and the piety of the later Mission Friends, according to Philip J. Anderson, *op. cit.*

¹⁵ Cf. Aelred of Rivaulx, *Spiritual Friendship,* Mary Eugenia Laker, trans. (Washington, D.C.: Cistercian Publications, Consortium Press, [c. 1166] 1974); Gilbert Meilander, *Friendship: A Study in Theological Ethics* (Notre Dame: University of Notre Dame Press, 1981); William Cheyn, *The Friendship of Christ* (n.p., 1718); Agnes M. Royden, *The Friendship of God* (New York and London: G.P. Putnams Sons, 1924); Henry Wright, *The Friendship of God* (n.p., 1882); and the extensive biography in Sallie McFague, *Models of God* (Philadelphia: Fortress Press, 1987), pp. 216-222, esp. n. 22.

¹⁶ Jones, "The Friends of God," p. 243.

¹⁷ Karl A. Olsson, "Covenant Beginnings: Mystical," *Covenant Quarterly,* 13 (1953), 46.

¹⁸ McFague, *Models of God,* p. 64.
¹⁹ *Ibid.,* p. 169.
²⁰ *Ibid.,* p. 161.
²¹ *Ibid.,* p. 158.
²² *Ibid.,* p. 159.
²³ *Ibid.,* p. 160.
²⁴ *Ibid.*
²⁵ *Ibid.,* p. 162.
²⁶ *Ibid.*
²⁷ *Ibid.,* p. 164.
²⁸ *Ibid.*
²⁹ *Ibid.,* p. 165.
³⁰ *Ibid.,* p. 174.
³¹ *Ibid.,* p. 179.
³² *Ibid.,* p. 187.

The Emigrants and the "Readers"

Two Neglected Groups in Cultural History

Gunnar Hallingberg

John Dewey wrote, with some irony I suppose: "The arts that have most validity for the greatest part of the population are not considered arts at all." A generation or two later a word of wisdom was heard from Marshall McLuhan: "When a medium becomes a depth experience, the old categories of classical and popular, or of highbrow and lowbrow, no longer obtain."

Popular culture was long overlooked by serious critics and among scholars in the history of literature, music, art, and drama. The academic tradition of criticism and research limited itself to elite art within an aesthetic context, innovative, aiming at discovering new symbols, a new "language" of art, new ways of recording human experiences. Popular art, on the contrary, was fabricated, created for profit, aimed at the big audiences. It was more or less considered to be a threat to the real culture. There was, and of course is, a conflict between art and egalitarianism.

As popular art and, in a wider sense, popular culture developed in the mass society, it became more and more important to focus on it as an object of study. Consequently, new areas and new groups within society were taken into consideration from a new point of view. These groups very often lacked the innovators, the great solo performances in the history of culture. However, they provided examples of good, original folk art (generally of rural origin) and also showed a marked place for products of modern mass society.

This essay addresses two areas of Swedish-American and, especially, Swedish culture: *the "emigrants"* and *the "readers"* (*läsarna*), sometimes sharing common experiences and developing similar forms of culture. Both groups have also been

almost totally neglected in standard surveys of Swedish literature, art, and music. From a more recent point of view, it
is possible to draw a most interesting picture of a cultural landscape without dramatic contours but with a great deal of plain
land, cultivated according to traditions and with love for
national heritage, language, and religious experiences.

I

The scholarly study of popular culture in the United States
dates back to the 1950s and '60s. Russel B. Nye's major survey
of popular arts in America, *The Unembarrassed Muse,* appeared in 1970. It is a book about literature, music, theater,
art, and the press in America during the nineteenth and twentieth centuries. But it is a book without chapters about the
famous early American authors and artists such as Ralph Waldo
Emerson, Edgar Allan Poe, Walt Whitman, Winslow Homer,
Aaron Copland, and George Gershwin. Personalities in this
book are not as important as they usually are in cultural history. Rather, Nye successfully describes cultural life *in terms
of function* with the public, placing the audience in the center
as much as the creators and performers. To Nye the influence
on the public of a certain piece of art is essential.

It is likely that the study of popular culture and its history
became important because of an increasing awareness of the
central position of mass media in American society. This had
to be studied and understood. Popular culture was the product of modern technology and a structure of the society, characterized by literacy, more leisure time, and more money to
spend on evening entertainment. This was certainly culture
for the millions, a culture adapted for the marketplace. Perhaps
this did not mean art according to traditional standards, but
popular culture was just popular, presented on a large scale
with great public appeal. The "unembarrassed" muse was seldom favored among the best critics but gained consolation in
tremendous support from large audiences.

The extensive research on popular culture has enriched
and widened the image of past American culture. During the
last decades, American culture has been described in extensive volumes, where "culture" is interpreted in a modern context, not limited to the fine arts. Neil Harris writes in the pref-

ace to the seven-volume work that he edited, *The American Culture:* " . . . in America, where physical mobility and ethnic diversity have been so crucial, this conception of culture is restricting. The interesting in our civilization is omitted if we confine ourselves to the formal arts." In his book *Popular Culture and Industrialism 1865-1890,* Henry Nash Smith explains and defends his selection of topics: "I am concerned here with the commonplace and the ordinary rather than with distinguished achievement . . . materials I have collected consist in large part of pseudo-ideas and stereotypes rather than challenging intellectual discoveries."

Popular culture is sweeping the country. When cultural historians in America make their surveys in order to find the sources and the direction of the movement, it might have something to do with their conviction that popular culture is something primitively American. It concerns "business as usual"—the marketplace rather than the academies. One prerequisite was the modern press, which had its greatest impact in America.

It is interesting to see how American culture was treated among Swedish cultural historians during the first part of the present century. Few, if any, were ready to credit the newspaper as a cultural phenomenon of special importance. Otto Sylwan—a highly respected professor of literature with an interest in publicity, and author of well-known handbooks—in his 1906 study of the modern press had some very definite judgments about the newspaper market in the United States. The press was, according to him, adapted to nerveless and naively sensitive people who desired action and thrilling news that was easy to understand. A more sophisticated writing and more elaborated language would only be wasted and even hamper sales. In possession of the world's best publishing technology, Americans, as part of a young and immature nation, had to be excited and touched by strong stimuli!

American literature was not taken seriously by Swedes until after World War I. Ruben G:son Berg wrote a book in 1925 about modern Americans, introducing writers such as Edgar Lee Masters, Sinclair Lewis, Theodore Dreiser, and Willa Cather. In a survey chapter about American literature in Sweden, he concluded that two groups of authors in particular attracted the Swedish public: the religious poets and authors for children and youth. Among these were James Fenimore Cooper and Jack London. While Ralph Waldo Emerson was known only to strictly limited groups, Ira Sankey was well-known: "The American influence is doubtless widest within the sects." Thus, "American" meant "popular."

Artur Lundkvist in his pioneer work *Atlandvind* (1932) stated, however, that modern literature in America was among the most fascinating in the western hemisphere. The yearly harvest of 10,000 published books did not consist only of best-sellers, he said. Bestsellers, religious books, children's litera-ture about Indians, thrilling stories, Nick Carter—that was America! Popular culture!

II

The scholarly interest in popular culture also draws attention to subcultures especially associated with the immigrant expe-rience. These are common in American society and collectively have been interpreted by images such as the "melting pot" or the "salad bowl." Among these many subcultures was the small but significant Swedish-American culture.

It is somewhat startling that Alrik Gustafsson in his *History of Swedish Literature* (1961) did not mention Swedish-Amer-ican literature at all. And yet he was himself a Swedish-Amer-ican, teaching Swedish literature at both Augustana College and the University of Minnesota. Though the intent of his book evidently was to introduce Swedish literature to an English-speaking academic public, one might have expected at least to find Henning Berger included, a Chicago novelist at the turn of the century and later a well-known Swedish author. More-over, not until recently has Swedish-American art been intro-duced in scholarly works (e.g. Birger Sandzén—while Carl Milles was merely considered to be a Swede honored with spe-cial assignments in the United States).

There is, however, a definite Swedish-American culture in the sense of literature, music, art, etc. The writers are many. They are listed in Ernst Skarstedt's *Pennfäktare* ("Scribblers"), first printed (in Swedish) in San Francisco in 1897 and revised and extended in a second edition, published in Sweden in 1930. Skarstedt quite honestly admitted that "not all our writ-ers have contributed to the improvement of our [Swedish] literature," but that, nevertheless, a considerable number of writers have contributed to the field of literature. He blamed the public for being uninterested, helping to explain the poor market for books in Swedish.

A national subculture will generally be very anxious to preserve customs and traditions as long as possible. Most of Skarstedt's writers, if not all, wrote entirely in Swedish. They were above all journalists, contributing to the many Swedish newspapers published in the new country.

There were also publishers, some influential—among them Engberg-Holmberg Publishing Company in Chicago. Their catalog in 1901 listed more than 300 books in nine sections. Most books were printed in Sweden and imported to America. The largest selections were: theology and church history (83 items); Christian narratives (80); textbooks and language (30); music (30); and poetry (25). Engberg-Holmberg was also the agent for the publishing company of the Evangelical National Foundation in Sweden. In 1909 the publishing company advertised several of Zakarias Topelius's novels, Esaias Tegnér's longer poems (*Fritiofs saga,* also in English translation), and books by such contemporary popular writers in Sweden as Vilhelm von Braun, Sigurd (A. Hedenstjerna), and Herman Bjursten. It is interesting to see that several English language authors were advertised in Swedish translations. Among them were Charles Lamb's *Tales from Shakespeare* and a book about American rhetoric. Engberg-Holmberg was also the publisher of a literary calendar, *När och fjärran* ("Near and Far").

In the early 1960s North Park College acquired the library of the Idrott Cafe in Chicago. When I assisted the librarians in classifying the books—all in Swedish—I found an excellent collection of what we now consider Swedish classics with first editions of major works by Selma Lagerlöf, Verner von Heidenstam, Gustaf Fröding, and others.

The preservation and maintenance of the Swedish cultural heritage was a primary concern for most of the first generation of Swedish-Americans. Consequently, innovations were not particularly prevalent. Provocative, radical literature in the native language was not to be expected against a background of ethnic consciousness in a foreign country. But the publishing ventures and the mostly mediocre new writers were not unimportant when seen in the general context of cultural history. Eager to maintain and pass on to the next generation the language of the old country, the writers, publishers, and librarians provided reading for a specific public. Three writers deserve special recognition as examples of the types of literature within the Swedish-American subculture.

Henning Berger lived in Chicago from 1892 to 1899, and upon his return to Sweden published a series of novels and a collection of short stories based on his impressions of America. He is generally mentioned, if only briefly, in handbooks and surveys of Swedish literature as one of the turn-of-the-century generation: Hjalmar Söderberg, Hjalmar Bergman, Sara Lidman, et al. He belongs, therefore, to the established group of Swedish authors—notably the only Swedish-American. After a most promising beginning his writing, however, declined and he was accused of superficiality and lack of interest in moral and philosophical as well as social problems. He did not really qualify as a character writer. The circulation of his work was limited and reprints are rare. Today he is almost forgotten.

Leonard Strömberg moved to America in 1895 and never returned permanently to Sweden. He was a popular writer with a very wide audience. About two dozen editions of his most popular novels appeared. Series of selected novels were still reprinted and advertised in the 1960s. Older people in Sweden with roots in the Swedish folk movements will generally remember at least some of Strömberg's books.

Strömberg was a Methodist minister who spent most of his life in Oakland, Nebraska. He wrote—and generally preached—in Swedish. Once a year, sometimes even more frequently, he mailed a book manuscript to his publisher in Uppsala, Sweden. The plots always took place in Sweden, in a setting familiar to him from his youth. They caught on with his public, which he managed to keep loyal and faithful for a long time. In the 1920s he was considered to be Sweden's most widely read fiction writer!

The secret behind Strömberg's incredible success was probably that he sensed what his readers wanted. Rita Strombeck has argued in her dissertation on Strömberg that he became the Swedish Horatio Alger. Strömberg's novels could be seen as a typical example of popular literature, with ingredients of love, tension, a little nostalgia, and good moral education. Strömberg wrote "good books" that were by no means boring. He does not, however, as an immigrant have a place in Sweden's literary heritage. But from the wider perspective of popular culture and Swedish-American subculture he achieved great fame.

Likewise, *Gustaf Nathanael Malm,* from Svarttorp near Jönköping, is never mentioned in any Swedish history of literature. He moved to America in 1889 and settled in Lindsborg, Kansas, where he first started to learn painting with Birger Sandzén as his teacher. According to Skarstedt, he painted and sold thirty altar paintings for churches. Later, he turned to writing but was also interested in music and participated actively in the famous Messiah choir at Bethany College. His classic novel, unique in theme and language, was *Charlie Johnson, svensk-amerikan: Verklighetsbild ur folklivet bland svenskarna i Vestern på 1890-talet* (Chicago, 1913). This book was unknown in Sweden. Malm managed to recreate the mixed language used by first-generation Swedish-Americans. Moreover, his book is both a humorous and plausible story about farm life in Kansas. It has value as a novel as well as a cultural document.

In addition to the above writers, another phenomenon in popular culture with Swedish-American origin (perhaps similar to Strömberg) was *J. A. Hultman*—"the Sunshine Singer." Born in Sweden (Småland) but raised in America, Hultman became one of the most frequent travelers between Sweden and America during the first forty years of this century. He was a writer, composer, and musician, but above all a singer and preacher. In Sweden, his popularity was enormous. Both in Sweden and America he published collections of hymns and songs. The Swedish *"Solskenssånger"* were published in numerous extended editions and eventually numbered 500 songs.

III

Hultman, together with Strömberg and Malm, is also representative of the second neglected area in the history of culture that I wish to examine in this essay. The "readers" (*läsare*) were people who had been "born again" during the revival movements in Sweden beginning in the mid-nineteenth century. They derived their nickname from the central place given

to reading. The ability to read was not common in the rural
population in the early 1800s. In addition to Luther and other
spiritual writers, this group was above all reading the Bible.
Here they improved their vocabulary and acquired a treasure
of myth and epic that could be used in public speaking. The
readers were often preachers, and they were always listeners.
In Sweden they were representatives of the philosophy developed by the Danish reformer Grundtvig, which emphasized
the tremendous power of "the living word."

The readers had a reputation for social radicalism. They
often questioned traditional, established institutions—above
all the state church and its dominant theology. They promoted
freedom of speech and insisted on their rights to arrange meetings (conventicles) without permission from the parish minister. In their own societies (later churches) they invited believers to services of Holy Communion, a practice that the authorities judged illegal. They avoided conventional worship and
wanted freedom, personal decision, and commitment. Their
radicalism gained them support also among modern secularized
liberals. Revivalism and liberalism had much in common and
formed a new alternative in Swedish politics, preparing for
the democratic breakthrough in the early 1900s. This is fairly
well-known.

The cultural history of the readers is less well-known. Not
until recently have more profound scholarly studies been available (Kussak, Selander, Bernskiöld). It is a general opinion that
revivalism did not cope well with either the old folk culture
or the established, academic "high" culture. This is undoubt-
edly true, at least to a certain degree, but in the light of increasing interest in forms of popular culture, the "readers" as a
subculture should be of particular interest.

When revivalism became organized in associations and
societies (i.e., the Evangelical National Foundation in 1856 and
later the Swedish Mission Covenant in 1878) a unique culture
began to develop. Most obvious was the rapid development
of a press with wide circulation, indicating a considerable sensitivity among the readers for modern means of mass communication and for marketing. This was a time when demand
grew for more reading, and it was rather inexpensive to produce printed material. New music found a ready market. Song-
writers like Oscar Ahnfelt, Lina Sandell, and Nils Frykman

became well-known throughout Sweden and North America. Swedish readers very soon learned to add English and American imported music to their own repertory. As early as the 1870s and '80s songs by Ira Sankey, P. P. Bliss, and others were translated and in wide use, while Frykman emigrated to Minnesota and continued to write and compose songs in a more Americanized manner. Pointing to a timeless pattern of popular culture, Hans Bernskiöld characterizes Frykman with these words: "Like a successful composer of song hits, Frykman succeeded in giving old, well-known models and formulas a new characteristic profile which was perceived as something new." The free church movement in Sweden created a subculture, which may remind us of the Swedish-American subculture, in that both held in common many of the same democratic and reformist impulses.

It is more important to emphasize that the two cultures were "popular," aimed at the masses, not trained in the appreciation of "high culture." The free church culture had little ambition to renew Swedish literature, art, and music. Rather, it was satisfied if artists, writers, and publishers could create an atmosphere of identification and meaning among the particular and growing group of people called readers. Books and newspapers were to inform about the progress of revivalism all over Sweden—as the Swedish-American press delivered news from the old country and about newcomers in Minnesota, Illinois, and Nebraska. Novels and poems were to reflect thoughts and feelings among people ready to start their new lives, whether as settlers in Kansas or converted participants in the building of a small chapel in some village in Småland. In each case this literature was to edify and encourage people. This was a particularly important task for the hymnwriters and composers.

While the Swedish-American subculture would be seen against the background of an American cultural marketplace, the free church culture in Sweden had certain antecedents. Its background could be found in the established tradition that dates back to medieval times with its church and court-related culture. The state church had been the cultural center since the Reformation. The local pastor was also the highest public officer in the parish. Generally he was also the only one with some acquaintance with books and cultural life. Many of the

most important authors were church leaders (i.e., Esaias
Tegnér, Johan Olof Wallin, and Frans Michael Franzén) while
others (such as Johan Henrik Kellgren, Viktor Rydberg, Erik
Gustaf Geijer, and Olof Dalin) held positions in governmen-
tal offices, state universities, academies, and state institutions
of art. Later in the 1800s it became more common to have
the burgeoning press as a platform (i.e., C. J. L. Almqvist, Viktor
Rydberg, and August Strindberg). Quite a few prominent representatives of Swedish culture were born and reared in par-
sonages all over the country. "Pastors' kids" had opportunities
to study early and to get in touch with culture, something
denied most young people.

The Swedish culture as it appeared in academies, universities, theaters, museums, and galleries had its established
values presented on the cultural pages of newspapers and magazines as well as in literary anthologies and handbooks. In a
short survey of Swedish literature for the Swedish *folkhög-
skola,* Karl Warburg, famous scholar and critic, concludes the
discussion with Viktor Rydberg and Carl Snoilsky. Where is
Strindberg? He is missing.

Strindberg was still an outsider. He did not belong to the
cultural establishment and was never invited to be a member
of the Swedish Academy. He was a leader among those who
were radical, critical of traditional culture, and lacking in
respect for accepted values. He formed an alternative culture,
by degree more and more included in the establishment and
finally capturing it, replacing old artistic and political/social
values with the new. These radical opponents would later be
recognized as those who inaugurated a new epoch. Strindberg
is the best example in literature, followed by others in the
1890s such as Gustaf Fröding and Selma Lagerlöf. Their counterparts in art and painting were the members of *Konstnärsför-
bundet,* today considered to be one of the most glorious chapters in Swedish art history.

If the readers were considered to be radical and opposi-
tional, they certainly did not identify themselves with young
authors from the 1880s or radical painters from the 1890s!
They could be radical and liberal in politics and social life,
but when it came to literature, art, and theater they were conservative, even uninterested. They did not enter into the tension between conservatism and radicalism in culture, the cre-

ative dialectics in cultural life.

In his youth, P. P. Waldenström, one of the founders of the Swedish Mission Covenant, wrote a famous novel, or rather an allegoric tale, entitled *Squire Adamson* (1862). In Sweden this was one of the most widely read books for nearly a century. Waldenström was a gifted writer, but he was totally uninterested in fiction. He even warned against it in a very provocative way. In addition, he gained a reputation for bigotry and lack of sensitivity for art when in the parliament he protested against Oscar Björk's paintings (with some nudes) in the state opera house.

Waldenström's attitude toward culture was, rightly or wrongly, considered to be typical for free church people. It is true that what we generally mean by "culture" for a long time did not affect the readers. They formed an alternative culture with many of the same characteristics as the popular culture. Later the attitude changed. There is even reason to believe that it changed rather dramatically, from indifference, if not resistance, to involvement and even commitment to the popular culture. The history of this development can not yet be written because of a shortage of detailed in-depth studies. Recently, however, some scholarly works have been written in the field of literature, music, and art.

IV

I would like to conclude this essay with a tentative proposal for a broad survey of free church culture in Sweden as a subculture phenomenon. In a somewhat parallel though limited study, Paul R. Messbarger explored American Catholic popular fiction. It is interesting to learn that Catholics in America consciously formed a distinct subculture with at least nominal religious designation for activities such as parochial education, art, philosophy, and even Boy Scouting. This occurred in the late 1800s, simultaneous with the present discussion of "emigrant" and "reader" cultures. Catholic fiction "by, about, and for Catholics" was consciously supported by the church, which realized that the novel in America since the 1860s was established as such a popular and engaging literary form that it was necessary to deal with it seriously. The first step was to try to prevent people from reading fiction. The church showed open hostility, primarily for moral reasons.

By the turn of the century, however, Catholics had accepted the novel. By 1900 more than a hundred American
Catholics had written and published at least one novel. Paper-
back editions were available as Catholic bestsellers. Messbarger
notes, however, that this conscious effort to supply good Catholic literature resulted in "a harvest of mediocrity." Nevertheless, the Catholic reader learned much about social adjust-
ment, a code of behavior, and a sense of a particular Catholic
cultural heritage.

An additional step in the development of Catholic fiction
in the United States was assimilation, beginning with the claim
that the exclusiveness of the Catholic faith reveals itself in the
superiority of Catholic culture. "Therefore Catholic art must
be superior to non-Catholic!" This step never had any equivalent in the reader culture.

Among the readers in Sweden there are at least four iden-
tifiable steps from indifference and resistance to responsibility and participation. These steps also mark a development
over the course of a century from subculture to assimilation.
Today it is very doubtful whether we can speak of a free church
culture with significant values. The existence of a particular
Swedish-American culture is highly dubious as well.

1) The first period of Swedish revivalism was characterized by a remarkable development of the print media and
music. An increasing appetite for reading was met by the revivalists in newspapers (mostly weeklies) and tracts. Papers like
Hemlandsvännen and *Göteborgs Weckoblad* not only carried
sermons and edifying reading; they also contained news and
entertainment, travelogs, short stories, and biographical
sketches. Editorials on political topics appeared frequently,
together with letters to the editor. Reports from the mission
fields communicated knowledge about the world at a distance
and stimulated interest in foreign missions. This was the time
when Livingstone and Stanley drew the attention of a whole
world to Africa and when London was the obvious center of
world missions. The Swedish rural population was exposed
to the world through the free church press.

2) In the second period, beginning around 1900, revivalism became more firmly organized in denominations and free
churches. Publishing companies were founded. In 1905 pub-

lishers joined together in a special organization to serve common interests. In his dissertation about the literary development in the Swedish Mission Covenant, Åke Kussak writes about the existence of "an alternative literary system." Annual calendars and Christmas magazines abounded in sentimental and nostalgic pictures of Christmas traditions with a romantic national feeling. Lyrical poems were published everywhere. The readers got their own beloved poets, among them Carl Boberg. His poems were deeply felt and attracted a wide audience. Also they could be looked upon as some kind of lyrical utility product. The numerous programs in the growing youth movement created a constant demand for poetry to recite in public. This kind of poetry is a characteristic component of popular culture.

Though Waldenström was very negative toward any kind of fiction, his fellow believers tended more and more to mix Bible reading and fiction. Three female authors enjoyed great popularity among the readers: Runa, Betty (both pen names), and Anna Ölander. Among the men, Leonard Strömberg soon rose to top the bestseller list. These authors and poets (like Boberg) created a market for "pious" literature. They were good representatives of popular culture. Behind the marketing of good entertainment were also the efforts to get an alternative to the secular book market. Hall's Publishing House in Jönköping started a new magazine for short stories and advertised it as good entertainment. But the publisher also called upon subscribers to participate in a common crusade against destructive literature.

The call to crusade was often heard during the first four decades of the twentieth century. The target was, for a while, the "Nick Carter literature" from America. In its efforts to stop the distribution of these books, the revivalists benefited from very active resistance within the labor movement. Later the weekly magazines became the prime target, with their novels and short stories considered to be of a low moral standard. In a debate book published by *Missionsförbundets förlag* (the Swedish Covenant Publications) in 1931, such weeklies were labeled "a giant parasite" threatening the life of fiction writing. Åke Kussak has studied the Christian alternatives to the secular and "immoral" writing in magazines. He found a large number of short stories published in the denominational papers, particularly the youth magazines. These stories were concerned with the Christian faith and how to become a Christian. They were written to win readers to the Christian faith.

3) The third generation of "readers" included an increasing number of well-educated people with at least the *student-examen* (college and university level). During these decades— the 1930s through the 1950s—special centers and programs for adult education were organized within the free church movement. The Free Church Student Association (FKS), a member of the International Student Christian Movement, gained considerable influence in cultural issues. In membership, it was never large, but from time to time FKS virtually had a monopoly on cultural issues among the free churches. Its monthly magazine carried book reviews and essays about cultural topics. In the 1930s the influence of Frank Buchman's Oxford Movement was important. It reached even the secularized Swedish culture with a revivalist message. Famous authors became converted and functioned as a bridge between Christianity and culture. Another bridge was the Association for Christian Humanism. (It should be noted that humanism among Christians in Sweden never acquired the negative meaning it had and still has among many in the United States.)

The free church students and academicians found support and fellowship within these ecumenical movements. As a symbol of a more culturally oriented form of Christian faith, *Sigtunastiftelsen* offered a center for debate and creative efforts—a meeting place for Christian and non-Christians in the field of literature, art, and music established within the state church. The new generation of free church academicians reacted against the old subculture with all its restrictions and superficiality in the creative process. They tried to find a motive for a more profound participation in the formation of a true culture.

The leading person in this process was Erik Hjalmar Linder, a famous journalist, critic, and literary historian. In a precise formula he gave a generation of students a view of the Christian faith that opened the way for more involvement in cultural issues: Christianity creates culture unconsciously. In other words, it was not only possible but also desirable for a Christian revivalist to deal with culture! In responding to Christian imperatives, the Christian participates in the creation of culture, perhaps unconsciously. This, however, was much better and led to a more serious criticism than restrictive attempts to create an alternative subculture.

Attitudes toward the film medium among church members were restrictive, if not totally negative. The movies, above all the American film, reflected in form and content the weekly magazines. Crime and love, glamour and dancing, were frequently repeated themes that had little in common with the reader's way of life. The monthly magazine for culture, *Kristet Forum,* issued by the Free Church Christian Movement, incorporated film criticism, and gradually the "old" free churches became more open-minded toward the film, while the emerging Pentecostal movement remained negative.

4) Sweden has had television since 1956. The breakthrough of the new medium was fast and thorough. In a few years almost all Swedish homes had television sets. In 1969 the first and only channel for nationwide television was followed by a second, also run by *Sveriges Radio,* a public service corporation. Among the shareholders in the company is the Free Church Association.

With television, motion pictures invaded Swedish homes. A wave of popular culture of Swedish but above all foreign origin washed in. Even the Pentecostals had to give up their resistance. Today they work actively with television production with excellent equipment that can be compared to that of Swedish television itself.

As McLuhan argued, with television, old categories no longer apply. This is true as well concerning the relationship between established culture and sectarian subcultures. For the future it seems important to resist a threatening total dominance of international entertainment and commercialism. In its efforts to preserve ethical values and national patterns in Swedish television, the free church movement is not alone but in fellowship with other groups in Swedish society. Popular culture is gaining ground, but it is also an object of criticism and study.

Whether these older traditions of pietistic lifestyle and personal responsibility connected with the readers and their successors will play a significant part in future development remains to be seen. New subcultures are, however, unlikely in the modern mass-media society.

Bibliography

Berg, R. G:son. *Moderna amerikaner.* Stockholm: Gebers, 1925.

Bernskiöld, Hans. *Sjung, av hjärtet sjung: Församlingssång och musikliv i Svenska Missionsförbundet fram till 1950-talet.* Göteborg: Förlagshuset Gothia, 1986.

Gustafsson, A. *A History of Swedish Literature.* Minneapolis: University of Minnesota Press, 1930.

Harris, Neil, ed. *The American Culture.* Vol. 5: *The Land of Contrasts 1880-1901.* New York: George Braziller, 1970.

Kussak, Åke. *Författaren som predikant.* Stockholm: Gummessons förlag, 1982.

Lundkvist, A. *Atlantvind.* Stockholm: Bonniers, 1932.

Messbarger, P. R. *American Catholic Popular Fiction: Challenges in American Culture.* Bowling Green, OH: Bowling Green University Press, 1970.

Nye, Russel. *The Unembarrassed Muse.* New York: Dial Press, 1970.

Selander, Inger. *O hur saligt att få vandra: Motiv och symboler i den frikyrkliga sången.* Stockholm: Gummessons förlag, 1980.

Skarstedt, Ernst. *Pennfäktare.* Stockholm: Bonniers, 1930.

Smith, H. N., ed. *Popular Culture and Industrialism 1865-1890.* New York: Doubleday and Co., 1967.

Sylwan, Otto. *Den moderna pressen.* Stockholm: Bonniers, 1906.

Sweden's New Hymnals

J. Irving Erickson

"We shall have singing congregations again." "A great ecumenical achievement." "An excellent hymnal—characterized by openness and breadth."[1] "The new hymnal is the book of the year." "For the first time we have a hymnal that is appropriate to the time."[2] Such were some of the reactions to the introduction of *Den Svenska Psalmboken* (1986) in the Church of Sweden and *Psalmer och Sånger* (1987) in most of Sweden's free churches. But there were other reactions as well: "Don't touch our beloved old hymns!" "Let us be spared the meddlesome revisions." "The death of refinement."

The above statements were primarily concerned with the first part of each of the volumes which shared the same 325 hymns. Besides the Church of Sweden, fourteen groups were involved in the choice of these songs: Adventist, Alliance Mission, Baptist, Catholic, Free Baptist, Holiness, Liberal Catholic, Methodist, Örebro Mission, National Evangelical Foundation, Pentecostal, Salvation Army, Swedish Salvation Army, and the Swedish Mission Covenant.

The former songbook of the Church of Sweden was published in 1937. This was merely a revision of a hymnal that had been in use for more than a hundred years. Before the new collection appeared, there had been several trial supplements, the most important being *Psalmer och Visor 76* and *Psalmer och Visor 82*. The last hymnal of the Swedish Mission Covenant was published in 1951; in addition, there was a supplement of 138 songs in 1978, *Herren Lever*. This was produced in cooperation with four other free church groups.

In 1978 the Church of Sweden hymnal committee was joined by representatives of the aforementioned groups. They had taken the name *Sampsalm,* the root *sam* denoting union or togetherness. After considering several alternatives, the full committee decided to produce a basic collection with supplements or supplemental sections for the diverse groups.

The selection of the 325 basic hymns did not come easily. If this was to serve all fifteen churches, the songbook would have to include some of the pietistic, revival, and gospel songs used by the free churches and still loved by many members of the State Church. The main objection came from some of the Church of Sweden musicians, especially the members of the Royal Academy who were intent on retaining high musical standards. "Not a few were either undecided or directly opposed to their inclusion,"[3] wrote Per Olof Nisser, one of the committee members, in his comprehensive review of the volume and history of its development. In at least one church, when the advent song *"Gå, Sion, din konung att möta"* ("O Zion, Acclaim Your Redeemer") was introduced, the organist walked away from the console. The song is a reworking of an American text set to a rhythmic tune by James McGranahan.

It was songs like this and some of the contemporary material that prompted the statement that the new hymnal meant the death of refinement. But this is not new in the history of hymnody. Isaac Watts was under the same accusation when he was able to break the hold of the metrical psalm on the hymnody of his day. The Wesleys met the same kind of criticism a few years later. But what of the prediction that "We shall have singing congregations again"? It is too early to evaluate that statement, but preliminary reports indicate that the new books have created a new interest and excitement.

A comparison of the collections in each of the previous and new volumes should aid us in our evaluation. About 360 songs from the 1937 publication have been retained in the new (51 percent). Of this number 170 have been untouched, except for minor revisions reflecting changes in language and grammar. In several cases stanzas have been deleted. The remaining 190 have undergone more or less revision. Sixty-four texts have new first lines, and there is a special index to identify them.

The process of revision received nationwide attention when the committee published examples of reworked texts, and the church annual meeting of 1982 allowed time for discussion of the proposed changes. Space does not permit further consideration of the process, but an example of the reworking can be seen in the first line of the last stanza of "Wheresoe'er I Roam" by Rosenius. *"Följ mig, huldaste, uppstungna hjärta"* ("Guide me, most gracious, pierced heart") becomes *"Endast du, Uppståndne, kan mig frälsa"* ("Only you, the risen one, can save me").

A great number of the hymns retained are of the German chorale type. At least 20 percent have the stamp of Johann Wallin, either as originals or revisions. Wallin was largely responsible for the former hymnal which was used by the church for more than a century. Besides being the editor of the original 1819 edition, his name was still on 40 percent of the texts in the 1937 edition. Other well-known former Swedish hymnists represented by ten or more lyrics in the new book are Nataneal Beskow (1865-1953), Johan Eklund (1863-1945), Frans Franzén (1772-1847), Haqvin Spegel (1654-1714), and Jesper Svedberg (1643-1735).

Nearly 300 entries can be said to be new, not having appeared in a Church of Sweden collection before. Quite a few are of recent origin. The most prominent among the contemporary writers are Anders Frostenson (pastor and poet), Britt Hallqvist (theologian, writer, and translator), and Olov Hartman (pastor, author, and translator). Frostenson has contributed fifty original texts and more than a hundred translations and/or revisions. Hallqvist has eighteen originals and seventy-nine translations and/or revisions. And Hartman has nineteen originals and several translations and/or revisions. Some of the new songs were translated into English by Fred Kaan and published by Stainer and Bell Ltd. in *Songs and Hymns from Sweden.* Olle Engström's introduction to the collection gives us a good description of the new songs:

> . . . characteristic of the new texts is that they are not abstract theology in rhyme, as was so often the case in the past. They proclaim the presence of God in the Living Christ and the Spirit in the everyday life of men and women—even in the cities. There are more pavements, there is more smell of hectic rush hours than ever before in hymnbooks, where the only city that was mentioned was the heavenly Jerusalem. The troubled hearts of men and women

in this era of frustration, and God's concern not only
for uncertain and desolate individuals but for the
whole of creation . . . these are among the main
themes that occur.

Some of the new material is personal and subjective. One
comes across the personal pronouns *jag* (I), *mig* (me), and *min*
(my or mine) quite often. There are several texts based on biblical stories and parables. In hymn 156 Jesus meets his disciples on the shore after the resurrection. Number 384 is the
story of the feeding of the multitude. Mary's encounter with
Jesus in the garden is the story told in number 463. Jesus healing the blind man is depicted in hymn 264. This type of song
seems to be more prevalent than in the past.

In *Vår Nya Psalmboken,* Per Olof Nisser includes a chapter on the theology of the hymns.[4] He compares them with
the 1937 hymnal in respect to the conceptions of God, humanity, death and resurrection, the church and sacraments, and
creation and society. A brief summary of the chapter may give
us a better idea of the textual thrust of the songs. The views
of God are many-sided. While the holiness, majesty, transcendence, and otherness of God are present, now there is more
of an emphasis upon the love of God and his presence with
us through Christ. The new hymnal has a more balanced view
of humanity. The old tended to be pessimistic, with emphasis upon one's sinfulness and imprisonment. People still need
to be saved and to be freed from captivity but this is expressed
in more psychological terms. Frostenson once wrote that we
need hymns that help us know ourselves, our situation and
problems, and that will give us a meaningful pattern for our
lives. Freedom is a favorite theme, and this freedom allows
us to ask questions. Witness the following hymn phrases: "I
often have questions, Lord" (218); "I did not come here
because I believe" (532); "God, you went away" (592); "God,
are you dead?" (592). But the freedom to doubt, question, and
choose has its base in forgiveness, in being set free.

The picture of death as a homecoming has frequently been
depicted in hymns, but in the new texts it is more dramatic
and sensational. In hymn 630 Britt Hallqvist has God standing
on the threshold of his house saying, "Welcome, children!"
And in number 311 Frostenson says, "I shall tearfully cast

myself down on a shore that I have never seen. . . . I hear laughter from children at play, and I am a child in God's arms." The hymns in this category speak not only of death, resurrection, and the life to come, but about the journey as well. There is a resurgence of texts about the Christian as a pilgrim. One of the favorites among young and old is Bo Setterlind's "There Is a Way That Leads to Heav'n" (303).

A more self-searching and critical view of the church is seen in some of the new songs. This can be seen in Hartman's translation of "The Church's One Foundation" (57). In stanza four (which is omitted in most hymnals) the question is asked, "When deceit and power grow, where is the salt of the earth? Who helps and who heals when the whole world falls apart?" Then the prayer: "May the church become as before, a heart and soul, a refuge in the midst of trouble, and for truth a safeguard." There are only two baptismal hymns in the basic section, reflecting the practice of adult baptism in so many of the free churches. In its treatment of society the new hymnal takes note of the fact that Sweden is now an industrial nation. Hallqvist's morning hymn is a good example:

> The light breaks gently through the haze and smoke.
> Now the day's first hour begins with purpose and
>   order.
> On the way to the workshop, factory, and school
>   we receive a call
> That we should serve each other and share our bread
>   from God.

The international situation is often referred to, and we are admonished to work for peace in the world. About the trial volume, *Psalmer och Visor 76,* Olov Hartman wrote: " . . . this is the first Swedish hymnal that has questioned the status quo."[5] God is praised for the wonders of creation, but all creation is suffering. We have polluted the atmosphere and the seas. Both humankind and creation are in need of redemption, and several songs look forward to the morning when "there is a new world, when the air is clean and the bottoms of the seas are visible. When the poor rejoice at the message of liberation, when oppression is ended and captives are freed" (637). Nisser ends the chapter by citing several hymns, old and new, that praise God for the wonders of creation.

The music for the new texts is quite varied, composed
by about fifteen contemporary musicians. Some of the settings
are much like traditional hymn tunes. Others are like pop, folk,
and romantic songs. And there are some that demonstrate
exceptional musical artistry and originality. Not all of the tunes
are easily sung by the congregation but are more suitable for
solo or choir use. On the whole the songs are singable with
a moderate range and a lower than usual tessitura. The affin-
ity between text and tunes is commendable.

The 1937 *Psalmbok* had included about twenty hymns
from the Moravian, pietistic, and gospel songs traditions, half
of which were by Lina Sandell. The basic section of the new
volume has at least fifty of that type, with thirteen originals
and one translation by Sandell. The next greatest number is
by Nils Frykman with six texts. Among the other Pietists represented are Joel Blomqvist, Carl Boberg, Emil Gustafson, and
Carl Rosenius. Missing in the basic section are the texts of
Anders Rutström—*"Lammets folk och Sions fränder"* (411
in *Psalmer och Sånger*) ("Chosen Seed and Zion's Children")
and *"Kom, huldaste förbärmare"* (442 in *Psalmer och Sånger*)
("O Savior, Thou Who for Us Died"). Could it be that Rutström
is still *persona non grata* in the Church of Sweden? It should
be noted that *"Som en härlig gudomskälla"* (known here as
"He the Pearly Gates Will Open") is included in the basic section. The original tunes are used for these songs. Many are old
Scandinavian folk melodies and some are American gospel song
tunes. Among the Swedish composers are Oscar Ahnfelt, Joel
Blomqvist, Theodor Söderberg, and Gunnar Wennerberg.

By 1885 many of the nineteenth-century gospel songs had
been translated into Swedish. The main translators were Elizabeth Ehrenborg-Posse (1818-1880), Fredric Engelke (1848-
1906), Erik Nyström (1842-1907), and Gustav Palmqvist (1812-
1867). Nyström's texts were published in a popular collection
entitled *Sånger till Lammets lov* (Songs of Praise to the Lamb).
Only two of that type were included in the 1937 volume—
"More Holiness Give Me" by P. P. Bliss and "There Is a Gate
That Stands Ajar" by Lydia Baxter. These are retained in the
basic section of the new hymnals with the addition of the
following: "Come to the Savior" by G. F. Root; "Hallelujah,
He Is Risen" by P. P. Bliss; "Just As I Am" by C. Elliot; "O
Boundless Salvation" by W. Booth; "Savior, Thy Dying Love"

by S. D. Phelps; "We Praise Thee, O God" by W. B. Mackay; "What a Friend We Have in Jesus" by J. Scriven; and five hymns by Fanny Crosby. Most of the original musical settings have been retained.

The old volume had included only a dozen or so of the standard American and English hymns like Heber's "Holy, Holy, Holy," Stone's "The Church's One Foundation," Toplady's "Rock of Ages," or How's "For All the Saints." There were two each by Isaac Watts and William Cowper but none by Charles Wesley. All that were in the old hymnal are included in the new with the addition of at least eighteen hymns. Among them are Newton's "Amazing Grace," Alexander's "Once in Royal David's City," Williams's "Guide Me, O Thou Great Jehovah," Brooks's "O Little Town of Bethlehem," two additional texts by Watts, and four by Wesley. All of Wesley's songs are in the first section. In most cases the familiar musical settings are used.

The composer whose name appears on more hymns than any other is Johan Crüger. Thirteen of his tunes are used, some of them three, four, or five times. More than 60 percent are in the second section, indicating the strong hold of the chorale style on the Church of Sweden committee. The names of other earlier German composers and sources appear frequently. But there are also names of many contemporary musicians listed in the composer index. Those making the greatest contributions are Roland Forsberg, Harald Göransson, Egil Hovland, Trond Kverno (Norwegian), Oskar Lindberg, and Karl-Olaf Robertson.

In many cases where the same tune is used in the new hymnal as in the old, there is a change in rhythmic structure. The 1937 publication had changed most of the songs into chorales. An example is Hastings's music for "Rock of Ages." In the former edition all of the notes are even quarter or half notes:

In the new version the original rhythm is restored:

For several of the hymns the original melodies have been rein-
stated. An example is the use of Bradbury's setting for Sandell's *"Herre, samla oss nu alla"* (81) ("Now Before Thee,
Lord, We Gather") instead of the chorale type seventeenth-century tune by W. Wessnitzer. The diversity of rhythmic structure is more noticeable in the first section of the hymnal but
it extends into the second section as well. Some would say
that the changes represent a lowering of musical standards but
it is clear that the committee wanted the new collection to
represent many musical tastes. The music of the contemporary
composers demonstrates a wide variety of musical styles.

The arrangement in each of the sections is quite conventional but the second part has four additional divisions:
1) hymns in other Nordic languages—Danish, Finnish (repeated
in Swedish), and Norwegian; 2) psalms and canticles; 3) Bible
songs and canons; 4) liturgical songs. Division two has
one- or two-line stanzas primarily from the Psalms. Most of
the musical settings are by Egil Hovland and Trond Kverno.
In division three there are songs much like the biblical praise
choruses that are popular in North America. One is from a
Maranatha songbook—"Seek Ye First the Kingdom of God"
by Karen Lafferty. All of these have guitar chords, and it should
be noted that chords are provided for many songs throughout
the volume.

As we noted at the outset, the hymnal has its critics. Perhaps those who object to extensive revisions of old familiar
texts are the most vocal. As is true whenever a new hymnal
is introduced, certain favorites are missed. One of the omis-
sions was *"Fadernas kyrka"* (the church of our fathers). The
reaction was so heated that a single sheet was provided to
attach inside the back cover. The new numbering was also a
target of criticism. For more than a hundred years *"Var halsad
skona morgonstund"* ("All Hail to Thee, O Blessed Morn")
had been number 55, and now it is 119. The people should
welcome the variety of textual themes and musical styles. No
doubt many will enjoy the more rhythmic melodies, the joyful
contemporary songs, and the favorite older ones that had not
been included in the former songbook. And now at ecumenical
gatherings the Swedes will have a single collection of hymns
from which to lift their voices together in praise to God and
to challenge each other to faith and service.

Psalmer och Sånger is the new hymnal for nine of the free church groups. As we have already noted it shares the same 325 hymns with *Psalmboken*. The second section includes 458 songs, making a total of 784. The churches sharing this hymnal are: Adventist, Alliance Mission, Free Baptist, Holiness, Methodist, Swedish Baptist, Swedish Salvation Army, Swedish Mission Covenant, and Örebro Mission. In 1978 five of these churches were involved in the publication of *Herren Lever,* a collection of 138 new hymns and songs. Many of these are in the new volume. The last hymnal of the Swedish Covenant, *Sånger och Psalmer,* appeared in 1951. The new hymnal retains only 38 percent of the 788 hymns from that volume.

The second section shares about a hundred songs with the second section of *Psalmboken,* which means that the two volumes have a total of 425 hymns in common. In order to make room for the new material, several of the pietist and revival songs were deleted. There were sixty-six Sandell texts in the old book and twenty-nine are in the new. Frykman had twenty-seven in the old and has fourteen in the new. There are a few additions in the gospel song category, including Fanny Crosby's "To God Be the Glory" (327) and "Blessed Assurance" (359). The Methodist influence is seen in the addition of nine texts by Wesley.

The second section has the greatest number of all new songs. Many of them were written by Anders Frostenson and Britt Hallqvist. The former is responsible for twenty-eight originals and twenty-three revisions and/or translations, and the latter, for eighteen originals and eleven revisions and/or translations. Among other contemporary writers are Olov Hartman, Arne H. Lindgren, Margareta Melin, Eva Norberg, and Göte Strandsjö. The most prolific of the composers are Torgny Erséus, Roland Forsberg, Egil Hovland, Lars Lindberg, Karl-Olof Robertson, and Gunno Södersten.

There is a section of thirty-one songs at the end of the regular hymn selections entitled *Psalterpsalmer och andra sånger ur Bibeln* (hymns from the Psalms and other songs from the Bible). These are akin to the selections in the divisions in *Psalmboken.* In fact, they have eighteen songs in common. Many of the musical settings are by Egil Hovland, Torgny Erséus, and Gunno Södersten.

The index of first lines includes all stanzas. There is an

index of writers and composers with brief identifying statements. The placement of the indexes about two-thirds of the
way through the book has generated some criticism. The
remainder of the volume (almost 400 pages) is devoted to Bible
readings and other worship aids. The total number of pages
is 1,324, a rather hefty volume. This, too, has caused some
unfavorable reaction.

It is too early to assess the general acceptance of *Den
Svenska Psalmboken* and *Psalmer och Sånger.* One wonders
whether the committees have been too bold in the introduction of so much new material. To drop 62 percent of one's
hymnody as the Swedish Covenant has done seems ill-advised.
The policy of extensively revising many of the texts is also
questionable. One can understand the attempt to bring the language in line with modern usage and grammar but to replace
whole phrases and interchange lines is "an attack on memory."[6] It seems that severe revising is less urgent when there
are so many new texts. One argument advanced for the revision of hymns is that it may result in a more meaningful engage-
ment of the singer with the hymn. One advantage that the new
hymnals have is that they were preceded by many trial publications, and the churches were involved in the process of change.
Another advantage was the care with which the new volumes
were introduced and promoted. Special study sessions were
provided to acquaint people with the new collections.

The committee is to be commended for the idea of a union
hymnal. For a whole nation to be able to sing from the same
collection is unique indeed. The process has created interest
among Christians and non-Christians. A cartoon depicts one
Swede confronting a friend saying, "Why are you so upset
over the new hymnal, Gustav? You never go to church." To
which Gustav answers, "Ya, I know." Dare we hope that the
new hymnals may stimulate a return to the church and God?

Endnotes

[1] Per Olof Nisser, *Vår Nya Psalmbok* (Stockholm: Verbum, 1987), back
cover.
[2] Rut Stenlund Gröhn, *"Hostens Viktigaste Bok," Svensk Veckotidning,* 46:44 (October 1987), 8-9.

[3] Nisser, *op. cit.,* p. 153.
[4] *Ibid.,* pp. 166-192.
[5] *Ibid.,* p. 190.
[6] Gracia Grindal, "Where We Are Now," *The Hymn,* 38 (1987), 23.

The Pietist Schoolman

Zenos E. Hawkinson

When David Nyvall resigned his position as assistant to Fridolf
Risberg in the Swedish division of Chicago Theological Seminary, his purpose was to free himself to work toward a Covenant school. What it cost Nyvall to become the Covenant's
schoolman is to be found in Karl Olsson's wryly accurate
assessment reflecting to some degree his own experience—as
well as that of the legion of educated Pietists during recent
centuries who have struggled to found and maintain schools
for the children of their fellowships:

> [Nyvall] left security, status, and almost ideal work-
> ing conditions (which would have permitted him
> to carry on his beloved studies) for insecurity, pov-
> erty, frequent hostility to educational enterprise, a
> great deal of personal envy of the educated, and an
> exhausting schedule of speaking, writing, teaching,
> and administering. He did this because he believed
> in the cause of the Covenant and in Covenant edu-
> cation. He never seems to have regretted his step.[1]

Some of this exigency was inseparable from beginnings.
No one lives affluently when capital is scarce and tradition
thin. What Europe's wandering scholars had suffered during
the twelfth- and thirteenth-century infancy of the universities,
later schoolmen would have to endure in their turn.[2]

Time and stereotype being what they are, one hesitates
to mention Henry Dunster of Harvard and David Nyvall of
North Park in the same breath. But no one familiar with the
records can doubt that the Massachusetts Bay Puritan schoolman and the Covenant schoolman would have had much to
compare with each other, including their forced retirement

from office—Dunster (in 1653) because conscience led him
to confess publicly his position as a Baptist, Nyvall (in 1905)
because conscience compelled him to remain a convinced and
honorable Pietist. But overdue tuitions and payment in kind
were their daily experience, though 250 years separated their
professional lives.[3]

The quickening of Euro-American Protestantism we now
call Pietism was on one of its many faces Lutheran.[4] This line
runs from Johann Arndt's *True Christianity* (1605-09) to
Philipp Jakob Spener's *Pia Desideria* (1675) to Spener's pro-
tegé, August Hermann Francke, pastor and professor in Halle/
Glaucha (1692-1727). Francke wrote:

> I found among the poor people such coarse and
> dreadful ignorance that I almost did not know where
> I should begin to bring to them a firm foundation
> of their Christianity. . . . So many people went
> about like cattle without any knowledge of God and
> divine things, but in particular that so many children,
> on account of the poverty of their parents, neither
> attended school nor otherwise enjoyed any good
> upbringing, but rather grew up in the most shameful
> ignorance and in all wickedness so that with advanc-
> ing years they became of no use and therefore gave
> themselves over to stealing, robbery, and wicked
> deeds.[5]

Francke began by inviting the poor to devotionals in his
parsonage, where he distributed alms. When in 1694 an unex-
pected sum appeared in the alms box, he used the money to
begin a school for poor children, went on to establish an orphanage, a free lunch program for needy university students,
a home for widows, a series of new schools for middle- and
upper-class children, and the Canstein Press, which in the
course of its work printed and distributed more than two million Bibles and other edifying literature. Taken together with
the powerful impetus to world missions, these were the Halle
Foundations, exemplars to a quickly growing circle of Christian progressives.

Francke the preacher was frequently in hot water with
high-church Lutherans; Francke the educator and philanthropic
entrepreneur remained in good favor with influential layper-

sons at the court of Brandenburg who usually responded generously to his pleas for moral and financial support. Pietist
schoolmen usually enjoyed more sympathy from kings than
from archbishops.[6]

They were also well-received by Americans. Stung by
orthodox disdain for the New World as "the outer darkness"
into which the worthless servant of Matthew 25:30 was to be
cast, Cotton Mather (M.A. Harvard, 1681) wrote enthusiastic-
ally to Francke in 1717 about the Halle Foundations, declar-
ing that "we Americans here live beyond Ultima Thule, in a
country unknown to Strabo and Caesar, but not unknown to
Christ," and went on to defend the ecumenical spirit as something deeply shared by "American pietists," among whom he
included himself.[7]

Let us remember that Halle was not the only foundation
of the 1690s; so also was Yale College,[8] and William and Mary.
Obviously the curve of educational concern was rising, not
only among Pietists but among people of other theological
views and in both hemispheres. Whatever labels we use, the
Bay Colony Puritans had a concern that Francke shared, and
that they had moved to satisfy in the New World sixty years
before. As Morison says:

> The common school system of early Massachusetts
> was intended to teach boys to write, cipher, and
> read the Bible, and that it did. Are we too sophisti-
> cated to admit that reading the Bible may be of some
> use to a people in forming their character, or in-
> structing their taste? [9]

As for Harvard College, its first college laws included the
requirement that every student must be instructed that:

> the main end of his life and studies was *to know God
> and Jesus Christ* . . . and therefore to lay Christ in
> the bottom, as the only foundation of all sound
> knowledge and learning.[10]

That the Harvard founders were Puritans and university
trained was equally clear; their passion for an educated ministry
was at the root of their decision to banish Anne Hutchinson
and her party. Had the Hutchinson view prevailed, thinks Morison, there never would have been a Harvard.[11]

Whether German or English, the Pietist schoolman as a type necessarily reflected the character of Pietism as a Christian movement.[12] The Pietist schoolman was usually a university graduate profoundly discontent with the state of the church and determined to see it reformed. He was mainline in theological conviction but hungry and thirsty for living faith experienced in the company of others. He tended to place less emphasis on creed than on Bible, less on erudition than on pastoral care, less on the authority than on the responsibility of the pastoral office. The Pietist schoolman was urgent about his responsibility to the children of common people. Francke loved to say that his duty was twofold: God's glory and neighbor's good. Francke's mentor, Spener, looked forward to "better times in the church," being deeply rooted in a confidence that serious biblical awareness and a new spirit of lay ministration would soften the rigid doctrinal orthodoxies into which the territorial churches had fallen since Luther and Calvin.[13] Nor did Spener hesitate to recommend that Christians debate their theological opponents in the spirit of the Good Samaritan.

Spener's godson, Nikolaus Ludwig Graf von Zinzendorf (1700-1760), equally at home in Germany, Britain, and America, breathed ecumenical generosity and educational innovation:

> Zinzendorf would have nothing to do with the prevailing form of religious education which sought to mold all the children into the same pattern and to demand of them the same inward experiences in a set progressive order. He recognized the manifoldness of life and the individuality of the child. He opposed the tyranny of schemes and methodism. As long as the child is "walking with Jesus" he is being nurtured in the best possible of all schools: "In Herrnhut we do not shape the children," he wrote; "we leave that to the Creator." He was against coercive measures in any branch of the child's education. The modern conception of "teaching as meeting" was implicit in his whole approach.[14]

Zinzendorf's daughter maintained the family tradition in America by opening a school for girls at Ashmead House, Germantown, Pennsylvania, in 1742, attended among others by George Washington's niece, Eleanor Lee.[15]

Eighteenth-century Enlightenment winds blew good news for children and others in need of instruction. To the Pietist concern for an educated ministry and a ministering laity, we may add an increasing secular awareness of the social values of education. Rousseau's *Émile* was first published in 1762. Johann Heinrich Pestalozzi (1746-1827) read it while training for the Lutheran priesthood in Switzerland; together with the memory of his grandfather's careful pastoral attention to the education of his parish children in the canton of Zürich, *Émile* persuaded him of his vocation to children. In 1774 Pestalozzi opened an orphanage to teach neglected children useful life skills, based on pedagogical convictions centered on the natural growth of the child, and illustrated in *Leonard and Gertrude,* a novel first published in 1781.[16] His boarding school at Yverdon, founded in 1805, attracted European attention, not least from the founding father of the *Kindergarten* movement, Friedrich Froebel (1782-1852), whose father was an Old Lutheran pastor in Thuringia.[17]

From Pestalozzi and Froebel, and their enthusiastic advocate, the German reform philosopher Johann Fichte, as well as from his own dismal experiences as a schoolboy, the powerful leader of the Danish national renaissance, Nikolai F. S. Grundtvig (1783-1872) took inspiration and direction. Grundtvig, seriously at odds with the prevailing rationalism of Danish theological faculties, believed with Froebel that all education must be religious at its base for it to be productive. Against the prevailing pedagogical practice, he desired a method and content for school instruction more natural to the learner. Education, said Grundtvig, must have as its goal "man first, then Christian."[18] Grundtvig was no jovial Enlightenment optimist:

> He had learned from his own experience that human
> life without Christ is "to worse than the grave cast
> out":
>> "In and of itself, the soul
>> Severed from life's spring,
>> Like a river cut off from its source,
>> Sooner or later runs dry."
> And separated from life's spring man had become.

> Only in Christ did the spring gush forth anew, in
> Christ as he was found in the living word in the con-
> gregation.[19]

Nor did his vision stop with the education of children. He saw
all around him young people and adults who had no hope of
a university matriculation, but who for their own sakes and
for the future of his beloved Denmark needed access to educational stimulus. His answer: a school for people, eighteen
years and older, based upon the same sense of natural and practical order that Pestalozzi and Froebel had advocated for children. Thus were born the "folk high schools,"[20] the first at
Rödding in North Schleswig in 1844, the second under
Christen Kold at Ryslinge in 1850.[21] The folk high school idea
spread quickly to Norway and Finland, less quickly to Sweden.
Today these schools number more than three hundred
throughout Scandinavia.[22]

The first national provision for common schooling in Sweden dates from 1842, the year in which George Scott was
driven from Sweden, handing over his infant religious
monthly, *Pietisten,* to his young assistant, Carl Olof Rosenius
(1816-1868). The very word "Pietist" was so obnoxious to
high-church Swedes that Archbishop Wingård pleaded with
Scott to choose another title.[23] The journal, as Rosenius shaped
it, was itself a schooling in biblical piety for the growing conventicle movement in the Swedish countryside, for which
Rosenius became, by degrees, mentor and prophet.[24] More perhaps than any other, Rosenius led his people back to Luther,
and through Luther to serious biblical study of narrative and
argument. It is not an exaggeration to call him the biblical
schoolmaster to the *läsare* movement; he did not begin it, he
instructed it. Around Rosenius gathered Swedish priests and
laity with a passion for church reform, the circle that would
produce in 1856 the National Evangelical Foundation, almost
—if not quite—a bow back to Spener.

Among the humbler of this circle was P. A. Ahlberg
(1823-1887), between 1861 and 1875 the master of Ahls-
borg—a school in Vetlanda, Småland, for boys, colporteurs,
and candidates for the North American ministry. Ahlberg
remembered his own school days: "To read and to weep—flog-
gings and long lessons—clarified mostly with the cane."[25]

Clearly Ahlberg's Vimmerby schoolmaster had not heard of
Zinzendorf, Pestalozzi, or Grundtvig; nor, possibly, would he
have listened had he heard. But we have Erik August Skogsbergh's recollections of happy days with Pastor Ahlberg (even
though he thought Ahlberg too much bound to the law), getting homiletic instruction some years before his emigration
in 1876 to Chicago.[26]

That Pietism as a folk movement could create its own
schools was demonstrated by the widow Maria Nilsdotter of
Vall, Värmland, when she began a Sunday school on her farm
in 1850, and some years later expanded it into an orphan-
age-school with the support of her son Carl Johan and others
in the Karlskoga parish. No Francke in either education or
connection, her instincts ran in the same directions and her
energies dominated the landscape around her.[27] Schools
remained a central concern to Carl Johan Nyvall as he pro-
gressed through his tutelage as colporteur for the National
Evangelical Foundation, to itinerant preacher, to founding
spirit of the Värmland Ansgar Society, to one of the handful
of founders of the Swedish Mission Covenant in 1878. David
Nyvall believed that his father's foremost concern in the establishment of the Covenant was to assure organizational support for schools.[28]

David Nyvall at sixteen sent off a letter to his father's great
friend Paul Peter Waldenström, asking advice on the best way
to become a poet. Waldenström replied immediately:

> If you follow my advice, you will not fantasize away
> your time with novels and such stuff, but will set-
> tle yourself down to those studies demanded by a
> proper and basic *Studentexamen*. If God intends you
> to be a poet, you cannot become one without study,
> and if someday you become one, you will find in
> God's will rich fields for the greatest poetic gifts if
> you wish wholly to serve the Lord.[29]

Thus began a seminal relationship between a visionary boy
and the linguist-theologian-free church preacher which would
continue through bright and stormy weather on two continents. Nyvall, reflecting, declared that his studies under Waldenström at Gävle revealed a teacher of unequalled clarity:

His way of paraphrasing and condensing Norbeck's *Dogmatics* was astonishing in its effect. The most unimaginable became self-evident as he worked with it, and as a rule it took him one line to clarify what the book took ten lines to obscure.[30]

But clarity for the living future might be another matter. We do not know why David Nyvall entered medical studies at Uppsala; we do know that he appeared in Chicago during the summer of 1886, distressed and forlorn. He and his father explained only that he was visiting. But the visit turned into an emigration, the visitor into a greenhorn in search of his own promised land. He was, however, not alone. The river of Swedes flowing into America was at high flood. Moreover, a generation of predecessors had worked their way through the confusions of American life and had formed the North American Covenant in 1885, not without the influence of Nyvall's father.

Some confusion remained. Like other religiously serious Swedes, the Covenanters had to face the educational question presented by the absence in America of a state church and its associated institutions. Ethnicity, theology, and fellowship went into the search for an appropriate form.[31]

The Covenant at its organizational meeting in 1885 had accepted a generous offer from American Congregationalists to provide theological training for ministerial candidates in a Scandinavian department at Chicago Theological Seminary. Was this "Risberg School" an adequate solution? Fridolf Risberg, personally selected in consultation with Waldenström by C. A. Björk, thought so and remained faithful to his original understanding with the seminary until the department was disbanded in 1917. Others were not so sure. Some complained that the selection and admission of ministerial candidates were not under Covenant control. Others, including Nyvall, looked in vain for educational opportunities for Covenant young people without ministerial vocation.

That is why Nyvall, after two happy years as Risberg's assistant during 1888-1890, returned to Skogsbergh's school in Minneapolis, a school for immigrants begun in 1884:

It was a humble enterprise, to be sure. We gathered in an empty store in a then outlying part of the town

where Lindblade taught English and Business and
I taught, in Swedish, everything that I could persuade anybody to learn. . . . It was, in all its poverty and its almost total lack of organization, an independent school, standing under obligation to no
other denomination and absolutely free to accept
students and adopt methods that seemed best fit-
ted to the ends in view. The work was not in vain.[32]

It might have been Halle/Glaucha two centuries earlier, another
attempt at "God's glory, neighbor's good." Nor did it stop
for the Covenant with Nyvall.

Karl Olsson, coming to the North Park presidency in 1959,
chose to grapple with traditional Pietist themes in his inaugural
address titled "Divine Foolishness and Human Learning."[33]
"Is it possible," he asks, "that Paul has anything to say to
schoolmen?"

At the center he places the traditional *Wiedergeburt* of
Pietism, quoting Blaise Pascal's journal of midnight visitation:
"FIRE—God of Abraham, God of Isaac, God of Jacob, not of
the philosophers and scholars. Certitude." Against this incom-
mensurable experience, Olsson places Paul's complaint that
Jews are seeking for a sign, Greeks for wisdom. "If the pursuit of a sign or the pursuit of learning is thought to control
human history, then God has become a captive God devoid
of sovereignty and freedom."

Where then is the solution? Some schools, embarrassed
by traditional theology, have become secular. Others have
become moralistic and doctrinaire. "This school," says Olsson,
"adheres to its Christian heritage not merely because it desires
the redemption of man but because it desires the redemption
of learning through the foolishness of God."

God will continue, no matter how much we may
protest, to choose the foolish to shame the wise, the
weak to shame the strong, and the low, the despised,
and the nothing of this world to bring to nothing
the things that are. So inscrutable is his wisdom and
his ways past finding out. *To him alone be the glory
now and forever.*

It is in the nature of the inspiration that took Pietism as

its form that its work is never finished, not at least until God's kingdom is completed. That work required, and requires, the schoolman, the one whom Nyvall called the skylark—on whose wings one first discerns the dawning of the new day.

Endnotes

[1] David Nyvall and Karl A. Olsson, *The Evangelical Covenant Church* (Chicago: Covenant Press, 1954), p. 64, n. 21.

[2] The term "schoolman" is traditionally derived from these medieval teachers of philosophy and theology. It is used in this paper to describe the later adaptions of this educational tradition and is not intended to be exclusive in language or tone; rather, it recognizes the metaphor and self-understanding of the specific historical contexts.

[3] Dunster (1609-1660) M.A. Magdalene College, Cambridge, emigrated to Massachusetts Bay in 1640 and was immediately appointed president of Harvard. Samuel Eliot Morison, *Builders of the Bay Colony* (Boston: Houghton Mifflin, 1930), pp. 183-216, presents a lively and loving portrait. The reluctance of the Massachusetts General Court to remove him from office is clearly documented. Nevertheless, antipedobaptism was considered unacceptable radicalism, especially in the leader of Harvard.

[4] One should not neglect, however, Chasidism as well as French Jansenism. See Martin Buber, *The Origin and Meaning of Hasidism,* Maurice Friedman, ed. and trans. (New York: Horizon Press, 1960); and F. Ernest Stoeffler, *The Rise of Evangelical Pietism* (Leiden: E. J. Brill, 1965).

[5] Quoted in Gary R. Sattler, *God's Glory, Neighbor's Good,* (Chicago: Covenant Press, 1982), p. 48. This work offers a concise description of Francke's world-famous "Foundations" (pp. 47-67).

[6] The University of Halle was itself a foundation by Frederick III of Brandenburg. Compare the experience of N. F. S. Grundtvig with Christian III of Denmark, and of P. P. Waldenström with Oscar II of Sweden.

[7] Ernst Benz, "Ecumenical Relations between Boston Puritanism and German Pietism: Cotton Mather and August Hermann Francke," *Harvard Theological Review,* 54 (1961), 165, 171. One may suspect diplomacy in Mather's language without entirely discounting his willingness to be identified with Francke's efforts. The point of contact between the two was the court chaplain to George of Denmark, Prince Consort of Queen Anne, Pastor Anton Wilhelm Boehm, who played a role in London uncannily parallel to that played in Stockholm in the 1830s by the Wesleyan pastor George Scott. For a full treatment of Mather and Pietism, see Richard F. Lovelace, *The American Pietism of Cotton Mather: Origins of American Evangelicalism* (Grand Rapids: Eerdmans, 1979).

[8] With an original grant from Elihu Yale obtained through the good offices of Cotton Mather! See Roland Bainton, *Yale and the Ministry* (New York: Harper and Row, 1957), pp. 6-9.

[9] Morison, *Builders of the Bay Colony,* p. 187.

¹⁰ Quoted in Samuel E. Morison, *The Founding of Harvard College* (Cambridge: Harvard University Press, 1935), p. 251.

¹¹ *Ibid.,* pp. 171-180, for Morison's discussion of the real options.

¹² Debate during the past generation about the boundaries of Pietism has stabilized our categories. An excellent summary of the present understanding is in F. Ernest Stoeffler, "Pietism: Its Message, Early Manifestation, and Significance," *Covenant Quarterly,* 34 (1976), 3-24. The reader will do well to bear in mind Stoeffler's opening sentence: "Historical movements have fuzzy edges."

¹³ Spener's vision of the Pietist program is concisely summarized in K. James Stein, *Philipp Jakob Spener: Pietist Patriarch* (Chicago: Covenant Press, 1986), pp. 93-103. See also Manfred W. Kohl, "Spener's Pia Desideria—The *Programmschrift* of Pietism," *Covenant Quarterly,* 34 (1976), 61-78.

¹⁴ A. J. Lewis, *Zinzendorf the Ecumenical Pioneer* (Philadelphia: Westminster Press, 1962), pp. 172f.

¹⁵ *Ibid.,* p. 174. Lewis quotes E. E. and L. R. Gray, *Wilderness Christians,* p. 331: "Many twentieth-century educational programmes were inaugurated in eighteenth-century Moravian schools. Parent-teachers' meetings, community-school associations, educational and vocational guidance, and student participation in school management were common practice as early as 1750."

¹⁶ A. Pinloche, *Pestalozzi and the Foundation of the Modern Elementary School* (New York: Scribner, 1901), is a reasonable summary. See also Eva Channing, trans. and ed., *Pestalozzi's Leonard and Gertrude* (New York: D. C. Heath, 1885). The pastor "no longer allowed the children to learn any long prayers by rote, saying this was contrary to the spirit of Christianity, and the express injunctions of their Saviour" (pp. 156f).

¹⁷ Robert B. Downs, *Friedrich Froebel* (Boston: Twayne, 1978).

¹⁸ Hal Koch, *Grundtvig,* Llewellyn Jones, trans. (Yellow Springs, Ohio: Antioch Press, 1952), pp. 151-165. Jones freely translates one of Grundtvig's poems: "If we do not feel in our hearts,/We are sprung of heaven's race,/If we cannot feel with sorrow,/That we have become debased,/Then we only make mock of the word/That God will redeem us and give/Rebirth as his own children."

¹⁹ *Ibid.,* p. 152.

²⁰ Not to be understood in the sense of American secondary schools. These were to be adult education foundations, small residential schools built around the idea of mutual communication and practical educational purpose. "High" meant, therefore, only "advanced," while "folk" implied that anyone, without discrimination, was to be admitted who might find the experience useful. Grundtvig himself founded no schools, though he projected many.

²¹ Roar Skovmand, "Grundtvig and the Folk High School Movement," in Christen Thodberg and Anders P. Thyssen, eds., *N. F. S. Grundtvig: Tradition & Renewal,* Edward Broadbridge, trans. (Copenhagen: Det Danske Selskab, 1983), pp. 321-343.

²² Was it Grundtvig's passionate insistence on the importance of the

Danish mother tongue that inspired the pedagogically revolutionary discoveries of Jens O. H. Jesperson (1860-1943), a linguist who insisted that foreign languages must be taught as children learn their own, by using it, even before they know what they are saying? One of the scandals of American education in the twentieth century is that few Americans (outside the Peace Corps) have paid much attention to Jesperson's methods.

23 Gunnar Westin, *George Scott och hans verksamhet i Sverige* (Stockholm: Svenska kyrkans diakonistyrelses bokförlag, 1929), p. 622.

24 Karl A. Olsson, *By One Spirit* (Chicago: Covenant Press, 1962), pp. 52-58, provides a graphic description of the conventicle practice during these years. By 1855 *Pietisten* had a monthly circulation of 7,000, compared to *Aftonbladet* (the most popular liberal paper in the country) at 4,000 (Erland Sundström, *Trossamfund i det svenska samhället* [Stockholm: Tidens förlag, 1952], pp. 70-71). And that figure needs a multiplier; the paper was often shared, one subscriber per conventicle!

25 E. J. Ekman, *Den inre missionens historia,* (Stockholm: E. J. Ekmans förlagsexpedition, 1896-1902), II:2, p. 1141.

26 E. August Skogsbergh, *Minnen och upplevelser* (Minneapolis: Veckobladets tryckeri [1923]), pp. 51-58.

27 David Nyvall, *My Father's Testament,* Eric G. Hawkinson, trans. (Chicago: Covenant Press, 1974), pp. 28ff., 63-73.

28 *Ibid.,* pp. 153-158.

29 The letter in Waldenström's hand is reproduced in David Nyvall, *"Waldenström som lärare,"* in A. Ohlden, ed., *Lector P. Waldenström,* (Uppsala: J. A. Lindblads förlag, 1917), p. 65. It is dated 18 September 1879.

30 *Ibid.,* p. 67.

31 Swedish Americans had already expended tremendous energies in establishing appropriate schools. A listing of surviving schools might be a helpful reminder:

Augustana, Rock Island, Illinois (1860)
Augustana, Sioux Falls, South Dakota (1861)
Gustavus Adolphus, St. Peter, Minnesota (1862)
Bethel, St. Paul, Minnesota (1871)
Bethany, Lindsborg, Kansas (1881)
Pacific Lutheran, Tacoma, Washington (1890)
North Park, Chicago, Illinois (1891)
Upsala, East Orange, New Jersey (1893)
Trinity, Deerfield, Illinois (1897)

An incomplete listing of colleges not surviving includes:

Ansgar, Knoxville, Illinois (1875-1884)
Martin Luther, Chicago, Illinois (1893-1895)
Texas Wesleyan, Austin, Texas (1911-1931)
Trinity, Round Rock, Texas (closed 1929)
Walden, McPherson, Kansas (1907-1912)

To these add a substantial number of secondary institutions. See, for instance, Emeroy Johnson, "Swedish Academies in Minnesota," *Swedish Pioneer Historical Quarterly,* 32 (1981), 20-40.

[32] Quoted in Leland H. Carlson, *A History of North Park College,* (Chicago: North Park College, 1941), pp. 24f. Nyvall had spent 1887-1888 with Skogsbergh in Minneapolis.

[33] The text is printed in the current number of *Pietisten,* 3, No. 1 (1988); it was also published separately following the inauguration in 1959 by North Park College.

The Covenant and the American Challenge
Restoring a Dynamic View of Identity and Pluralism

Philip J. Anderson

More than any other people in the world, Americans speak often and easily about pluralism. A nation comprised of almost total immigrant stock with varied beliefs, behaviors, and values confronts these complexities in every area of life. Despite efforts to describe these differences and attach labels in order to provide personal and group identities, the word "pluralism" all too often becomes a glib way to mask the confusion, and a deterrent to serious investigation of the issues. At the same time, the need for transcendent identities is crucial to the health and well-being of a people. What is a serious challenge for the nation is no less one for American churches.

The reality of this dilemma is especially apparent in the Protestant churches. The most notable quality of the Reformation is its diversity, recognizing that people think different thoughts even when they seek to witness to the same gospel. It is distinctive that Protestantism accepts these ambiguities as part of its heritage, as both a sign of health and a symptom of illness. A Protestant must always seek to discern the difference. Such diversity has occurred because Protestantism has been a movement that consciously has assumed the burden of relating its message directly to the concerns and problems of people in specific historical contexts.

The history of Protestantism, then, has been the pluralistic endeavor to take its formal principle (the supremacy of the Bible) and its material principle (justification by grace through faith) and apply them to the inherited body of tradition, liturgy, dogma, and churchmanship, as well as to specific times and places. In addition to schism with the Roman Catholic Church, the hostilities between the Lutheran, Reformed, Anglican, and left-wing Reformation movements are all too painfully known to students of history.

Protestantism, however, was still in a profound way a unified movement of protest, and in recent decades scholars have endeavored to identify a transcendent "Protestant principle." Because of its dependence on the biblical message, Protestantism contains the divine and human protest against any absolute claim made by a relative reality, even if the claim is made by a Protestant church. A clear statement of this point comes from Paul Tillich:

> What makes Protestantism Protestant is the fact that it transcends its own religious and confessional character, and that it cannot be identified wholly with any of its particular historical forms. . . . Protestantism has a principle that stands beyond all its realizations. It is the critical and dynamic source of all Protestant realizations, but it is not identical with any of them. It cannot be confined by a definition. It is not exhausted by any historical religion; it is not identical with the structure of the Reformation or of early Christianity or even with a religious form at all.[1]

This kind of discussion of Protestant unity and diversity is very helpful to an understanding of the Swedish setting that forms the background of The Evangelical Covenant Church. The Lutheran reform in Sweden, its controversies with Catholicism and Calvinism, the renewal that came through various forms of Pietism, the Anglo-American influences of the nineteenth century, and many other aspects of Swedish religious life indicate the pressures of a growing pluralism. A small yet significant portion of this history gave birth to the Swedish Covenant in 1878.

It was in North America, however, that unbridled, disestablished pluralism alternately fascinated and horrified the Swedish immigrant. It was in the American context, far more than in the Swedish and Continental antecedents, that the diversity of the Covenant was to blossom. Prior to the middle of the nineteenth century, America was already infused with a variety of religious faiths (though essentially Protestant), but the subsequent tides of immigration assured a pluralism quite independent of preconceived theory. The boundless frontier and unrestricted immigration led to the American religious pattern described by adjectives such as pluralistic, voluntaristic, individualistic, competitive, democratic, pragmatic, activistic, revivalistic, and enthusiastic. North America seemed committed to the principle that the Christian tradition must be pluralistic, with each denomination claiming for itself, by voluntary identification, the truth once and for all delivered to the saints. This may have changed somewhat in the present ecumenical age, but as Sydney Ahlstrom has said (paraphrasing Goethe), the drive for these churches was "the North American opportunity to begin anew without being hindered by custom or misled by tradition."[2]

There is something else, however, equally apparent in these diverse, disestablished North American churches, and that is a primordial sense of Christian tradition, particularly among those whose origins were never truly sectarian. The immigrant especially found it difficult to abrogate tradition, what Jaroslav Pelikan has called the living faith of the dead— not the dead faith of the living—the continuous link to the church's catholicity. North America was better (as the letters home consistently said), but the immigrants sought to preserve many of the traditions of the homeland and to allow them to grow in the new environment. Of course, that would not be easy, and the transition from generation to generation proved to be times of testing and change. Yet in many immigrant churches time served to deepen this primordial sense of the Christian tradition with both a particular and universal rootedness, despite the fact that American culture would tend to work against such identification and even pressure the pluralism to be resolved in some new synthesis or vague national sense of a "civil religion."

The purpose of this essay is to examine from the perspective of the historical sources the diversity and unity within the North American Covenant, and the models proposed in recent times to make the pluralism more understandable and, perhaps in the desires of some, even manageable. This examination is necessary for a number of reasons. Only through attention to the sources can the complex story be told and, above all, the self-understanding of the actors in history be preserved. Only through careful historiography can issues of influence be distinguished from cardinal matters of identity. And only through a critical nurturing of the Covenant's history (in the context of a dependence on the biblical witness) can the denomination authentically perpetuate from generation to generation, from old to new, the heart of its understanding of the gospel and the church, without being bound by the past or denying full ownership of the tradition to those who come from widely varied backgrounds and experiences. A non-creedal, biblically based, and relationally oriented church has only its history to maintain this identity in the fresh openness of the present and future, and thus serve as a trustworthy beacon.

The essay suggests three areas of further exploration (beyond the constraints of the space here) to aid in the quest for understanding the Covenant's identity and pluralism. The first section will propose a number of general areas of historical research necessary to any judgment about the denomination's past, and when taken together provide a critical historical framework. Second, the essay will explore recent attempts to describe and manage the church's pluralism by creating types and circles, and will try and show that such efforts have not only failed to maintain integrity with historical evidence but are inadequate to the desired task and misleading. The final section will propose, in a preliminary way, a constructive model to understand this past and present diversity. It grows out of the historical sources themselves and forces the student of Covenant life to understand persons, churches, events, and issues in a descriptive language that takes seriously the story of each. It defies typing and labeling, and preserves the church as a dynamic, living whole—as opposed to other models that, contrary to motive, render the church static by artificially separating persons, churches, events, and issues into sterile categories. Only then can the pluralism of the church truly be understood, the creative dialectic of its life be maintained, and the prospects of a future of commitment and mission be enjoined by all its members.

I. *Ad Fontes*

J.W. Burgon: Mr. President, give me leave to ask you
a question I have sometimes asked of aged persons,
but never of any so aged or so learned as yourself.

Every studious man, in the course of a long and thoughtful life, has had occasion to experience the special value of some one axiom or precept. Would you mind giving one the benefit of such a word of advice?

Routh, after thought: I think, sir, since you come for the advice of an old man, sir, you will find it a very good practice always to verify your references, sir!

Martin Routh (1755-1854),
President of Magdalen College, Oxford[3]

The above (somewhat humorous) quotation, well-known to scholars in the English tradition, is the axiom by which historians construct the basis for any argument. It simply calls attention to the care with which sources are not only marshaled but double-checked and verified for accuracy. It is the only way to approximate and reconstruct a past known solely by the sources, and thereby becomes the basis for a consensus of understanding or substantive disagreement. The Covenant has benefited from historians who throughout its history have labored in the records, manuscripts, books, sermons, correspondence, diaries, and newspapers generated by more than a century of denominational life. None have probed deeper or more comprehensively, with keener insight, than Karl Olsson. His significant writing in Covenant history sets a high standard of historical research and lays a foundation upon which others may build.

The ongoing task, particularly in relation to the church's pluralism, requires significant research in at least four major areas of church history beyond basic Covenant sources. This section can only be suggestive of bibliographic issues, but outlines that which is indispensable to any generalizations about the Covenant tradition.

The first is the broad field of Reformation studies and the medieval context of the transformation that occurred throughout Europe in the sixteenth century. It has been commonplace in older denominational histories, especially those growing out of the Lutheran or Reformed traditions, to be bound by stereotypes derived from either confessional dogma or centuries of interdenominational polemics. Consequently, Luther,

Calvin, and others have rarely been allowed to speak for themselves as their views have been absorbed and adapted by the multitude of ecclesiological offspring that claim them.

In the past half-century a renaissance of scholarship has occurred, of unprecedented thoroughness and sophistication, based on the availability of sources. Major studies have appeared that give a full picture of Luther's life and seriously call into question older generalizations about his use of philosophy, his debt to the mystical tradition, his two-kingdom theory, his role in the peasant revolts and attitude towards radicals and Jews, his ethical system, his view of conversion and the Christian life, and many other aspects of his theology.[4] Studies of John Calvin and other major reformers have yielded similar results.[5] The Anabaptists, the left-wing of the Reformation, have often been relegated to the backwaters of sectarian religion, and only in recent years have major studies of these movements restored them to the central discussions of modern church history.[6]

A significant result of these efforts has been the crucial ability to distinguish Luther from Lutheranism, Calvin from Calvinism, etc., thus enabling similar studies of the varied traditions as well as allowing these great figures of the church's history to have a contemporary and prophetic voice. My point here is that any examination of the Swedish church and the issues that gave rise to free church movements in Sweden and the North American setting requires keeping abreast of the burgeoning Reformation scholarship.

A second area of research, particularly germane to Covenant history, is the significant work over the past generation on Pietism and the free church tradition. Pietism, a movement of renewal within many European established churches, has until fairly recently been subjected to a variety of popular prejudicial judgments, equating it with overly emotional, prudish, and subjective spirituality. The early Karl Barth said it well: "Better with the Church in hell than with the Pietists, of a higher or lower type, in a heaven which does not exist."[7] Recent studies, however, have delineated the richness and importance of the Pietist renewal, noting its public and social character in the work of mission and evangelism (as well as inner and communal convertive piety), and have made it possible to relate the work of Spener and others to those denominations that trace their roots to Pietism, and to see its significance in light of the varied responses to Protestant Orthodoxy during the Enlightenment.[8] In addition, studies of the Moravian and Wesleyan movements have explored an influence which is of vital significance to Covenant history.[9]

It especially has been the case that sweeping generalizations have been made about the free church tradition, its origins and characteristics—which in fact are extremely varied and complex. Prior to the disciplines of twentieth-century historiography, denominational historians and apologists were eager to trace some kind of uncritical, vertical lineage back to a foundational source, be it the Apostles and other persecuted saints at the hands of the establishment (sectarian), the Anabaptists (historic peace churches), or the Puritans (Reformed). Some of these generalizations still persist. On the basis of substantive research (of a more horizontal nature), these issues can now be seen more clearly in their complexity and interrelatedness, especially as they pertain to manifestations of renewal and protest in specific times and places which led to separation from established churches.[10] This is all the more important for understanding the history of these groups in the American setting which the first amendment of the Constitution guarantees a priori to be composed entirely of free churches. Greater insight into the free church tradition has often been a product of the research in the radical Reformation and Puritanism, the latter receiving more attention than any other field of historical study in the past fifty years.

With the Covenant's origins as a Swedish church in North America, the third area of crucial scholarship involves immigration and ethnicity studies. This is a highly rigorous discipline which continues to produce pioneering work in all areas of the immigrant experience. Major surveys by Hansen, Handlin, Higham, and Bodnar have been augmented by numerous studies of particular ethnic groups and their relation to others.[11] The subject of Swedish immigration alone continues to expand and deepen at a prolific rate.[12]

Scholars are generally agreed that no institution in immigrant America exhibited more discord than the church. It was far from being a simple transplant of some homeland tradition. The immigrant experience itself required that those who left be oriented in some prior fashion towards the modern goals of autonomy, self-realization, and mobility. Timothy Smith has persuasively argued that it is fallacious to see ethnicity as synonymous with nationality and hence anachronistic in the immigrant. Peoplehood (ethnicity) was far more important than nationality (citizenship), and what began in the homeland, often in religious renewal, caused these immigrants amidst complex economic and cultural rivalries to look to their religious leaders, not as custodians of a secure past but as agents of change.[13] This area of research is absolutely necessary to any probing of Covenant history, because it demonstrates the complex challenge to choose among competing patterns of belief and behavior, and its effects on immigrants in all periods of American history—providing a religious perspective to what Higham has called the need for "integrative pluralism." Of equal importance is the way that such studies assist in understanding the tangled issues of assimilation and the transition from one generation to another in an ethnic community.

The final research area to be noted is the largest and perhaps of most importance to the question of pluralism in the Covenant. Even just a half-century ago, American church history was only emerging as a specialized discipline; today it is a well-defined and flourishing sub-specialty of the church historian. The student of the North American Covenant must at least be at home in this literature which ranges from the diversity of the Colonial and Antebellum periods to the post-Civil War explosion of religious pluralism. This development witnessed a continued expansion of the frontier populated by a growing number of immigrants who not only challenged the Puritan-Episcopal-Methodist dominance of American Protestantism but brought huge numbers of Catholics, Greek and Russian Orthodox, Jews, and others to be legitimate heirs of religious freedom in the new land, contributing to the competitive and voluntaristic proliferation of denominationalism.[14] Of course, this resulted in new forms of nativism and zealous nationalism in attempts to reinforce older preconceptions of a Protestant America.[15]

A sub-specialty within this sub-specialty of church history, however, requires more than just a passing acquaintance with the sources. The broad evangelical experience in America, rooted in the awakenings of the eighteenth and nineteenth centuries, has taken on much greater complexity in the twentieth.

Growing concern for orthodoxy in doctrine over and against the threats of modernity and the perceived liberalism of the mainline Protestant traditions have caused evangelicalism in America to fragment even further into polemical camps, eroding the general evangelical ecumenism of the earlier awakenings. Dispensationalism, premillenarianism, fundamentalism, neo-evangelicalism, and a host of other movements and agendas moved to center-stage for many American evangelicals. A word that formerly had been an adjective and most closely associated with the confessional Lutheran and Reformed traditions, now became a noun and the subject of endless categorizing about its true ontology.

During the past two decades, scholars of the American church have undertaken to study and understand this phenomenon and to locate their own and other traditions within this increasingly cultural faith.[16] Institutions, churches and parachurches, and major evangelical presses have lent their weight and resources to this task. Some of its major characteristics, which come from the insights of these scholars, will be noted in the next section as a further illustration of American evangelicalism's influence on Covenant pluralism, especially the increased tendency to interpret both in strongly Reformed categories.

The four areas of research outlined above (in addition to strictly Covenant historical sources) are not intended to be exhaustive of the possibilities of historical understanding of relevance and benefit to Covenanters. They do, however, underscore the necessity to attend faithfully to the sources and see the Covenant story as part of a larger one. Moreover, it is the sources that enable the church to construct and critique models of its pluralistic life together.

II. Is the Covenant Going in Circles?

Karl Olsson's historical writing has consistently addressed the issue of diversity in the Covenant. He has utilizied a dynamic image of the "center" and the "periphery" to describe these forces that worked together for denominational interests, and those that tended to be either content with more local concerns or even adversarial towards denominational leadership and institutions.[17] Recently, he has explored the question from the perspective of inclusion, control, and affection.[18] In developing these images, Olsson has written in the context of the dynamic character of the historical sources.

During the past decade more specific models have been proposed to describe through generalizations the pluralism of the Covenant. In each case, the models are sociological (and to a lesser extent theological) in their descriptions yet remain unsupported by research data. Consequently, they are phenomenological (as important as that may be), and even though they tend to caricature, many Covenanters initially find a way to locate their own experiences. My contention is that when analyzed and tested by historical evidence, as well as seen in light of experiences that seek to get beneath the surface of things, it is difficult to substantiate these models.

The first such model was proposed in 1979 by Lloyd H. Ahlem, former president of North Park College and Theological Seminary. It describes four types of Covenanters: 1) Swinging Conservative; 2) Traditional Conservative; 3) Traditional Covie; and 4) Mainline Protestant.[19] Though the descriptions of each type might bear some experiential recognition, they tend to be value-laden statements, hardly inclusive or nuanced. Besides, the tongue-in-cheek generalizations diminish whatever value they might have. They may serve to promote discussion but can in no way be seen as a description of reality. Rarely would the life stories of individual Covenanters, upon adequate reflection, fit any one of the four types. The attempt in Ahlem's conclusion to locate within the types North Park faculty members, national leadership, and new membership and growth, as well as the comment that all histories are written around the Traditional Covie (a diminishing group), is especially caricaturing. In my judgment, models such as these are counter-productive to the task of finding unity in the midst of diversity, much less encouraging of serious and substantive discussion.

The second and far more influential model was proposed by President Milton B. Engebretson to the Council of Superintendents in 1982. Clearly dependent on Ahlem's types, the president sought to describe three circles of Covenant life, the point of which was to try and describe two dominant historical groups in the church and an emerging third party that has difficulty relating to the formers' agendas about origin and identity beyond their own local experiences. Since these circles have since taken on a certain life of their own, and have become the basis for revisionist hypothesizing about Covenant history, it is worthwhile to quote Engebretson's description in full:

> The First Circle. These are the Covenanters who are thought of and sometimes think of themselves as the ethnic purists among us. . . . In a sense the devotees of this circle claim to be the rightful owners and interpreters of the heritage. . . . Theologically they cling to Lutheranism as closely as possible but have problems with Luther himself. Pietism in its arcane form suits them best. They are wonderful people and are crucial to the mystique, image, and future mission of the Covenant.
>
> The Second Circle. These are practically all the rest of the Covenant from coast to coast with the exception of those later to be defined as the third circle. They, too, think themselves to be the true descendants of the early Covenant fathers. . . . They claim the heritage with the same fervor as those of the first circle, but interpret it differently. They tend to blend more with the evangelical conservative on the American scene. They also tend to emphasize Reformed theology more than the Lutheran. They probably have some basis for this since the Swedish church . . . prizes its membership in the World Alliance of Reformed Churches. This group can be characterized as more growth conscious and risk-taking than the members of the first circle. Again, they are good people—the ones who usually control the vote and too often in history have had a case against the Covenant which in reality is a case against the First Circle.
>
> The Third Circle. This is the curious composition of fine people who are flocking into churches like Arvada, Rolling Hills, Hillcrest, Redwood City, Burnsville, and a number of others. They have no other investment in the history or heritage of the

Covenant than that offered and emphasized by the local church to which they belong. Many of these are ready to enroll in either the first or second circle. Their only real problem with the Covenant is that it tends to place too much emphasis on its ethnic origins. Included in this group are the ethnic churches—Blacks, Koreans, Latins, and Assyrian groups.[20]

These circles share with Ahlem's types the same sort of sociological generalizations without supporting data. They do, however, grow out of the vast experience in local churches of the former president. Likewise, then, they are phenomenological descriptions; the experiences are real as are the pluralistic patterns in the church. Leadership, in an attempt to understand the issues, tends also to want to name and label the diversity. The experiential character of the circles invites a ready identification from some people, a sort of "find yourself in the circles" exercise. But will they stand up to the test of evidence and reflection, and can they serve the common task of finding unity without demanding a synthesized uniformity? The motives behind the creation of types and circles are good ones, I believe. Their initial usefulness, however, must not be confused with an accurate description of reality. Isaiah Berlin's analysis of Leo Tolstoy's view of history, namely, the Greek poet Archilochus's tension between the hedgehog and the fox ("The fox knows many things, but the hedgehog knows one big thing"), is relevant here for it shows the limitations of generalized typologies:

> Of course, like all over-simple classifications of this type, the dichotomy becomes, if pressed, artificial, scholastic, and ultimately absurd. But if it is not an aid to serious criticism, neither should it be rejected as merely superficial or frivolous; like all distinctions which embody any degree of truth, it offers a point of view from which to look and compare, a starting point for genuine investigation.[21]

What follows in this section is not necessarily an attempt to jettison the circles (though I do believe the less reference to them the better), but rather a desire to further genuine investigation beyond what can only be seen as a starting point, not "the" starting point since historical reflection about this diversity has always been present in Covenant life. In another context, Paul L. Holmer has described the effects of disjunctive thinking which depends on categorizing issues. He says, "Much of what passes for 'understanding' comes by placing a thing in a category. We seem rather confident that to put something in the right category is to understand it, at least a little." To those involved this can seem exhilarating, but Holmer concludes that while we can argue within pre-established categories, the arguments for them and from them are extremely difficult to substantiate.[22]

Within each of the circles, Engebretson seeks to be descriptive and affirming, never unjustly critical. In that same spirit, I would like to suggest by illustration the weaknesses of the descriptions, the unfortunate static polarization that results, and the constraining effect of the circles that impedes a constructive understanding of the church's pluralism. It is true that those described in the first two circles have by and large nurtured the heritage and the ethnic roots (but even here one does not want to generalize too strongly), though they may have disagreed about aspects of their meaning. But that does not make one an "ethnic purist" or exclusive in one's attitudes towards new people; many recent Covenanters have broad sympathies, even identities, with what is described in the first two circles, and ethnicity is not an issue for them. Moreover, there really are no ethnic purists; scholars of immigrant culture will distinguish very carefully between Swedish elements and their complex transformation in the Swedish-American setting, becoming something uniquely American.

Other claims require much closer scrutiny. The statement about Luther and Lutheranism in the first circle is hardly true; if anything, history suggests just the opposite. Covenant people (regardless of circle) in the early days had a strong self-understanding of emerging from a Lutheran tradition. Their problem was with *Lutheranism* as a distortion in some points of biblical faith as they sought to assert their own convictions about the supremacy of the Bible over the creeds and confessions, and the believers' church over the folk church. And in so doing, they relied heavily upon the statements of Luther. Like many others in the past, they used the fresh insights of

Luther to critique their Lutheranism in light of his *sola scrip-
tura* principle.[23]

Likewise, the statement about the preference for Pietism
is equally confusing and misleading. Many Covenanters have,
in scholarly and other ways, nurtured the church's rootage
in the movement. North Park Theological Seminary has
received notice as a center for Pietist research and publication. That is a neutral historical issue. Engebretson says: "Pietism in its arcane form suits them best." Pietism, by definition, is never arcane (though some later expressions of the
movement may have become so), because it is always public
in its expression of the Christian faith active in love. If one
were to substitute the word "archaic" (perhaps that was
intended in reference to Spener and Francke?), that would only
serve to worsen the caricature of the attempt to understand
a formative historical relationship.

The second circle seeks to describe stronger affinities to
fundamentalism and conservative evangelicalism and to locate
them historically. While this is a major area of the church's
pluralism to explore, once again the description is problematic.
What does it mean to emphasize Reformed theology more than
the Lutheran? Most of these early Covenant people (ascribed
to this circle), and their successors, would have been unable
to utter truly distinctive Reformed doctrines. There is, however, something else at work in this "reformed" influence
(which I do find valid and important), which will be explored
below. It is especially questionable to make this assertion by
citing the position of the Swedish Covenant and its membership in the World Alliance of Reformed Churches. This is a
post-World War II decision and is principally derived from
the church's desire to relate ecumenically and in mission to
many of its free church counterparts around the world. It has
little to do with theology or doctrinal perspectives that would
cause a revision of the church's history.[24] Though some leaders
of the Swedish Covenant may wish to push this connection
with Reformed theology, it is usually done in, for example,
a Barthian perspective and not in any significant interaction
with historical sources (Barth, incidently, would be an enemy
to most circle two people as currently described). One questions too the statement that this circle has usually controlled
the vote at Annual Meetings; if that were true, it is unlikely

that it would have such a "case" against the first circle. The decisions at meetings such as Omaha (1928) suggest otherwise. It also describes a bipartisan character to the church's politics (which the circles want to establish) which is, even when it may appear, sporadic at best and not very predictable (e.g. women in ministry or abortion). Finally, to label the second circle churches more "growth conscious and risk-taking" than members of the first circle requires specific judgments about which congregations fit these categories, and then marshaling supporting data. I wonder if the assertion would prove to be a valid one?[25]

A brief comment needs to be made as well about the third circle and its attempt to describe new Covenanters whose experience tends to be understandably local and, reflective of most Americans today, rootless and ahistorical. I do not believe that their "only real problem with the Covenant is that it tends to place too much emphasis on its ethnic origins." Many of these tensions have to do with older Covenant (and equally American evangelical) issues about localism and denominationalism, inclusion and exclusion, affection and disaffection, control and powerlessness (to use Olsson's images), in which ethnicity, though a valid issue of tension, becomes a convenient catch-all symbol. When compared with other immigrant churches in America, a strong case can be made for the Covenant doing rather well with the ethnicity issue, and being far more poised to proclaim its message of good news and incorporate in healthy ways all sorts of people into the family of faith. If some of the present-day ethnic (e.g., black) churches in the Covenant continue to be frustrated with the denomination, it has less to do with the "Swedishness" than with a church that reflects many of the values of middle to upper-class America.

In summary, the circle terminology needs to be transcended if the church is to understand the complex interrelated character of its pluralism. It is insufficient to label the historical tension by creating a polarity between circles one and two (and their "cases" against each other), and somehow locating new Covenant people outside these intramural squabbles. Though the intent is to be descriptive in a dynamic way and take the patterns of the church's diversity seriously, the circles are destined to be static labeled categories that place people, churches, and issues into boxes—and if inattentive to the relational stories of each (which is at the heart of the Covenant), the circles may become rather bald tools of management, for example, in the matching of pastors with congregations.

There is a certain irony to this, as well. I believe that the effect of the circle categories tends inevitably towards an exclusive rather than inclusive understanding of the Covenant's life together, unless one hopes that a synthesis of the two circles in the new third will bring about inclusion, a process I find unrealistic. Consequently, its pragmatism runs counter to what Karl Olsson has rightly described as the genius of Engebretson's presidency—the structuring of a spirit of functional unity.[26] A model born of that passion and commitment at the very least raises serious questions.

It is also necessary briefly to address another side of the circles theory, and this is the use President Paul E. Larsen has made of it as a basis for developing an argument about the convergence of Lutheran interiority and Reformed covenantalism in Covenant history. While space does not permit a fuller critique of the argument, I would like to raise a number of questions and make some observations from an historian's point of view.

Larsen's starting point is the polarity of the first two circles (the language is static), and though he cautions against simple stereotypes and states that few Covenanters would fit neatly into any of the circles, he uncritically accepts the circles and acknowledges his indebtedness by saying that "Engebretson locates the source of the divergence not in the modernist-fundamentalist tension but in the earlier Lutheran-Reformed tensions."[27] I have commented on the difficulty of the second circle having any self-conscious Reformed understanding. If this wing of the Covenant was truly Reformed in disposition, it would exhibit many of the same characteristics ascribed to the first circle: commitment to the value of the confessions; a greater retention of the practice of infant baptism and some understanding of Christ's real presence through his Spirit in the Lord's Supper (rather than a merely Zwinglian view); worship that in many ways values the pericope, the church year, confession and affirmation of faith; and a much more highly structured, hierarchical form of church government, in addition to the congregational polity of Baptists and others.

The argument seeks to locate the Reformed contribution to Covenant identity by looking backwards from 1885 to trace a vertical lineage. There are a number of historiographical problems with this approach, since the links, and their strength and effect, are difficult to establish from the sources. Too much appears to be made of Spener's contact with Labadie, and while Reformed Pietism's relation to the German movement is well known, it should not be forgotten that Spener always viewed himself as a dwarf on Luther's back, and his theology remained Lutheran.[28] The connections made with Puritan writers like Baxter and Dutch covenantal theologians are also well known, but wide kinds of *influence* are too readily made narrow issues of *identity*.

A good example of this is the assertion that "the idea of the free church is clearly Reformed. When it occurs in the Lutheran tradition it invariably does so as a result of Reformed influence."[29] Scholarship of the free church tradition has demonstrated that this comprises only one theory about origins, one that does not even achieve the consensus of most historians. In fact, after a lengthy discussion of the various theories of origin, Donald Durnbaugh chooses to quote from Luther's preface to the *German Mass* (1526) as the most concise definition of the characteristics of the tradition, the same passage used repeatedly by Covenant forebears to justify their actions.[30]

Many of the characterizations about the origins of the free church ideal, and the relation of the Reformed tradition to Pietism and the free churches, come from a dependence on Ernst Troeltsch. In his monumental *Social Teaching of the Christian Churches* (1911), Troeltsch cautioned that his arguments concerned only the European setting and should not be applied to American churches. And though his pioneering work continues to influence sociologists of religion, his views (like those of Tawney and Weber) have been subjected to probing criticism. H. Richard Niebuhr, in his intoduction to the 1960 American edition, cautions against reading Troeltsch's conclusions in any propositional fashion, and being overly dependent on his categories of church, sect, and mystical types.[31] Jaroslav Pelikan has noted that one of Troeltsch's most memorable phrases was "to be historical is to be relative." "Viewed in this light," says Pelikan, "the work of the church historian is to debunk the work of his predecessors and to destroy the golden calves of historical tradition.''[32] When taken together, such comments suggest that one should use Troeltsch with caution, especially in his historical judgments which predate the significant research on all these topics.

Another area of needed exploration in the sources is the relation of federal covenantal theology to the Covenant Church. These connections cannot be drawn historically, so one is compelled to extrapolate from one to another. Johannes Cocceius's redaction and extension of Calvin's implicit covenantal thinking certainly served to broaden and soften the Dutch hyper-Calvinism of the seventeenth century (yet its chief contribution was eventually its incorporation into scholastic Reformed theology); and the contributions of leading Puritan divines like William Ames (Cocceius's teacher) are significant for English and American theology.[33] But the fact remains that federal theology comprised only an aspect of the Reformed tradition which in time produced its own scholastic tendencies, even in England and America where federal theology flourished most.

In this light, to press too tight a connection with a nineteenth-century movement in Sweden that was evangelically ecumenical and Lutheran (even the Anglo-American influences in Sweden were not overtly federalist) in character is questionable, and narrows rather than broadens the tradition. Covenantal theology existed within the tight constraints of double predestination; Swedes had long since expressed their preference for Melanchthon's semi-Pelagianism rather than Luther's own views of election. The North American Covenant clearly has followed suit; certainly, few in the second circle (as described) would have been comfortable with that central pin of covenantalism. They might even have seen it as blatantly contrary to the good news of the gospel. Both circles were, for the most part, Waldenströmian in the early years.

The claim that these Reformed antecedents influenced directly or indirectly the Swedish renewal comes from arguments like the following. First is the conviction, which has already been discussed, that conventicles and the believers' church are wholly Reformed ideas and that they could not have been arrived at indigenously (with, of course, some outside influence) from Lutheran Pietism or the Swedish milieu. Second, the membership of the Swedish Covenant in the World Alliance of Reformed Churches is also cited, but this too is problematic from an historical point of view. Finally, the reference in C. J. Nyvall's diary to reading a history of the Scottish free church, as well as Baxter's *Saints Everlasting Rest* and a biography of Wilberforce, is noted as evidence that the Swedish Covenant was modeled after the Scottish example.

This opens an interesting area of historical discussion. The example of Thomas Chalmers and the formation of the Free Church of Scotland in 1843 was of great interest in Sweden; in fact, the Scottish presence was first felt three decades earlier in the formation of various Bible societies in Sweden. In the 1850s, the Scot, James Lumsden, formed several important Swedish friendships, among them Carl Axel Torén of Uppsala, T. N. Hasselquist (future leader of the Augustana Synod), H. J. Lundborg, and especially Peter Fjellstedt—who suggested in 1855 that Sweden adopt the Scottish model.[34] The Swedes were intrigued by the model, and the Scots were helpful in the formation of the Evangelical National Foundation within the State Church in 1856 (thus having close links with Rosenius), but they consistently distanced themselves from the Reformed theology and polity. In fact, once in America early Augustana leaders lost all interest in it. It is not surprising, then, that in February 1866 Nyvall was reading a history of the Scottish movement; it would have been standard reading for someone in his position. More importantly, his diary records that a few days later he met with Lundborg (then the leading proponent of the Scottish model, though he later would modify his views) and discussed the latter's plans for the Ansgar Society and the Swedish Church, to which Nyvall voiced his dissatisfaction.[35]

Consequently, I find the argument for a dialectic between Lutheran interiority (historically an inadequate generalization) and Reformed covenantalism (ultimately a narrowing of the Reformed tradition) much more a "thought experiment," to adapt Kierkegaard's phrase, than a description of historical reality. It will remain so unless it can be demonstrated from the sources a part of the record and of a people's self-understanding. Although I recognize Larsen's concern to see the idea of "covenant" as a biblical, sociological, and theological concept that transcends historical particularities, and one that can be a basis of creative discussion for the future, the life of the church is historical and the direction of the argument tends to resolve the above dialectic in the third circle, suggesting not only a Hegelian synthesis but historical determinism. If circle one at its best is Lutheran interiority, and circle two at its best is Reformed covenantalism, the fruits of the convergence will be reaped by circle three. Ultimately, the circles paradigm controls the argument.

Rather than this type of convergence, John Weborg's comments about Pietism make a similar point without the need to isolate a Reformed emphasis. Weborg notes the "convergence of the faith believed (*assensus*) and the 'believing' faith in the life of the Christian. The convergence of these two factors yields a life that has a consequence of faith and practice."[36] This concern is well-expressed in a variety of traditions, such as Lutheran Pietist, Reformed Pietist, Dutch Precisionist, English Puritan, and Continental Anabaptist. Although the circles seek to establish a polarity, or "two traditional parties," it is extremely doubtful that any case can be made for seeing the Reformed tradition as an equal pole to the Lutheran in terms of Covenant origins.

There is, however, an historical way to look at these questions and see the character of a "reformed" (not "Reformed") influence on the North American Covenant. Though the antecedents to 1885 are important, the historical task demands a forward look at the experience of an immigrant church over the course of a century. There is no real polarity between Lutheran and Reformed; rather, an immigrant community composed of essentially Rosenian Pietists encountered a dominant American tradition which espoused doctrinally and culturally many reformed characteristics, especially in the evangelical churches. It is notable that many major historians, such as Sydney Ahlstrom and Winthrop Hudson, have consistently structured the story of American religion in Puritan and post-Puritan categories.[37] The teaching of American church history in most seminaries reflects this interpretation. Only recently in these surveys have other important evangelical traditions, such as the Wesleyan and holiness, begun to receive the attention they merit. Moreover, the place of evangelical immigrant churches has yet to get a balanced hearing that might deter the ready absorption of their stories of origin and life into the controlling historiography.

Interpretation of evangelicalism in America during the past century has often been dominated by a reformed agenda. Some time ago, Martin E. Marty wrote in *Christianity Today* about the "baptistification of the American church," the tendency in many evangelical and mainline churches to move towards more conservative, low-church, nonliturgical and nonsacramental styles of belief and practice. Scholars have also begun to see the "Presbyterianization of evangelicalism," especially among those whose own traditions relate only indirectly, in terms of origin, to the broader reformed agenda. Here the role of Princeton theology and emerging fundamentalism was crucial to a growing tension within many evangelical churches. Donald W. Dayton says: "By the 'Presbyterianization of evangelical historiography' I mean the tendency to interpret and even rewrite 'evangelical' history according to the categories of this tradition." Dayton has noted the effect of the Princeton intellectual tradition of Warfield and Hodge on theologians in other churches who were looking for systematic frameworks (e.g., Strong and Wiley), as well as the fact that "in the conflicts over biblical authority in the late nineteenth century . . . many conservative revivalist groups were looking for a lifeboat and climbed aboard the Princeton theology to ride out the storm." "They stayed on this lifeboat so long," Dayton continues, "that many forgot that they didn't really belong there and gradually took their own identity from this shared experience. Thus contrary to most interpreters of the history, many evangelical groups were not originally committed to 'inerrancy' formulations of the doctrine of scripture but began to adopt them under this influence." He also highlights the remarkable impact of the Keswick movement and "the victorious Christian life" on American evangelicals. Dayton, concerned for his own Wesleyan tradition, concludes:

> And finally the sociologists have taught us that beliefs contribute to the creation of social realities. The Presbyterian description of what "evangelicalism" is has become so strong that it creates its own reality—it serves to draw people in its own direction . . . [so that they] act in accordance with that self-understanding, betraying in the process the dis-

tinctive witness of their own tradition.[38]

If we apply this argument to Covenant history and identity, we can see the tensions within at least the first two generations over many of the same issues, particularly since the early Covenant was so intimately tied to an encounter with dispensationalism, premillenarianism, the Moody style of evangelism and worship, and eventually fundamentalism—all of which have strongly reformed qualities. Several historians of the American church (who have no connection to the Covenant) have looked upon Covenant history as a good case-study of the exceptions to these dominant movements and interpretations. Frederick Hale, for example, has studied the Covenant and The Evangelical Free Church, both conservative evangelical immigrant churches emerging from a common history, to test Ernest Sandeen's thesis about the Darbyite dispensational, millenarian, and Princeton origins of fundamentalism. Hale concluded that the Free Church—in its Swedish, Norwegian, and Danish backgrounds—became strongly fundamentalist in doctrine because of its broad adoption of Anglo-American characteristics, while the Covenant—especially in the years prior to World War I—grew out of a more indigenous Swedish Lutheran movement of renewal which interacted with Anglo-American influences in a more critical manner.[39]

A leading scholar of fundamentalism, Joel Carpenter, has noted its (and its heir, neo-evangelicalism's) tendency to consider "the 'evangelical Calvinist' wing of American Protestantism as the normative mainline." It adds the Wesleyan-Arminian, Disciples-Christian, Lutheran, and Pietist traditions "only as afterthoughts and virtually ignores many others." Carpenter considers the important role of immigrant churches as "one of the great and relatively unexplored ironies of American religious history," and notes that as late as the 1960s spokespersons for neo-evangelicalism, such as Harold Ockenga and Harold Lindsell, were still defining evangelicalism as if it were exclusively Reformed in theology. Carpenter comments as well about the Covenant and this reformed agenda:

> Fundamentalist beliefs and emphases penetrated these varied traditions with uneven success. Some communions *with close previous affinity to American churches* [emphasis mine], such as the Swed-

ish Baptists, became thoroughly part of the fundamentalist movement. Others, such as the Swedish
Evangelical Mission Covenant, the Mennonite
Church, and the Dutch Christian Reformed Church,
had both affinities and strong antagonisms towards
aspects of Fundamentalism. They had been penetrated by the movement while struggling to assert
a unique and substantially different identity.[40]

This reformed agenda in neo-evangelicalism can also be
traced to the 1940s and '50s as the new movement divorced
itself socially from older fundamentalism while retaining a high
commitment to the doctrines and epistemology forged in the
older controversies. Carpenter has shown that the roots of
neo-evangelicalism "were in the generally Reformed wing of
North American Evangelicalism: the Baptists, Presbyterians,
and Congregationalists."[41] The institutions established during
this period, most notably Fuller Theological Seminary, reflected that Reformed preoccupation during the first two decades (with accusations of heresy, apostasy, and softness of doctrine being flung in the direction of the mainline institutions
their leaders left, and frequently at each other), years which
were formative to many of the concerns today in the evangelical community.[42]

I would submit that this is the far more important issue
of historical investigation in order to understand the abiding
influences of the reformed traditions on the North American
Covenant, and the challenges to its self-understanding and
identity. It helps to explain why Swedish Covenanters do not
refer to themselves as "evangelicals" (only as evangelical Christians), and are almost totally perplexed by many issues (doctrinal and otherwise) in the North American Covenant. It also
adds legitimate credence to many of the descriptions that Engebretson sought to locate in the second circle. For example,
these second circle people and churches (as described) would
have had difficulty relating to a notion of Reformed covenantalism that seeks to transform as well as redeem the world. In
the Covenant, rather, the protest against "the social gospel"
was so strong that the greatest concern was to save souls before
the world met its just apocalyptic end, and to speculate about
whether the saved would have to endure the tribulation or

be spared by a secret rapture. This, in fact, is part of the "great reversal" by which Timothy Smith, David Moberg, Donald Dayton, and others have described the evangelical movements of the nineteenth century which were major carriers of social reform impulses, yet in the twentieth century joined the denouncers of those participating in ministries of the social gospel as "liberals" who had given in to "modernism." I wonder, therefore, in light of the above recent historiography about the reformed character of much of American evangelicalism, whether the need to legitimize an equally Reformed pole of the Covenant may be motivated by these kinds of perceptions.

What then are the issues, including several of a reformed nature, that have led many Covenant people and churches occasionally to feel distanced, even alienated, from a center? There needs to be another model (one that emerges from the sources and makes it difficult to label and categorize) that can contribute to an understanding of this pluralism, these patterns of diversity that are real and need to remain dynamic with unresolved dialectics, and yet reinforce a foundational sense of unity in the gathered body of Christ.

III. The Forces Within

Perhaps the most obvious question left unaddressed by the circles theory, and consequently most problematic to a sense of denominational unity, is how the three circles relate to each other. We continue to affirm that the church is one. Do the circles overlap? If so, how much? At which points? In other words, the circles attempt to describe pluralism but do little to affirm unity, unless one sees the necessity of some Hegelian synthesis at work. The problem then of explaining the "three in one" is not unlike the trinitarian mystery which requires some new generation of Cappadocian fathers to find the right language.

Really we are not left with three circles. If the wholeness of the church requires a single circle, in fact we have something more like a pie that is cut into three slices. But how big are the slices? How do they relate to each other? They no doubt share in common the same ingredients (being an apple pie, for example) but the slices still sit there physically isolated from each other, dependent upon whomever is doing the cutting.

Obviously, this image is also an unsatisfactory one. Paul Larsen's solution to the question of unity is one of trying to introduce a new framework in covenantal theology which should
be compatible with the past (even if it was not a conscious
image for Covenant people) because it is the biblical story of
origin and destiny. The church, however, remains historical,
and there must continue to be a way, as Karl Olsson has done,
of seeing the historical diversity in dynamic ways that do justice
to the sources of Covenant history. A concern for the past
should not be seen as the "incessant fussing about denominational roots."[43]

The image must be dynamic, like Augustine's description
of the visible and invisible church within a circle as the *corpus mixtum*. It must be made up of forces that interact with
each other in some relational fashion, because that is the nature
of life itself—above all in the church. One may wish to consider much or most scholarship on Covenant history as confined to circle one interests, but that risks casting aspersion
on the professional integrity of how sources are used. Such
judgments must be made from a similar investigation of the
sources, and though it is asserted that there are two polar interpretations of Covenant history in the first two circles, there
has yet to appear a challenge to long-standing Covenant historiography based on equally rigorous use of the sources. The
revisionist character of the circles cannot at present be a substitute for the patient work of scholars like Karl Olsson whose
images of center and periphery, inclusion, control, and affection remain the best way to describe the meaning of the Covenant's pluralistic life together.

Although space does not permit the full development of
a dynamic model that meets the above criticisms, I would like
to propose another perspective, one that preserves the lively
character of the issues, arises from the sources, and allows a
way to see any aspect of Covenant life, past and present. Its
very nature resists labeling and forces one to address people,
churches, issues, and events in their own stories and meanings. I have repeatedly used it in my teaching of Covenant history where it has proven its helpfulness and durability. It does
not explain away the diversity but allows it to stand in all of
its creative tension, in the midst of which the church's
self-understanding and identity are tested.

The image is a familiar and common one, and was first
suggested by David Nyvall as he sought to describe the pluralism of the early Covenant by commenting on its two most
important and well-known leaders, C. A. Björk and Erik August
Skogsbergh:

> Among his equals Björk [the Covenant's first presi-
> dent] lifted his head above the rest. He had a much
> more immediate influence over those who stood
> next to him than he had over the crowd. In this as
> in many other things he was the opposite to Skogs-
> bergh [Minneapolis pastor and Nyvall's brother-in-
> law], the evangelist from Värmland, who was strong
> with the crowd and somewhat lacking in the per-
> suasive powers over those next in command. Björk
> towered at the conferences where his will could be
> organized into official decision. Skogsbergh had the
> ear of the people between the conferences. He was
> largely an independent and somewhat vaguely sup-
> ported by public opinion. *Together they represented
> a centripetal and a centrifugal power within the
> Covenant which was jointly beneficial* [emphasis
> mine].[44]

The model is one of seeing the life of the Covenant as a
whole (within a single circle, if you will) comprised of centripetal and centrifugal dynamics which together are "jointly
beneficial." The value of the image is that it is a living one;
it allows the perimeter to expand and contract, as well as per-
mits the center to move. It demonstrates the dangers of centrifugal forces so strong that they fling themselves beyond the
mutually established perimeter out into some orbit of their
own, and centripetal forces so powerful that they cause the
center to collapse in upon itself.

During its history, the Covenant has always lived with the
tension between those concerns and activities that tended
towards a strong denominational center and leadership (centripetal) and those that tended to value more highly congregational autonomy and local leadership (centrifugal). Regional
concerns often found themselves somewhere in between. The
heart and will of the denomination, however, has been constitutionally expressed in the Annual Meeting, for better or

worse. Since the church in its first seventy-five years was especially prone to controversy, its diverse expressions can easily
be interpreted by varying degrees of these images. And though
the past quarter-century has been far more tranquil, many older
issues still persist in questions of denominational identity,
which get added to more current issues involving the character
of the church's growing pains in a new generation composed
of many people whose experiences are primarily local and not
necessarily predisposed to strong denominational ties. In a
way, the Covenant's polity insures that these loyalties will
always be competing with each other to some extent. Health
and balance lie in the constructive interaction of the centripetal and centrifugal. Sometimes this relationship may even be
symbiotic, a biological description of two dissimilar organisms
living together when the association is mutually beneficial, a
kind of functional unity.

A full narrative discussion of how Covenant history might
be seen through centripetal and centrifugal dynamics needs
to appear elsewhere, but I can at least suggest the character
of such an approach. At times either dynamic can be seen as
a corrective to the other or in the best interest of the whole
church. Judgments cannot be made here, which need to occur,
about the character and implications of so many of these issues.
But in these dynamics we see at least two important developments. First is the the structural ecclesiological growth of an
infant church; it had no choice but to move forward into an
uncharted future, maturing beyond the youthful idealism of
a revivalistic mission society.[45] That this would produce tension is hardly surprising, when it was the attempt to bring
churchly union to the fragmented and scattered Mission
Friends that gave rise to the Covenant in the first place. Second, in these dynamics we can see the character of the challenge of American religion and culture, as described above,
and ways in which so many aspects of evangelicalism, fundamentalism, and neo-evangelicalism (with many of its "reformed" qualities) influenced the denomination, and tested
its theological underpinnings.

Before 1920, the kinds of centripetal and centrifugal tensions can be seen in the following: a commitment that a denomination is no faction over and against the "free" dispensational
assault on such views; the development of the role of the

Annual Meeting and ministerial credentialing over and against
the pattern of autonomous congregations and itinerant evangelists; the function of the national executive committee (Björk)
over and against local and regional interests (Skogsbergh); the
need for regional associations and Covenant stewardship over
and against the American Home Missionary Society and the
generosity of the Congregationalists; the necessity of a Covenant school over and against the convenience of Chicago
Theological Seminary; Chicago and conflicting interests of
some of its leaders over and against geographical distance and
regional competing interests; denominational newspapers and
publications over and against independent presses (for example, Conrad Bergendoff found it almost miraculous that the
Covenant could even survive as a body with a paper like
Missions-Vännen complicating its work for almost seventy
years);[46] the interests of the church and North Park over and
against the gold controversy, and its effect on Nyvall, Björk,
Högfeldt, and others; the establishment of Covenant mission
fields over and against the independent competition from Fran-
son's Scandinavian Alliance Mission and other agencies; the
establishment of ambitious benevolence ministries over and
against a persistent shortage of trained workers and adequate
funds. These are only suggestive of the interplay of forces, and
the "over and against" language is not intended to indicate
polarity but rather varying degrees of tension. Some issues were
very distinct, others far more gray and ambiguous.

The period since 1920 can be seen in similar ways with
many older issues carried over. Here the centripetal and centrifugal dynamics might look like: the strength of young peoples' organizations over and against the tragic loss of many
in the second generation because of assimilation and continued
ethnic provincialism; the transition to English and the establishment in the 1920s of English congregations over and against
the slowness and pain of the transition (at least a decade behind
Augustana); the need to find fresh means of evangelism and
mission over and against the closing of immigration and the
Americanization of the church; the work of Nyvall, Nils Lund,
and others over and against the criticisms of Gustaf F. Johnson,
A. B. Öst, and others; the concomitant crisis for North Park
and higher education over and against the elevation of Bible
schools as the only "safe" education; continued denomina-

tional structuring over and against the perception that renewal fires had died and that the Covenant's future was questionable without fresh revival; the development of strong regional conferences and programs of home mission over and against continuing localism, independency, and the influx of pastors from outside the Covenant without proper credentialing;[47] the Committee on Freedom and Theology over and against the Doughty case; the Survey Commission and new constitution of 1957 over and against varied "state's rights" opposition; the desire for strong Covenant youth organizations over and against the unprecedented rise of parachurch groups; a coordinated budget and capital fund campaigns over and against the local interests, moods, and commitments of congregations. To these might be added concerns about worship, preaching, Christian education, spiritual formation, church music, evangelism and church growth, management, and the roles and responsibilities of clergy and laity—the possibilities are endless.

I have tried to argue that this type of historical investigation makes labeling totally undesirable, if not impossible; rather, it forces a faithfulness to the issues of history as well as an awareness of the present. The circle designations break down when one considers just the following: Axel Mellander's "turning" on Nyvall during the gold scandal, to the detriment of North Park and the church; the description that Björk represented the churchman and Skogsbergh the evangelist (a useful comparison to project forward), when Björk was also concerned about evangelism and Skogsbergh about the denomination—it is the dynamics and degrees that are telling here; the Northwest Conference Ministerium bringing a resolution in 1927 that resulted, in part, in the Omaha controversy, and yet seven years later taking the initiative to defrock A. B. Öst because he persisted after the Annual Meeting had acted on the charges; the strong and mediating leadership of T. W. Anderson, who worked against factionalism while taking a strong stand on denominational loyalty. Those pastors who signed the 1965 petition at Des Moines represented not only "circle two" in its historic protest against North Park, but included those whom some might consign to "circle one." Obviously, there was wider concern from some about issues of balance and fairness not necessarily related to Omaha and its aftermath. Attitudes about abortion or women in ministry freely cross circle lines. And some newer fast-growing congregations show little interest in helping support other new churches in their area, while elsewhere such cooperation is evident; or they seem reluctant to contribute to denominational budgets and campaigns while others give generously. What might that say about "circle three" and denominational commitment? It says that the centripetal and centrifugal dynamics are alive and well, even in new churches. Many "circle one and two" congregations have helped parent these new "circle three" churches (e.g. Frontier Friends). This list too can be considerably expanded.

One can only surmise that Covenant people and churches, though fitting many kinds of patterns, respond to issues and relate to each other in a more complex manner than the circles suggest. Karl Olsson has commented on the athleticism required of present Covenant leaders to keep impulses moving quickly from center to periphery and vice versa.[48] I would only add that these impulses frequently move across a field highly charged with centripetal and centrifugal forces that will defy any categories we attempt to create.

Finally, it needs to be added that perhaps the Covenant's greatest contribution to North American religion is its inclusion of all who confess Christ in the context of biblical and theological freedom tested and nurtured by the life and wisdom of the covenanted body of Christ. This offers a true *via media,* as it did in Sweden and America in the nineteenth century. The Covenant's history is crucial, not constraining, to the realization of this cardinal fact of identity. I disagree that the Covenant "shorn of its ethnicity and traditional culture, plunges into its second century."[49] I prefer to believe that a healthy living organism such as the church moves confidently and deliberately into the future, affected and challenged by change but secure in its identity because it grows out of a living tradition whose head is Christ. Otherwise, there is only Protestant principle without Catholic substance; the material principle of the Reformation collapses into the formal principle alone.

David Nyvall suggested another fruitful image which complements well the challenging closing sections of Paul Larsen's *The Mission of a Covenant:*

On a well-equipped ship there is an anchor as well
as sails. They both serve the welfare of the sailor,
the anchor insuring his conservation, his safety, the
sails provided for his progress, including his goal,
his home. The anchor does not mean rest, and the
sails do not mean just unrest. . . . I would hate to
sail without an anchor, and certainly I cannot sail
with the anchor alone. Sails and anchor are one in
purpose, largely. Sails make an anchor very much
needed, and an anchor makes sails very much
wanted. We do not all the time want them equally
bad, but we always need them both, and we need
one in proportion as we want the other. The more
sails we have up, the more sure we are to have the
anchor ready. We think of the anchor when we put
on sails. And it is when we are lowering the anchor
that we are longing for sails. Why, then, should there
be any quarrel between the anchor and the sails?[50]

The nautical image is a beautiful and ancient one for the
Church. Any concern for the seaworthiness of the vessel, however, cannot ignore the ship's original crafting and life of service that has shaped her character—the tales of the seas
traversed, the storms weathered, the pain of mishap and
mutiny, damage and loss, the heroic efforts to rescue mariners
of misfortune, the exotic ports visited, the sooty docks and
tons of cargo carried in her holds, the officers and crew who
served and loved her and knew every nook and cranny. Paul
Larsen attempts "to predict the Covenant's second century
by proposing to build it . . . to lay its keel on Christ, the Scriptures, and the believing community."[51] To this I add my whole-
hearted support, with one caveat in defense of history and
the tradition of shipbuilding. A keel is laid only once in the
life of a ship; the vessel can be refitted and rebuilt to do the
work demanded of the present, the keel can even be length-
ened or shortened. But to lay a new keel is to scuttle the old
ship and start over. The keel of the Covenant was in one
important sense laid in 1885; a seasoned seaworthy vessel
enters its second century eager, in whatever way necessary,
to do the work of the kingdom today. But in an even more
important sense (to borrow once again an image from Augus-

tine about the Church as an ark), the keel was laid in eternity, in the providential work of God's gracious plan for his creation—and here is the Covenant's insoluable tie to the one, holy, catholic, and apostolic Church.

Endnotes

[1] Paul Tillich, *The Protestant Era* (Chicago: University of Chicago Press, 1957 ed.), pp. 162f.

[2] Sydney E. Ahlstrom, "Tradition in Transit and Tension: the Continental Inheritance in America: the Lutheran Experience," *Encounter,* 20 (1959), 332.

[3] Jan Morris, ed., *The Oxford Book of Oxford* (Oxford: Oxford University Press, 1978), p. 236.

[4] Bibliographic references are numerous concerning Luther's life and theology. See, for example, the excellent bibliography appended to Eric W. Gritsch, *Martin—God's Court Jester* (Philadelphia: Fortress Press, 1983), pp. 263-280. Cf. also Steven Ozment, ed., *Reformation Europe: A Guide to Research* (St. Louis: Center for Reformation Research, 1982), pp. 59-83; and Roland H. Bainton and Eric W. Gritsch, eds., *Bibliography of the Continental Reformation* (Hamden: Archon Books, 1972), pp. 57-106.

[5] See, for example, the bibliography in the most recent biography of Calvin by William J. Bouwsma, *John Calvin: A Sixteenth Century Portrait* (New York: Oxford University Press, 1988), pp. 295-302. Cf. also Ozment, *Reformation Europe,* pp. 211-232; Bainton and Gritsch, *Bibliography,* pp. 161-184; and John H. Leith, *Introduction to the Reformed Tradition* (Atlanta: John Knox Press, 1977, 1981).

[6] The standard work remains George Hunston Williams, *The Radical Reformation* (Philadelphia: Westminster Press, 1962). See also Franklin H. Littell, *The Origins of Sectarian Protestantism: A Study of the Anabaptist View of the Church* (New York: Macmillan, 1964 ed.); Ozment, *Reformation Europe,* pp. 135-159; and Bainton and Gritsch, *Bibliography,* pp. 124-158.

[7] Reported in Andrew Drummond, *German Protestantism Since Luther* (London: Epworth Press, 1951), p. 79.

[8] See especially Dale Brown, *Understanding Pietism* (Grand Rapids: Eerdmans, 1978); F. Ernest Stoeffler, *The Rise of Evangelical Pietism* (Leiden: E.J. Brill, 1965); Stoeffler, *German Pietism During the Eighteenth Century* (Leiden: E.J. Brill, 1973); K. James Stein, *Philipp Jakob Spener: Pietist Patriarch* (Chicago: Covenant Press, 1986); Gary R. Sattler, *God's Glory, Neighbor's Good* (Chicago: Covenant Press, 1982); Karl A. Olsson, "The Influence of Pietism on Social Action," *Moravian Theological Seminary Bulletin,* Fall 1965, 45-56; and Stoeffler, ed., *Continental Pietism and Early American History* (Grand Rapids: Eerdmans. 1976).

⁹ John R. Weinlick, *The Moravian Diaspora* (Nashville: Abingdon, 1959), esp. pp. 112-143 for the Moravians in Sweden; Weinlick, *Count Zinzendorf* (Nashville: Abingdon, 1956); Clifford W. Towlson, *Moravian and Methodist: Relationships and Influences in the Eighteenth Century* (London: Epworth Press, 1957). Also see Howard A. Snyder, *Signs of the Spirit: How God Reshapes His Church,* forthcoming from Zondervan, for a helpful discussion of the interrelationship of Pietism, Moravianism, and Methodism.

¹⁰ Donald F. Durnbaugh, *The Believers' Church: The History and Character of Radical Protestantism* (New York: Macmillan, 1968), esp. pp. 3-33. See also Gunnar Westin, *The Free Church Through the Ages* (Nashville: Broadman Press, 1958); Franklin H. Littell, *The Free Church* (Boston: Starr King Press, 1957); and Durnbaugh, *Every Need Supplied: Mutual Aid and Christian Community in the Free Churches, 1525-1675* (Philadelphia: Temple University Press, 1974). For an insightful discussion of how vertical and horizontal approaches pertain to denominational historiography, see Patrick Collinson, "Towards a Broader Understanding of the Early Dissenting Tradition," in C. Robert Cole and Michael E. Moody, eds., *The Dissenting Tradition: Essays for Leland H. Carlson* (Athens: Ohio University Press, 1975), pp. 3-38.

¹¹ Marcus Lee Hansen, *The Atlantic Migration 1607-1860* (New York: Harper and Row, 1940, 1961); Hansen, *The Immigrant in American History* (New York: Harper and Row, 1940, 1964); Oscar Handlin, *The Uprooted* (Boston: Little Brown & Company, 1951, 1973); John Higham, *Strangers in the Land: Patterns of American Nativism 1860-1925* (New York: Atheneum, 1955, 1963); Higham, *Send These to Me: Immigrants in Urban America* (Baltimore: The Johns Hopkins University Press, 1975, 1984); and John Bodnar, *The Transplanted: A History of Immigrants in Urban America* (Bloomington: Indiana University Press, 1985). Cf. also Rudolph J. Vacoli, "The Resurgence of American Immigration History," *American Studies International,* 17 (1979), 49-66; and Thomas J. Archdeacon, "Problems and Possibilities in the Study of American Immigration and Ethnic History," *International Migration Review,* 19 (1985), 112-134.

¹² For example, see George M. Stephenson, *The Religious Aspects of Swedish Immigration* (Minneapolis: University of Minnesota Press, 1932); H. Arnold Barton, ed., *Letters from the Promised Land: Swedes in America 1840-1914* (Minneapolis: University of Minnesota Press, 1975); Harald Runblom and Hans Norman, eds., *From Sweden to America: A History of the Migration* (Minneapolis: University of Minnesota Press, 1976); Nils Hasselmo, ed., *Perspectives on Swedish Immigration* (Chicago: Swedish Pioneer Historical Society and University of Minnesota, 1978); Sture Lindmark, *Swedish America 1914-1932* (Uppsala: Studia Historica Upsaliensia XXXVII, 1971); J.I. Dowie and E.M. Espelie, eds., *The Swedish Immigrant Community in Transition* (Rock Island: Augustana Historical Society, 1963); and four decades of articles published in the *Swedish-American Historical Quarterly.*

¹³ Timothy L. Smith, "Religion and Ethnicity in America," *American Historical Review,* 83 (1978), 1155-85. Cf. also Jay P. Dolan, "The Immi-

grants and their Gods: A New Perspective in American Religious History,'' *Church History,* 57 (1988), 61-72; Dolan, "Immigration and American Christianity: A History of their Histories," in Henry Warner Bowden, ed., *A Century of Church History: The Legacy of Philip Schaff* (Carbondale: Southern Illinois University Press, 1988); Smith, "Religious Denominations as Ethnic Communities: A Regional Case Study," *Church History,* 35 (1966), 207-26; and Nathan Glazer and Daniel P. Moynihan, *Beyond the Melting Pot* (Cambridge: Harvard University Press, 1963).

[14] Standard histories of the American church remain Winthrop S. Hudson, *Religion in America* (New York: Macmillan, 4th ed., 1987); and Sydney E. Ahlstrom, *A Religious History of the American People* (New Haven: Yale University Press, 1972). For the inclusion of Canada, see Robert T. Handy, *A History of the Churches in the United States and Canada* (Oxford: Oxford University Press, 1976). On historiographical questions, see Jon Butler, "The Future of American Religious History: Prospectus, Agenda, Transatlantic *Problematique," William and Mary Quarterly.* 3rd ser., 42 (1985), 167-183.

[15] Robert T. Handy, *A Christian America: Protestant Hopes and Historical Realities* (New York: Oxford University Press, 1971, 1984); Higham, *Strangers in the Land;* and Will Herberg, *Protestant-Catholic-Jew: An Essay in American Religious Sociology* (Garden City: Doubleday, 1955).

[16] The literature on the history of evangelicalism in America has exploded in recent years. For the two most comprehensive bibliographies, see William G. McLoughlin, ed., *The American Evangelicals 1800-1900: An Anthology* (New York: Harper and Row, 1968), pp. 1-26; and Leonard I. Sweet, ed., *The Evangelical Tradition in America* (Macon: Mercer University Press, 1984), pp. 1-86. See also David F. Wells and John D. Woodbridge, eds., *The Evangelicals: What They Believe, Who They Are, Where They Are Changing* (Nashville: Abingdon, 1975); James Davison Hunter, *Evangelicalism: The Coming Generation* (Chicago: University of Chicago Press, 1987); and Douglas W. Frank, *Less Than Conquerors: How Evangelicals Entered the Twentieth Century* (Grand Rapids: Eerdmans, 1986).

[17] Karl A. Olsson, *By One Spirit* (Chicago: Covenant Press, 1962), *passim;* and Olsson, *A Family of Faith* (Chicago: Covenant Press, 1975), *passim.* Also of interest is Olsson's discussion of the "three kinds of thinkers in the early Covenant" (speculative, traditional, and intuitive) in "Covenant Beginnings: Doctrinal," *Covenant Quarterly,* 13 (1953), 107ff.

[18] See especially "The Covenant Constitution and Its History," *NARTHEX,* 3 (1983), 5-25, 42-6; and Olsson, *Into One Body . . . by the Cross* (Chicago: Covenant Press, 1985-1986).

[19] First presented in a paper to the Covenant Leaders' Consultative Congress, the description was later printed in the *Covenant Companion,* June 1, 1980, p. 27. It is also printed in Paul E. Larsen, *The Mission of a Covenant* (Chicago: Covenant Press, 1985), pp. 15f. Ahlem says it was written "with a minimum of research and a sackful of impressions."

[20] Quoted in Larsen, *Mission of a Covenant,* pp. 16f. William R. Haus-

man, former president of North Park College and Theological Seminary, also presented a paper to the Council of Administrators attempting to critique and refine the circles. The weakness of the paper was the continued typing of Covenant people with little reference to historical and theological matters. Its value was in in the more balanced and positive phenomenological descriptions of the three types: 1) Biological Sons and Daughters; 2) Adopted Sons and Daughters; and 3) Good Neighbors and Prospective In-laws. The caricaturing of people without careful attention to their individual stories, however, shows the dependence on the models of Ahlem and Engebretson.

²¹ Isaiah Berlin, *The Hedgehog and the Fox: An Essay on Tolstoy's View of History* (New York: Mentor, 1957), pp. 8f.

²² Paul L. Holmer, "Contemporary Evangelical Faith," in Wells and Woodbridge, *The Evangelicals,* pp. 87-90. A poignant critique of the exclusive character of types, though in a far different context, was graphically made in the North Park College yearbook about Covies, Blacks, Jocks, and Freaks (*Cupola,* 1972, p. 199).

²³ Karl Olsson and other historians have consistently noted this relationship, though not to the exclusion of other non-Lutheran influences. See especially my "The Läsare and Luther, or What Does Värmland Have to Do with Wittenberg?" *Covenant Quarterly,* 41 (1983), 31-48; and C. John Weborg, " 'Lutherans in Their Theology': Luther and the Covenant Church," *Explor,* 8 (Spring 1986), 23-30.

²⁴ Paul Larsen also echoes Engebretson's observation about the World Alliance of Reformed Churches and adds the curious phrase "to this day," as though this Reformed affiliation is long-standing in the Swedish Covenant (*Mission of a Covenant,* p. 22).

²⁵ My own discomfort with the experiential descriptions of these first two circles, in particular, is directly related to my own lifelong journey in the Covenant Church. As one who has been labeled "circle one," though raised in the congregation (First Covenant Church, Minneapolis) that is usually labeled the prime "circle two" example, I simply cannot fit my own pilgrimage into these circles or identify in any substantive way with the descriptions, either from a personal or a professional point of view. I have tested my own ambiguity with many other Covenanters (old and new), some of whom were initially attracted to the circles schema, and in virtually every case we share a similar dilemma about relating the circles to our own life stories and the Covenant churches in which we have had a home.

²⁶ Olsson, *Into One Body . . . by the Cross,* pp. 377-447.

²⁷ Paul E. Larsen, "The Convergence of Covenantalism and Interiority," *Covenant Quarterly,* 44 (1986), 14.

²⁸ See Stein, *Philipp Jakob Spener,* pp. 60ff. Stein notes that while in Geneva, Spener "registered several criticisms of the Reformed Church" (p. 61). The argument that Lutheran Pietism was dependent on antecedents in Reformed Pietism and especially Puritanism has been advanced most strongly by Stoeffler, *Rise of Evangelical Pietism.* Many scholars, however, have been unconvinced by this approach. For a persuasive critique of Stoeffler on this point, see the review by Egon W.

Gerdes, in *Concordia Theological Monthly,* 39 (1968), 197-201.

²⁹ Larsen, "Convergence of Covenantalism and Interiority," 21; cf. also 15-17. This statement is modified somewhat in *Mission of a Covenant* (p. 53) to recognize Anabaptist origins, as well.

³⁰ Durnbaugh, *The Believers' Church,* pp. 32f.; Anderson, "The Läsare and Luther," 41.

³¹ H. Richard Niebuhr, "Introduction," *Social Teaching of the Christian Churches,* 2 vols. (Chicago: University of Chicago Press, 1960), pp. 7-11.

³² Jaroslav Pelikan, *Obedient Rebels: Catholic Substance and Protestant Principle in Luther's Reformation* (New York: Harper and Row, 1964), p. 38. For a description of some of the reasons why theologians and church historians have discounted Troeltsch's theories (as well as bibliographic citations), see Durnbaugh, *The Believers' Church,* pp. 23-26.

³³ Larsen, *Mission of a Covenant,* pp. 22f.; and "Convergence of Covenantalism and Interiority," 15ff. See Keith L. Sprunger, *The Learned Dr. William Ames: Dutch Backgrounds of English and American Puritanism* (Urbana: University of Illinois Press, 1972); and Sprunger, *Dutch Puritanism: A History of English and Scottish Churches of the Netherlands in the Sixteenth and Seventeenth Centuries* (Leiden: E.J. Brill, 1982). Sprunger does not even mention Coeccius in this massive volume, and especially notes that though the English Puritans respected Dutch Reformed theology, they repeatedly criticized its lack of application in daily living—and here the precisionist faction of the Dutch church made a contribution (pp. 357ff.). John Leith mentions Coeccius only once, and notes that one of the weaknesses of covenantal theology ultimately for the Reformed tradition was its undercutting of the sovereignty of God and its conceiving of the Christian life in legalistic and rationalistic ways (*Introduction to the Reformed Tradition,* p. 119). Larsen also asserts that the separation of the Swedish Covenant can be linked to English Reformed figures. He argues that it was "left-wing covenantal Puritans like Milburne in England and Roger Williams in the colonies who developed the idea of the free church and the whole doctrine of the separation of church and state" ("Convergence of Covenantalism and Interiority," 16). This is not true. I assume that "Milburne" is a misprint for John Lilburne, the notorious Leveller during the English Civil War. He was hardly representative of Puritan arguments for separation, and like many others stood in a long tradition of English separatism going back at least to the Marian exiles, but strongly articulated by Robert Browne, John Robinson, and Francis Johnson. See B. R. White, *The English Separatist Tradition* (Oxford: Oxford University Press, 1971); G. E. Aylmer, ed., *The Levellers in the English Revolution* (London: Thames and Hudson, 1975); Christopher Hill, *The World Turned Upside Down: Radical Ideas During the English Revolution* (London: Penguin Books, 1972, 1975); and Pauline Gregg, *Free-Born John: A Biography of John Lilburne* (London: George G. Harrap & Co., 1961). Likewise, Roger Williams's separatism had a lengthy prehistory, including a famous confrontation with John Cotton in which he denied separatist views while in Salem. He too was heir to the established English theories oppos-

ing Erastianism, while adapting them to the new world. See Edmund Morgan, *Roger Williams: The Church and the State* (New York: Harcourt, Brace, & World, 1967). The most thorough study of covenant and contract as a social ideology is Michael Walzer, *The Revolution of the Saints: A Study in the Origins of Radical Politics* (Cambridge: Harvard University Press, 1965). For the introduction of federal theology into English Puritanism see Perry Miller, "The Marrow of Puritan Divinity," *Errand Into the Wilderness* (Cambridge: Harvard University Press, 1956), pp. 48-98; and for a critique of the effects of rationalistic federalism on American Presbyterianism, see Leonard J. Trinterud, *The Forming of an American Tradition: A Re-examination of Colonial Presbyterianism* (Philadelphia: Westminster Press, 1949), pp. 171ff.

34 Emmet E. Eklund, *Peter Fjellstedt: Missionary Mentor to Three Continents* (Rock Island: Augustana Historical Society, 1983); Eklund, "The Scottish Free Church and Its Relation to Nineteenth-Century Swedish and Swedish-American Lutheranism," *Church History,* 51 (1982), 405-418; and O. Fritiof Ander, *T. N. Hasselquist* (Rock Island: Augustana Historical Society, 1931), pp. 8, 10f., 22, 44.

35 David Nyvall, *My Father's Testament* (Chicago: Covenant Press, 1974), pp. 110f. It is also interesting to note that C. V. Bowman, Covenant president and strong articulator of the church's Lutheran origins, wrote his first book in 1906 on a history of the revival in Wales. Related to this, Larsen makes another statement that begs for clarification: "The Moravianism of Rosenius was clearly influenced by Reformed theology. It is also found in the Methodism of George Scott, because Wesleyan Arminianism is Reformed as well" ("Convergence of Covenantalism and Interiority," 21).

36 C. John Weborg, "Pietism: A Question of Meaning and Vocation," *Covenant Quarterly,* 41 (1983), 59. My critique of Paul Larsen's "thought experiment" focuses on only one part of his argument, and I wish in no way generally to extend this critique to other parts of *Mission of a Covenant,* much of which I find helpful and thought-provoking. I am above all concerned here with historiographical questions and fidelity to the sources lest revisionist Covenant history be uncritically accepted without firm foundation.

37 Cf. Hudson, *History of Religion in America;* Ahlstrom, *Religious History of the American People;* Ahlstrom, "Theology in America: A Historical Survey," in James Ward Smith and A. Leland Jamison, eds., *The Shaping of American Religion* (Princeton: Princeton University Press, 1961), pp. 232-321. For a discussion of how this relates to the Augustana Synod, see Ahlstrom, "Facing the New World: Augustana and the American Challenge," in *Centennial Essays: Augustana Lutheran Church 1860-1960* (Rock Island: Augustana Press, 1960), pp. 1-27; and especially "Tradition in Transit and Tension," where Ahlstrom states: "The essentially Reformed caste of American religious life and thought during the first two centuries of the country's history is, from an ecclesiastical point of view, the basic fact. I assume it to be so obvious as to make further elaboration unnecessary" (320).

38 Donald W. Dayton, "Yet Another Layer of the Onion: Or Opening

the Ecumenical Door to Let the Riffraff In," *The Ecumenical Review,* 40 (1988), 100f. The major point of Dayton's critique is to see from the sources that although the prevailing evangelical historiography (and popular interpretation) is to focus on the reformed matrix, in actuality the origins of evangelicalism and its current institutional expressions are to a significant extent rooted in the traditions of revivalism, millennialism, new school Presbyterianism and Congregationalism, and Keswick piety, not "in terms of the foreign categories of the orthodox traditions of Princeton." ("An Analysis of the Self-Understanding of American Evangelicalism with a Critique of Its Correlated Historiography," paper delivered to the Wesleyan/Holiness Study Project, Asbury Theological Seminary, January 28-30, 1988). For a good example of Reformed interpretation (in this case of public life), see Mark Noll, *One Nation Under God? Christian Faith and Political Action in America* (San Francisco: Harper and Row, 1988), esp. pp. 14-31.

39 Frederick Hale, *Trans-Atlantic Conservative Protestantism in the Evangelical Free and Mission Covenant Traditions* (New York: Arno Press, 1979); Ernest Sandeen, *The Roots of Fundamentalism: British and American Millenarianism, 1800-1930* (Chicago: University of Chicago Press, 1970); and George M. Marsden, *Fundamentalism and American Culture: The Shaping of Twentieth Century Evangelicalism 1870-1925* (New York: Oxford University Press, 1980).

40 Joel Carpenter, "The Fundamentalist Leaven and the Rise of an Evangelical United Front," in Sweet, *Evangelical Tradition in America,* pp. 267, 275, 288.

41 *Ibid.,* p. 259.

42 See especially George M. Marsden, *Reforming Fundamentalism: Fuller Seminary and the New Evangelicalism* (Grand Rapids: Eerdmans, 1987). This history notes many of the controversies of those early years, especially as "Neo-orthodoxy" replaced "Modernism" as the enemy in the minds of so many. Edward Carnell's problems and pleas for intellectual openness and toleration are well-known; and Bela Vassady, the Hungarian classical Reformed scholar of note brought to the faculty, eventually likened enduring this fundamentalist mentality as similar to having survived the Nazis and communists in Europe, and left when he was attacked for his constructive appreciation of Barth and his activities in the World Council of Churches (p. 111). It is also of interest that Paul S. Rees (then pastor of First Covenant Church, Minneapolis) was seriously considered for the position in evangelism at Fuller (and he was interested) in 1955, but was turned down because he was an Arminian: "The faculty nonetheless dearly wished to enlist him as a colleague. President Carnell, who ultimately opposed the appointment, saw himself and the faculty as caught in a truly tragic situation. *In order to protect the seminary for future generations, they wished to keep their Calvinist identity* [emphasis mine]" (pp. 120, 157).

43 Larsen, *Mission of a Covenant,* p. 18.

44 David Nyvall, *The Swedish Covenanters: A History* (Chicago: Covenant Book Concern, 1930), pp. 87ff. Nyvall, who knew intimately both these men as well as the church, in the pages which follow gave an hon-

est and realistic assessment of the implications of their leadership on the life of the fledgling church.

[45] Karl Olsson has described the reality of this need in a poignant parable of those who in a revival culture found it necessary to leave the church to hear the voice of God (*By One Spirit,* pp. 323f.).

[46] Conrad Bergendoff, review of Olsson's *By One Spirit,* in *Swedish Pioneer Historical Quarterly,* 14 (1963), 34; and in *Covenant Companion,* April 19, 1963, p. 8.

[47] Philip J. Anderson, " 'Invading America': Home Mission and Ecclesiology in the Northwestern Mission Association, 1928-1950," *Covenant Quarterly,* 44 (1986), 37-50.

[48] Olsson, *Into One Body . . . by the Cross,* p. 444.

[49] Larsen, *Mission of a Covenant,* p. 17.

[50] Nyvall, *Swedish Covenanters,* p. 10.

[51] Larsen, *Mission of a Covenant,* p. 134.

The Liturgy as Story and a Place for Stories

The Magnetic Field of the Gospel

C. John Weborg

Karl A. Olsson resigned his position as president of North Park College and Theological Seminary in 1970. He took up the position of director of leadership training with Faith at Work, developing both a theory and practice of relational Bible study. Great attention was given to "story," one's own as well as the stories in the Bible and how one can find oneself in the Bible stories. He wrote, "The first principle of relational Bible study is to make the story my story. This means being willing to enter the magnetic field of the character and incident as if they concerned me."[1] Two years earlier he had published *Come to the Party,* a largely autobiographical work making great use of the expansive and thickly populated narrative of Jacob and Esau, and of the elder brother motif in the parable of the prodigal son.[2] Having found himself in the Bible, the author of these works now invites others to do the same.

This is a twofold business. First, there are characters in the Bible who are a match for us. We do find ourselves in the Bible. Tenaciously, Olsson lets the humanity of these people stand in all their unvarnished and unfinished character. Grace starts there, with us, just as we are. It is amazing how like us they are or how like them we are! Second, we find ourselves, come to ourselves, and arrive at self-knowledge in "the magnetic field of the character and incidents." Since we see ourselves mirrored in these stories we come also to see that certain persons are more than just people. They become paradigms, primal shapes of reality. The elder brother in the parable of the prodigal son is a universal character. So is Adam. So is Mary, whom the great Dante extolled as "the sum of all that creation most can bless." At times these stories and the characters who populate them generate an irresistible magnetism, most of all the story of Jesus Christ. Anyone who keeps company with Jesus will eventually have to say with the Samaritan woman that "he told me all I ever did" (John 4) and yet not feel "told off." When we find ourselves in and with Jesus in the stories of his life, we are both found out and found and then we can begin to find ourselves.

The phenomenon of story is a thread of unity in Olsson's life and work. His academic disciplines, literature and church history, are shaped by and take the shape of story. His most recent work in evangelistic, relational theology takes its methodological clue from the epistemological, evangelistic, and edificational power of the biblical narrative, to say nothing of the narratives of the Church's doctors, martyrs, and saints. Stephen Crites's assertion that "stories, and the symbolic worlds they project, are not like monuments that men behold, but like dwelling-places. People live in them," confirms the worthwhileness of the attention given to stories by Olsson.[3] For that reason, I presume, stories create a magnetic field.

This essay will address some aspects of the liturgy as a story. Using Olsson's language, it will try to show that the liturgy is the magnetic field of the story of the gospel, inviting persons to be drawn to Christ. The liturgy itself is a story and a place for stories, a dwelling place it is hoped, and not just an aesthetic and anachronistic monument.

I

In 1900 the Covenant's Committee on Ritual issued a statement[4] about the nature of worship that was translated and published as an introduction to *A Book of Worship for Covenant Churches.*[5] The dominant ecclesiological motif is "the body of Christ." To the authors of the document, this motif is suggestive of two ingredients. The first is aesthetic: "the outward form of worship should be *reverent, festive, and beautiful.*" Whether prompted by classical Greek sculpture of the perfection and prowess of the human form or not, I do not know, but this document finds "beautiful worship" intrinsic to the praise of God and pleasing to him. The form of the human body and the harmony of its complex functions are a mysterious beauty. So are the form and function of the body of Christ.

The second ingredient is the relation of form to spirit, a relation also suggested by the body. Counting the scattered and the sustained treatments of this relation, my estimate is that nearly one-fourth of the document deals with the relation of body and spirit and/or form to freedom. The rest of it deals with the forms—singing, praying, the sacraments, etc.

The authors rely on two sources in order to explicate this relation. Interestingly, the first is anthropological: "Man is a spiritual-physical being," say the authors. Persons communicate both by words and symbols—King Immanuel enters through the Eyegate and Eargate into the city of Mansoul, as the citation from John Bunyan goes. People get themselves across to others and reveal their spirit by means of body language. We clap our hands when we are excited, or cover our mouths when we are chagrined. In distress, we affirm each other by words and a hug. These three are perceivable means by which we convey and confirm ourselves to each other. Naked words are not enough when the deep things of the human spirit need to be awakened and confirmed. "God," the authors say, "has not given us an abstract theoretical system for our salvation; he has given us perceivable means, the Word and Sacraments. Thus we have need for outwardly forms embodying our spiritual life if it is not to evaporate into mere opinions or an empty sentimentality."

The authors go on to argue that daily life and the Christian life necessitate certain formalities just for getting on with life, e.g. greeting people, saying good-bye, etc. In the Christian life the forms do much to awaken and maintain devotion. So we have here a simple yet sophisticated awareness of the epistemological, edifying, and enlightening power of symbols as vehicles of the Spirit, for just as the human spirit is an embodied spirit, so in matters pertaining to the divine Spirit embodiment is just as intrinsic. And the forms and symbols that embody the divine Spirit have their own ways of creating a magnetic field, drawing persons to Christ, the king who is servant and the servant who is king, to use a Barthian kind of language.

The second source for use of "body language" is the Bible, in particular the references to the Church as the body of Christ, found in 1 Corinthians 12 and Ephesians 4. This image suggests particularity yet commonality (many members, one body), diversity (all parts of the body do not have the same function), and interdependence (bones require muscles to move, muscles require a complex communication network, i.e. the nervous system, etc.). With roots both in Lutheranism and classical Pietism, Covenant people knew about the priesthood of all believers. "The church is not a chaotic heap of members but a body in which each member has his place and function." Thus "worship must be a free action and be so arranged that there is room for the free participation of the attendants." Yet "good order should be reflected in the worship of the church."

What this order looked like has been translated and annotated by the late Glenn P. Anderson. It combines what he calls the "churchly and the conventicle traditions." As one takes time to read the order of worship and compare it with the document under consideration, one will note the interplay of form and freedom; of objective, ecclesiastical, liturgical material and subjective, personal, and experiential material; of spirit released in bodily expression; of order providing "room for the free participation of the attendants," presumably in prayer, song, and story or testimony.[6] Thus room was given to each and all to exercise their priesthood, to do ministry, to understand the service as a whole, not just the sermon as the message, using the language of Ronald Magnuson.[7] When reverence, festivity, and beauty attend this complex activity, a magnetic field of immeasurable significance and incalculable power is set in motion.

II

Currently, we are eighty-eight years removed from the writing of the foregoing documents on Covenant worship. One major change to be noted is in the area of ecclesiology. Whereas the "body of Christ" was the controlling image in those documents, the controlling image in contemporary ecclesiology tilts toward "the people of God." Hans Küng writes, "The idea of the people of God is the oldest and most fundamental concept underlying the self-interpretation of the ekklesia. Images such as those of the body of Christ, the temple, and so on are secondary by comparison."[8] Avery Dulles is bold enough to say that this image is the principal paradigm in the documents of Vatican II,[9] although that statement has been challenged by some Catholics as being too simple a version of the story.[10]

Writers in both biblical testaments use this image. In Exodus 19:6 Israel hears its vocation this way: "and you shall be to me a kingdom of priests and a holy nation." In 1 Peter 2:9-10 it is said, "But you are a chosen race, a royal priesthood, a holy nation, God's own people, that you may declare the wonderful deeds of him who called you out of darkness into his marvelous light. Once you were no people but now you are God's people; once you had not received mercy but now you have received mercy." Echoes of the "no people . . . now God's people" can be found in Hosea 2:23 and Romans 9:25-26. Paul Minear's work, *Images of the Church in the New Testament,* isolates ninety-six such images of the Church, sixteen of which are variations on the image "the people of God."[11]

Twentieth-century persons need to be aware of the way "people" is used in the Bible. It does not refer to an aggregate of persons, such as when someone says, "Three hundred people were at the game." Biblically speaking, as Minear points out, "People in general do not exist; there are only particular peoples." Furthermore, "we do not use the word in the plural. By contrast, when the New Testament writers want to refer to all men either they speak of Adam, the representative man, or they speak of 'all the peoples.' Humanity is not visualized as a world-wide census of individuals, but as the separate peoples that, taken together, comprise mankind as a whole."[12]

What then may account for the fundamental character of the image "people of God"? No doubt it lies in the doctrine of election: this people is chosen by God, called by God for his purposes, and covenanted with by God as the people who are his own (Ezra 11:19-20; Jeremiah 7:23, 24:7, 30:22; Acts 15:14; Titus 2:14; and Revelation 18:4 for various uses of this term applied to the "people of God" in both testaments). This "particular people" has as a single explanation, "God called us." Once "no people," now "God's people," and all by God's free grace, compelled by nothing except his own sovereign desire to be in a concrete relation with "a people."[13]

Furthermore, this image is a commentary on the nature of God. Hendrikus Berkhof writes about the missionary God or about God's apostolate, whose major concern is not with the church but with the world: "the apostolate is not one of the many functions of the church, but the church is a function of the apostolate of God in the world."[14] One of the liabilities of the "body of Christ" language is its possibly too close identification with Christ, being so close, in fact, to some users of this language that they speak, using christological terminology, of the "hypostatization" of the Church, meaning that some sort of hypostatic union exists between Christ and the Church. If God is a missionary God, so are his people. They are both a result and a part of God's mission. What Berkhof seeks is a self-understanding on the part of the people of God that this people is identified with Christ's mission. Identification with Christ's mission will engender a prophetic sense of ministry, both in critique of the people of God and of the world, whereas the image "body of Christ" tends to engender the priestly ministry.[15] The prophetic critique is the necessary dialectical pole to counter the triumphalism often present in a priestly mode of life.

The bearing of this image on the thesis of this essay lies in the area of story. A missionary God seeks a people, covenants to be their God, they his people, and remains faithful to them even when the agreement intrinsic to it is broken. It is the classic love story: a proposal, the nuptials, the jilted spouse whose faithfulness is legendary, and who makes a new covenant. This people was at one time no people; now they are God's people. History is at the heart of this image. It is a real story when a "nobody" becomes a "somebody." And the story goes on as the outsiders try to become insiders, to own their own history, to make an archetypal story their story.

The process of becoming part of a new people is known only too well by Rahab and Ruth in relation to Israel and by Gentiles and other sinners in relation to the Church. It is harder to integrate converts than to win them, which is a sad commentary on the Church. In order for such to *own* their new story it must be *shared* by those who are its stewards. The image "people of God" connotes this purposeful, often painful process of blending histories and stories, which belongs to the Lord's people as a gift and task.[16] It is a task because the Lord's people seek and find the lost. It is a gift because the fruit of the seeking needs to be made one with those who went looking. The mission continues the story of the God who created the story because God himself went looking and then became a receiver of gifts.

III

Claus Westermann says that the fact that there is no word in Hebrew for "to thank" has never been properly evaluated. Because modern, often western, persons are so accustomed to living between the poles of "please" and "thank you," they are hardly aware that these terms are not common to humankind. As Westermann points out, in no modern language does "thank" have its own root; it is derived from other verb systems, as, for example, in German, *danken* (to thank) is derived from *denken* (to think).[17] If not thanks, then what does one do? One gives praise, which is not exactly the same activity as giving thanks.

Long before Westermann's work, Friedrich Heiler, in his monumental book *Prayer* (first published in 1932), had taken note of the absence of a word for "to thank" in many tribal languages. He noted that among the African Kiziba the words "thank you" were usually rendered as "Thou hast done it." For example, "O Waka, thou hast given me this buffalo, this honey, this wine." A Khond might say, "O God, thou hast rescued me."[18] The concreteness of the expressions stands out. Affectional language is less present than if the expression had been more "thank you" oriented. By contrast, the form of expression is a recital, a recounting of deeds done for one's benefit. The gods are praised by retelling their deeds back to them.

Based on Westermann's massive exegetical work, I can note the following distinctions between praise and thanksgiving. Praise actually elevates the one praised. Thanks bears no such connotation. Praise occurs in a group and needs a forum, whereas words of thanks do not and are offered in private as much as in public (Psalm 22:22, 40:9, 118:1). To offer praise requires a sentence; the offering of thanks does not. When one praises another, one looks away from oneself to the one praised; whereas when I give thanks it is *my* thanks I am offering, thus related more to the subject than to the object. Finally, expressions of praise are highly personal and spontaneous expressions giving exaltation to the one who has made a difference in one's life.[19]

To be more precise, the offering of praise among the Hebrew people was expressed in one of two forms of prayer: the *berekah* and/or the *hodayah*. The former or the "benediction" was a way of blessing God. It had five parts: 1) the stereotyped formula, "Blessed be the Lord," always in the passive voice; 2) other appellatives for God; 3) a relative clause using the third person singular of an active verb in the perfect tense expressing the grounds for praise; 4) the anamnesis or remembrance and retelling of God's mighty works (on a corporate level see 1 Kings 8:15-21, and on a personal level 1 Samuel 25:39); 5) petition based on the remembrance and retelling of God's deeds; 6) when used liturgically the prayer often closed with another blessing of God and a congregational "amen" (see Psalm 89:52, 41:13, and 106:48).

The *hodayah,* often translated as "thanks," is, as Paul Bradshaw seeks to make clear, more appropriately rendered as "praise." A major distinction between this form and the former is that the *hodayah* is expressed in the active voice and God is addressed in the second person, otherwise the form is nearly the same.[20] Recalling Westermann's stress on the personal character of praise and substantiated by the work of Harvey Guthrie, the point of this grammatical shift is no small matter.[21] The "personal" relationship to God finds itself expressed in the active voice of an "I" to someone in the second person, a "you" or a "thou." Since the purpose of this prayer was to express praise by recalling the concrete deeds of the benefactor, it took on the form of a confession, reciting the great deeds of salvation and deliverance. In this sense, the use of the active voice added another dimension, namely that of personal testimony, which was also a form of proclamation. Westermann and Guthrie recall us to the fact that this praise was offered amidst people, often with a festal sacrifice and joyous feast with family and friends (Psalm 30, especially v. 4).[22]

It is a long and complex story from this to the Christian Eucharist. But Bradshaw and Guthrie take the time to try to reconstruct the story in detail, namely how Hebraic in form and intent the Eucharist is, for its chief purpose is to praise and proclaim the works of God for us at a meal set among the friends of God, the brothers and sisters of our Lord Jesus Christ, "blended" by the Holy Spirit into one body. When the Eucharist is offered, it is in the active voice; only four times is God blessed in the passive (Ephesians 1:3; 1 Peter 1:3; 2 Corinthians 1:3; Luke 1:38). Perhaps the practice of some Catholics to have a Eucharist offered after receiving some blessing or deliverance is a contemporary example of offering praise, recounting a great story at a feast in the congregation as did the ancient Hebrews.

Praise proclaims and proclamation praises. When the story is told in the form of praise, characters are named and incidents are recounted as a "means . . . to enter the magnetic field of the characters and incidents" and those who hear the story can dwell there with the initial recipient of its benefits, appropriate those benefits, and add to the praise.

IV

Karl Olsson wrote that "the first principle of relational Bible study is to make the story my story." This theme recurs. From a theologian of liturgy: "A recurrent function of religious ritual is to put successive generations in dramatic touch with an archetypal story which accounts for the present order of the people or the world."[23] From a theologian of pastoral theology: "The great vocation of the minister is continuously to make connections between the human story and the divine story."[24] The same vocation applies to the liturgy, namely to provide a way for the human story, at whatever place and time, to be taken up into the divine story so that human praise and protest, lament and petition can be joined with and transformed by the love and sacrifice made by Jesus Christ.

Happily *The Covenant Book of Worship,* published in 1981, and *The Covenant Hymnal* of 1973, give a more prominent place to liturgy.[25] The service of Holy Communion II (pp. 120ff.) in the former, also included in *The Covenant Hymnal* (Reading 818), is called "The Great Thanksgiving" and follows quite closely the traditional eucharistic form of Sursum Corda (Lift up your hearts . . .), an ascription of praise to the Father for creation, and the Son for redemption by retelling the story; the Sanctus (Holy, Holy, Holy); the Words of Institution; the Epiclesis or the invocation of the Holy

Spirit; and a Doxology including a vow. The text omits a Preface. A distinctly eschatological note is sounded in the acclamation, "Alleluia! The Lord our God, the Almighty has come unto his kingdom," given after the communicants have been served.

A careful examination of the text will reveal the features noted by Bradshaw, Westermann, and Guthrie. It is the language of praise employing numerous sentences. The praise language is that of an "I" or "we" to a "thou" and is in the active voice with God addressed in the second person. It is done in the midst of a people gathered for a feast. And now to pick up a final observation from Westermann: to praise is to make a vow, to perform that for which a person has lauded God.[26] The text of Holy Communion II reads, "O God, who called us from death to life, *we give ourselves to you;* and with the church through all the ages we thank you. . . ."[27]

What follows is one of my own creations. It is meant to show how the ancient form frees the liturgist and the liturgy to create a magnetic field in order to draw our stories, our places and times, into the archetypal story. By making characters and incidents available for companionship and witness, the liturgy enables the ongoing story of God's providential care to be our dwelling place and for us to be a part of the people of God.

This service was written for the ending of the school year, 1982. It was a time filled with transitions for many people, e.g. the retirement from the deanship of North Park Theological Seminary of Glenn P. Anderson.

The Service of the Holy Communion

Leader: Father, all-powerful and ever-living God, we do well always and everywhere to give you thanks through Jesus Christ our Lord.

We praise you with greater joy than ever this Easter season, when Christ became our paschal sacrifice.

In him a new age has dawned, the long reign of sin is ended, a broken world has been renewed, and human beings are once again made whole.

The joy of the resurrection renews the whole

world, while the choirs of heaven sing forever to your glory:[28]

People: (Sing)
Holy, Holy, Holy, Lord God of hosts!
Heav'n and earth are full of thee!
Heav'n and earth are praising thee,
O Lord most high!

Leader: Loving God; Alpha and Omega, beginning and end, first and last, from whom we come and to whom we go: you are not transitory. We are. We know it all too well this evening: the coming and going—juniors, middlers, interns, seniors—all stages on life's way. We are mindful too of Glenn and Jeanette, servants of yours and ours for Jesus' sake. They too are in transit. Accompany them and us who know the vexing mystery that times and seasons have their endings.

People: But we are not alone in this. Thank you for bringing to mind the signs of your companionship:
    With Noah, who went out to build an ark on dry ground;
    With Abraham, in transit from Ur to a land unseen;
    With Moses, who left Jethro's flock to tend a people yet unformed;
    With Jonah, en route to Nineveh by way of a great fish.
    Most of all we thank you for your son's promise, "I am with you always, to the close of the age."

Leader: And now Father, with heartfelt thanks, we remember Jesus Christ. On the eve of his departure, he took bread and gave you thanks and praise. He broke the bread, gave it to the disciples, and said: "Take this, all of you, and eat it: this is my body which is given up for you."
    When supper was ended, he took the cup. Again he gave you thanks and praise, gave the cup to his disciples, and said: "Take this, all of you, and drink

from it. This is the cup of my blood, the blood of
the new and everlasting covenant, shed for you and
for all so that sins may be forgiven. Do this in
memory of me.''

People: Come among us in power and great glory.
By the power of your Holy Spirit, take these gifts
and us: unite us with one another and with all the
saints in heaven and on earth to praise your Name:
Father, Son, and Holy Spirit, one God, now and
always. Amen.

V

Having shown the liturgy to be a story, I want to make a final
observation. The liturgy is also a place for stories. The document on Covenant worship published in 1900 spoke of forms
as awakening devotion and of the form providing ''free participation'' for those at worship so that all of the parts of the
body were given both time and place.

In the fall of 1987 a remarkable chapel took place at North
Park Theological Seminary. The form of worship was rather
conventional: call to worship, hymns, scriptural reading,
prayers and stories to replace the sermon—that was the shift
in form. The Scripture reading was a blending of Psalms 41
and 42. After each strophe of the reading, the congregation
responded with Psalm 42:11b: ''Hope in God; for I shall again
praise him, my help and my God.''

Three stories followed. One was by an amputee giving
praise to God for sustenance during the long convalescence
following an accident; one was by a young widow who spoke
of the long but persistent recovery from grief; the last was by
a recovered alcoholic who started out according to Alcoholics
Anonymous: ''Hi, my name is Nick'' (an assumed name) only
to have three from the congregation say, ''Hi, Nick!'' Shades
of free-form is it not! After each story the congregation, led
by the storyteller, responded, ''Hope in God; for I shall again
praise him, my help and my God.'' With that the congregation owned the story and God was exalted on the praises of
his people, the people of God who know him in a personal
and covenantal relationship. The form and the freedom of this

service gave room for both personal as well as corporate expression, for the stated words and the spontaneous.

Arthur Weiser, commenting on Psalm 40:9-10, which concerns the public testimony given by the one praising God, says that "the testimony to God's gift of deliverance to the individual becomes the instrument of God's providential rule. God doing his work through human beings who place themselves at his service and spread his revelation abroad."[29] A tall order for a story! Yet reflection vindicates Weiser's point. A story can inspire hope and hold back a capitulation to hopelessness. A story does not guarantee that God works in the same way for all persons. But a story does declare that God acts, reveals himself, and comes to our assistance. There may be lament aplenty in this story of hope, for God does not always seem to act promptly or according to our expectation. Stories thus encourage people to wait, to rely on the encouragement of friends, and to speak truthfully to God in prayer, with protest as well as petition and praise. In this way, stories play a part in God's rule by engendering faith, hope, and love.

The liturgy as a story and a place for stories can create a magnetic field for the hearing of the Gospel. As a form of praise it is also a proclamation of the One whose story seeks to be our story long before we seek it for our story. Once we were no people; now we are God's people. How that comes about is the story worth telling by means of the liturgy as story and a place for stories.

Endnotes

[1] Karl A. Olsson, *Find Yourself in the Bible* (Minneapolis: Augsburg Publishing House, 1974), pp. 37-38.

[2] Karl A. Olsson, *Come to the Party* (Waco: Word Books, 1972).

[3] Stephen Crites, "The Narrative Quality of Experience," *Journal of the American Academy of Religion,* 39 (1971), 295.

[4] Originally published in *Förslag till kristlig gudstjänstordning* (Chicago: North Park College, 1900). Hereafter, *Förslag.* The translator was E. Gustav Johnson.

[5] *A Book of Worship for Covenant Churches* (Chicago: Covenant Press, 1964), pp. xiii-xxvi.

[6] Glenn P. Anderson, "Toward Understanding Worship in the Covenant Church," *The Covenant Quarterly,* 31 (1973), 27-44. See *Förslag,* pp. 3-5 and 6-11 for the service of Holy Communion.

7 Pastor of the Harbert Community Church, Harbert, Michigan.

8 Hans Küng, *The Church,* Ray and Rosaleen Ockenden, trans. (New York: Sheed and Ward, 1967), pp. 119-120, but see the entirety of part C, chap. 1.

9 Avery Dulles, S.J., *Models of the Church* (Garden City: Doubleday and Company, Inc., Image Books, 1978), p. 75.

10 For example, Herwi Rilchof, *The Concept of the Church* (London and Shepherdstown: Sheed and Ward/Patmos Press, 1981).

11 Paul Minear, *Images of the Church in the New Testament* (Philadelphia: Westminster Press, 1960), chap. 3.

12 *Ibid.,* p. 68

13 For further discussion of this aspect of the image, see Philip Hefner, "The Being of the Church," in Carl Braaten and Robert Jenson, eds., *Christian Dogmatics,* 2 vols. (Philadelphia: Fortress Press, 1984), II: 212-14.

14 Hendrikus Berkhof, *The Christian Faith,* Sierd Woudstra, ed. and trans. (Grand Rapids: William B. Eerdmans, 1979, 1986), p. 417.

15 For a perceptive discussion of these issues, see Christopher Butler, *The Theology of Vatican II* (Westminster: Christian Classics, Inc., 1981), pp. 62-67; and Dulles, *Models of the Church,* p. 57ff. A more philosophical analysis of the image "people of God" can be found in John Macquarrie, *Theology, Church, and Ministry* (New York: Crossroad, 1986), chap. 11.

16 As best I can recall, this phrase belongs to Alexander Ganoczy in *Becoming Christian: A Theology of Baptism as the Sacrament of Human History,* John G. Lynch, trans. (New York: Paulist Press, 1976). This is a remarkable book in that it offers a reading of baptism as an anthropologist might view it.

17 Claus Westermann, *Praise and Lament in the Psalms,* Keith R. Crim and Richard Soulen, trans. (Atlanta: John Knox Press, 1981), pp. 25-26.

18 Friedrich Heiler, *Prayer: History and Psychology,* Samuel McComb, trans. and ed. (New York: Oxford University Press, Galaxy Book, 1958), pp. 38-39. Among native Americans, the Paiute, for example, have no linguistic equivalent of "thank you." Instead the phrase *toki-wah* is used, which means "good in your heart." A Paiute explains, "When I don't ask or tell you, but you do something for me because you yourself want to, then that's *toki-wah.*" Malgorzata Niezabitowska, "Discovering America," *National Geographic,* 173 (January 1983), 78.

19 Claus Westermann, *Praise and Lament in the Psalms,* pp. 27-30.

20 Paul F. Bradshaw, *Daily Prayer in the Early Church* (New York: Oxford University Press, 1982), pp. 12-14; 32ff.

21 Harvey Guthrie, Jr., *Theology as Thanksgiving: From Israel's Psalms to the Church's Eucharist* (New York: The Seabury Press, 1981), pp. 10, 21, 23.

22 *Ibid.,* pp. 10, 190.

23 Geoffrey Wainwright, *Doxology: The Praise of God in Worship, Doctrine, and Life* (New York: Oxford University Press, 1980), p. 119.

24 Henri Nouwen, *The Living Reminder* (New York: Seabury Press, 1977), p. 24ff.

[25] Both are published by Covenant Publications in Chicago, Illinois.

[26] Claus Westermann, *Praise and Lament in the Psalms,* pp. 28-29. Look at Psalm 40.

[27] The last paragraph, italics mine. See also the story form of prayer for baptism in *The Covenant Book of Worship,* pp. 93-94.

[28] Preface is a traditional Easter Preface from the Roman Catholic rite.

[29] Artur Weiser, *The Psalms,* Herbert Hartwell, trans. (Philadelphia: Westminster Press, 1962), p. 338; see also pp. 224-25. No doubt one of the most powerful uses of story in the liturgical form of the Eucharistic Prayer is found in Antonio M. Stevens Arroyo, *Prophets Denied Honor: An Anthology on the Hispanic Church in the United States* (Maryknoll: Orbis Press, 1980), especially chapter 5. Sample eucharistic prayers are included showing ways of incorporating the primal events of tribal history into the story of creation or the thanksgiving for key figures in the story of the Latin American search for freedom. At the same time there is lament and even petition for North Americans who have often caused suffering and heartbreak for these people.

Together with All the Saints

The Rediscovery of the One Church through the Ecumenical Movement

Olle Engström

Karl A. Olsson, in many of his pioneering works in Covenant church history, has underlined the debts of our Covenant churches to earlier Christian tradition, especially Lutheran and Pietist. He has always emphasized that our churches are closely knit to earlier church traditions, not only in the initial stage of their history but ever since, while discovering and maintaining their own identity and characteristics.

Our churches were not born in a vacuum, nor do they live in a vacuum. They are surrounded by a "host of witnesses" (Hebrews 12:1), by churches stemming from different ages and different regions of the world.

The ecumenical movement has allowed churches to see each other, bringing them closer together. In another publication (*The Covenant Quarterly,* November 1987) I have tried to present, in a very brief, sketchy way, some of the most important elements of that movement as well as its history.[1] All churches, even those who have openly opposed the "official ecumenical movement" represented by the World Council of Churches (WCC), have been influenced by it.

I. The Basis for Christian Unity

The churches have come closer to each other not predominantly for practical reasons. More and more they have discovered that unity belongs to the very essence of the Christian Church. It was in the sign of that unity that the primitive church, a new fellowship across the ethnic, social, and economic borders of those days, challenged the whole Roman Empire. There were tensions and conflicts within the church from the beginning, as is the case today, but there was a strong sense of unity, prayed for by the Lord of the Church himself (John 17:21) and advocated in most of his letters by Paul, the apostle of mission and of unity.

Everything in that unity is related to Christ. He is the cornerstone in the one temple (Ephesians 2:20-21). He is the head of the one body, which is the Church (Colossians 1:18, 1 Corinthians 12). To be a Christian is to have been brought into that one body, being a member of a unique organism, related to other members whether we know it or not, whether we like it or not.

From the biblical point of view there is nothing that can be called "free churches." Certainly, Covenanters hold the view that the local church must maintain a certain independence, so that it might fulfill its missionary task by addressing the unique needs of people living in its own area. A certain independence is necessary as a guarantee for faithful ministry to the gospel. But that certainly does not mean freedom in the sense of total independence. Every church is related to other churches in the same community or far away. The interdependence of Christian churches is total. A Christian church in Minneapolis is related to churches in Mexico City, Matadi in Zaire, Mjölby in Sweden, and Minsk in the USSR. There is no way out.

The blood shed for us at Golgotha and handed to us as a gift as we celebrate Holy Communion is what gives nourishment to the whole body. It is the same blood in Minneapolis and in Minsk. When two women drink from the cup at the Lord's table in Minneapolis and in Minsk, they feel the pulse of the body of Christ, the heartbeat of Golgotha. How could they ever live as if they were not members of the same body, dependent upon each other? Above all, they are brought together by Christ himself.

"Free churches" do not exist if we take seriously the gospel. Christ's church is one, indivisible. Only as such can it be a sign of hope for a divided world, a challenge to all the disrupting and distorting powers of this earth. Those who proclaim only the independence of their own church or denomination are nothing less than heretics, weakening and betraying the vision of Pentecost.

We all tend to lose that vision as we become used to our own denomination, domesticated by it, making equal the horizon of our own church with the horizon of Christ's Church on earth. Over and over again we have to be reminded by the Holy Spirit to what fellowship we have been born, a fellowship that did not begin in 1878 or 1885 but centuries ago in Jerusalem. The ecumenical movement of our days is the rediscovery of that unity—joyous, triumphant, inspiring, but also full of challenges, frustration, and emotional disturbances because it touches so much of what is fundamental to our traditional lives as individual Christians or as churches.

II. Widened Horizons

As I have said in the publication mentioned above, we in the Mission Covenant of Sweden are grateful to God and to the leaders of our church at that time who made our Covenant one of the founding churches of the WCC in 1948. The WCC is not the ecumenical movement, it does not pretend to be so. There are other ecumenical formations as well. But no one would deny that the WCC is the most visible, influential, and extensive expression of the ecumenical movement. Permit me, in this *Festschrift* for a man who has meant so much in strengthening the relationships between our churches on both sides of the Atlantic, to share some experiences of the Swedish Covenant within the fellowship of the WCC.

We in the Swedish Covenant are grateful for all that we have learned through our sister churches in Congo, Zaire, Ecuador, India, and Japan; churches that stem from our own mission. We are also grateful for what we have learned from the member churches of the International Federation of Free Evangelical Churches, to which both our Covenants belong. But it is our association with the WCC that has meant more than anything else in the short history of our Covenant. Our membership in the WCC has brought us into contact with so many churches, founded through the ages, churches in so many different parts of the world, churches hitherto unknown to us.

By means of that fellowship we have come to know *the realities in which churches all over the world live*—the political, social, economic, and cultural realities. On one hand we experience our oneness in Christ; on the other we see the enormous differences as to the conditions in which we live and work. These conditions should be taken seriously. It cannot only be the manger in Bethlehem that interests us. It must also be the places and conditions in which Christ and the Church are born today. This is not Christmas romanticism. This is Christian fairness and realism.

The *political conditions:* here we are in the so-called "free world" with our almost unlimited possibilities to express our individual faith and to structure the life of our congregations without interference from the political authorities. Buildings, church magazines, mass media, public meetings, appointing our own ministers—everything is given to us, with some minor restrictions. In contrast are those churches living under political pressure, not only in the socialist dictatorships of Eastern Europe but under the dictatorships of all kinds of political colors, such as in the one-party states of Africa, where one has to be careful about what one says in the Sunday morning sermon, or in the dictatorships of Latin America. We should always remember that our freedom is exceptional, that Christian witness in many parts of the world includes the risk of being arrested, tortured, imprisoned, stamped out from the community of the wider society.

Can we in our comfortable quarters ever imagine ourselves in their situation? During my fifteen years as a member of the WCC Central Committee, three African bishops, members of that body, have been brutally killed by the rulers of their countries, so I know of what I speak. Pontius Pilate, King Herod, the Babylon of the Book of Revelation—they are still alive for many of our fellow Christians in a very real way.

One aspect of the political conditions is the more specific questions of *church and state.* We in Scandinavia, with our established state/folk churches, and you in North America, with your separation of church and state and its advantages and agonies, should consider the enormous spectrum of state-church relationships, with the daily fight for the freedom of the church that goes on in so many places. We in Sweden have learned much of the intricacy of this issue from brothers and sisters in the WCC member churches during Bible studies and in committee meetings and around dinner tables. It gives one plenty of stuff for intercession, I tell you!

The *ideological conditions:* it is very hard for churches to live in many Marxist-communist countries. But in a way, it is easier to know the enemy, to know the arguments and methods and the rules the enemy is setting for your life. It is sometimes more difficult for churches in societies colored by other religions to know how to handle the situation. I am not talking about fundamentalist Muslim faith of the Iranian type, sometimes rather similar in its methods to Marxist doctrinarism. I am talking of those countries, especially in Asia, where Christians are a minority in a religiously pluralist society and face more social pressures than political or legal ones. How can Christians in such situations act wisely, combining joyous Christian witness with due respect for the faith and life experience of others? [2] In so many ways we in "the Christian countries" could learn from them. They know the price they have to pay for their testimony much better than we in the West. When we warn them of the "risk of syncretism," they smile (sometimes they get angry) and warn us of the risk we run, confident as we are living in "a Christian society," apt to make compromises with our 'isms'—materialism, consumerism, colonialism. Not least for Swedes their words about "Western syncretism" have reminded us of the fact that we too live close to the Mountain of Temptations—and what a privilege it is to see one's situation more clearly with the help of fellow Christians, living at another side of that mountain.

Needless to say, the *economic conditions* are being made alive at almost every Bible study, as it belongs to the very basis of human life. We Westerners can abstain from bringing up the issue, but you cannot expect Christians from the poor sections of the world (and there are a few of them!) to leave those questions back home when they go to ecumenical conferences. They can teach us basic things about how one can live a rich and joyous life in the midst of poverty, how in that very poverty Christ has come closer to them than ever. We should certainly not romanticise poverty, but how can we learn from them the mysteries and gifts of shared poverty and at the same time discover the immense risks of affluence—affluence that distorts so much of Christian discipleship today?

The *cultural environment* in which churches live and work shapes them to a degree. Churches color the culture in which they live, but in most cases churches are more colored by the culture. Just take music! Even if during the missionary and ecumenical era churches have influenced each other, there is still an almost shocking variety of church music. Once you have heard the liturgy of a Syrian Orthodox church, or rhythms and melodies of a Kimbanguist church along the Congo River, or the music of the churches on the Fiji Islands, you know for sure that churches never grow in a vacuum but in a distinctive cultural milieu. That sometimes means frustration but more often richness. The enculturation of churches is an effect of incarnational theology. The Word becomes concrete cultural reality.

That encounter between the gospel and an already existing culture is not limited to aesthetic areas like music, church art, and architecture. It naturally goes deeper. It has to do with fundamental ethical and doctrinal questions. Take polygamy. For centuries firmly embodied into many African cultures, challenged by the first missionaries, sometimes in a very unsensitive way, it is now seriously considered by many churches as acceptable at least during a transitory stage where polygamous marriages have to be lived out as a responsible consequence of promises given by the husband.

There is the whole area of demons and exorcism, a central problem for so many ministers and evangelists in Asia and Africa in their pastoral counseling, and as we know today not only there: it has, to our own surprise, sometimes become a problem in some of our own congregations as a consequence of the teachings of "Christian demonologists."

For us Western Christians the encounter with Asian, African, Pacific, or Latin American cultural phenomena in the life of their churches can be a frustrating one. But at the same time, every such encounter makes us ask, "To what extent are we and our churches stamped by our own cultural characteristics?" We certainly do not live in some kind of "clean" and timeless Christian culture. We are colored not only superficially but deep down in our attitudes and habits by the cultural environment into which we happened to be born. The ecumenical movement is a permanent reminder of that basic insight.

Third World churches teach us lessons in this respect. The very basic fact that not all members are literate gives new dimensions to discussions about Christian education. And there are other forms of illiteracy. In all the communal, state, or municipal libraries from Leningrad to Vladivostok, not one book is available that gives Christian edification in the usual sense of that word. No Christian books are available in libraries.

There is one Bible for every third Baptist family in the USSR, an explanation of the fact that the church services last for hours as whole chapters of the Bible are read. These are differing cultural conditions, for sure, in comparison with ours. To summarize: the conditions under which churches in different parts of the world live are so different from each other that it takes at least two hours at a dinner table or at a common Bible study before we begin to grasp the very basic conditions of churches that are not just exotic but in a very real sense part of our own family.

How poor is the Church, if it is only like our own. How rich the Christian worldwide Church with all its different rhythms, organs, guitars, flutes, drums, architectural expressions, colors—from the minister dressed in a black gown in a Reformed church in Geneva to the beautiful, colorful Indian textile worn by a Pentecostal evangelist in Guatemala. Whatever can be said about the Christian Church, it is not monotonous. The task of the ecumenical movement is to make that worldwide Church not uniform but unified.

It has been a fascinating experience through the years in the WCC to witness that unification process taking place with parliamentary procedures (one aspect of culture!), which for many church delegates bring frustrations that lead to anger or resignation. Proposals, amendments, amendments to the amendment to the amendment. "Has 'amendment' something in common with 'Amen'?" Should we use the German, the Anglo-Saxon, or the Latin American way of chairing a meeting to get the unification process going? What is the relationship between Anglo-Saxon parliamentary procedures and those of Acts 15:28?

III. Discoveries in a Renewed Fellowship

The ecumenical movement of our century has made it possible for churches to meet each other. The alliance movements of the last century brought individual Christians together. The fact that today churches meet together is in a way a miracle. Many of them had never before met. The fact that the Orthodox churches of Eastern Europe, which had been isolated from the churches of Western Europe for nine centuries, are now participating in ecumenical organizations illustrates the breakthrough for Christian fellowship across denominational barriers. It is the greatest event in the church history of our time. But not only have East and West met; for the first time state/folk churches have come to take seriously denominations with quite a different ecclesiology. That can easily be illustrated by the fact that through the ecumenical movement Scandinavian folk churches take the free churches in Scandinavia more seriously than before. In the WCC these free churches have a platform that has contributed to greater mutual understanding at home.

In the initial stage of this new ecumenical encounter it was easy to understand that many churches were confused and frustrated by all the new things they experienced. That confrontation and that beginning of a dialogue led almost all churches to contemplate the question of their own identity. What does my own church represent in this new fellowship? What is the unique character of my own church?

The Mission Covenant of Sweden felt the need to summarize what it stands for. Despite our traditional hesitancy about written creeds and systematic descriptions of what the Covenant stands for, the need was felt for some kind of inclusive statement about our church to be used in the ecumenical fellowship. At the annual meeting of 1964 such a document was agreed upon and included in our constitution.

This led to a *stage of comparative theology,* when the churches compared each others' doctrines and teachings, worship forms, ecclesial structures, and so on. That was the case within the Faith and Order movement. From the very beginning it was clearly stated in the constitution of the WCC that each member church would be free to guard its own traditions, e.g. doctrine and worship. Not even a common concept of what should be meant by the term "Christian unity" was required.[3] But that comparative stage with its continuous statements on differences was soon overcome. Dialogue meant reconsidering and relearning.

A. *Doctrine*

The Faith and Order Conference at Lund, Sweden, in 1952 is a very good illustration of the comparative stage. Both in the prepatory material and in the final report the comparisons between the churches' different positions dominate: comparisons as to baptism, Holy Communion, ministry, and so on. In a way it brought together important raw material to be used in the continued dialogue.

Compare the Lund documents with those stemming from the Faith and Order Movement Conference in Lima, Peru, in 1982. Years of fellowship and serious theological work had carried the churches far beyond the stage of comparisons to a much more dynamic approach. The Lima document was the result of more than just the discussions within the membership of the WCC. In Lima representatives of the Catholic Church and of Baptist and Pentecostal churches, who are not yet members of the council, were also present.

The document on baptism, eucharist, and ministry (known as the BEM document) is not a consensus document, but in the preface of the report it is clearly stated that "the text represents the significant theological convergence which Faith and Order has discerned and formulated."[4]

Convergence is the result, and how could it be otherwise? Churches that have lived for centuries or at least for decades at some distance from each other—which provides good soil for prejudices, misinterpretations, and distortions to grow— have come to discover that even if many differences remain, a unity exists. This is the great and joyous discovery, which enriches their own lives.

In Sweden we have had the interesting experience that the BEM document has been studied not only in the local churches of the WCC member-churches but also far outside those churches. It is studied intensely at theological seminaries of nonmember churches. No other WCC document has been studied as widely and as thoroughly as the BEM document. As to its importance for the Swedish Covenant, it has meant much in the work that has now resulted in a new manual for ministers and church services. The report has also helped us to deepen our debate on doctrinal matters with the Church of Sweden (Lutheran), e.g. as to our openness for both forms of baptism, earlier not easy for the Lutherans to accept. As to the great classical themes of the BEM report there are still important differences. But what is most important is that so many have discovered how much the churches have in common.

Also, important new insights have been gained concern-

ing the *unity of the Church*. There might have been a few
dreamers of a unified church structure à la Rome. But even
they had to read the Toronto declaration carefully. Today one
might speak of a wider spectrum as to concepts of Christian
unity. On the one hand is the importance of the local unity
of Christians, of which the New Delhi Assembly spoke so con-
vincingly in 1961. On the other hand is some kind of national
and international manifestation of the unity of Christ in terms
of "conciliar fellowship," some kind of looser but visible manifestation of the unity we have in Christ. And still the prayers
and dreams continue that churches will merge and by means
of a renewed understanding testify to their unity in the one
Lord in an era of so much of disunity and destruction. The
talks about Christian unity in Sweden, recently resulting in a
partially common hymnbook for most Swedish churches, has
profited immensely from the material coming from the wider
ecumenical scene.

Still more dramatic are the discussions about *social ethics*.
Some Protestant churches, especially those belonging to the
Reformed tradition, have always been active in the social and
political arena. Others have another tradition. The Lutherans
with their teaching about the two realms (that of the secular
government and that of the church) have been much more
reluctant and inexperienced in that field. The Orthodox
churches of Eastern Europe have seldom come to grips with
the political issues as they strive for harmonization of the relationship between church and state.

In this new ecumenical fellowship, social ethics and common action lines have had to be discussed and decided upon
concerning an extremely wide range of issues: racism, poor-
rich/North-South, development, disarmament, and all the political issues, including the Middle East, South Africa, Central
America, Afghanistan, and so on. Those problems have been
tackled with the conviction that the gospel relates to all sides
of human life, not only to the spiritual dimension of it. And
there have always been member churches in the midst of hunger or in open repression that have urged the council to speak
up.

This has been a bewildering experience for many, to be
compelled to take a stand on issues of which their own church
has never before said a word. But this hammering out of some

kind of common belief in social ethics has been as enriching as it has been painful. Sometimes one has the feeling that the task to speak righteousness to those in power, which was once given to the Old Testament prophets, has now been given to a council of churches—a council that has only recently discovered each other. It seems a task almost too overwhelming. The resolutions of the council have often been controversial, and how could it be otherwise with nations and churches so emotionally involved in issues of importance for their everyday life?[5]

The Covenant of Sweden has always been active in the political arena through its members. It is a subject that has always been addressed in our church publications. But it is difficult, indeed, to imagine how that discussion in our church and in the wider church in Sweden would have developed if we had not had the privilege of referring to the experiences of the wider Christian family within the WCC.

B. *Worship*

We have become accustomed to the worship style and form of our own church. Most of us are probably rather happy about it, e.g. the efforts of Covenant churches to combine freedom and warm atmosphere with solemnity and a certain liturgical continuity.

We often discuss means of renewal of our forms of worship. Suddenly we meet brothers and sisters from Orthodox churches who smile at our efforts of renewal and refer to their form of worship dating back to the end of the fourth century with the great liturgical renewer of those days, the church father Chrysostom. "Why do you discuss all these changes? Our form has carried the gospel through centuries. Why are you so nervous about your forms?" Are they just blind and deaf in view of the needs of our time, or can we learn something from their confidence in the endless, joyous liturgical repetition of the great events in the history of salvation?

Or, as a contrast, watch the spontaneity and informality of the Pentecostal churches in Latin America that have brought the gospel to millions of people and brought them into the fellowship of the Christian Church. Observe the Kimbanguist Church of the Congo River, with its colorful celebration, the joyous singing, the direct preaching, its remarkable mixture of informality and order.

Once you have experienced the rich variety of worship within the Christian Church you can get new impulses for your own as it is seen in a deeper perspective. You begin to wonder to what extent the different forms of worship are merely reflecting the culture in which they are performed or whether they are derived from different interpretations of biblical material. Is it significant that in most Orthodox churches the participants in a service stand for two hours while we try to make the pews as comfortable as possible? What is there in the fact that most Reformed ministers dress in black, while Anglicans and many Third World churches use a variety of colors to the glory of God? What does it mean that most Lutheran ministers turn their back to the congregation while leading prayers and intercessions, while Catholic priests and most Protestant ministers face the congregation? The church service, the liturgy as drama, can be better understood if we have a deeper insight into the variety of forms now used in different churches.

C. *Ecclesiology*

In Europe, the tension between folk churches, most often closely related to the state, and the free churches, with membership of those who confess a personal faith in Christ, has been long and sometimes bitter. But times have changed. The secularization in Western Europe has made most folk churches reconsider their positions, at least demanding baptism as a condition for membership.

In Eastern Europe still more dramatic changes have taken place as an effect of the aggressiveness of the state and the party. The former folk church in East Germany, for example, has more and more become a church that discovers the pains and privileges of being a free church with members who are very much conscious of what Christian faith means in a society hostile to them and to the church.

It has been one of the most fascinating aspects of being a member of the WCC to be able to witness this change and to testify to our own efforts of being a fellowship of believers—not exclusive, but open to the wider society.

D. *Mission and Evangelism*

The North American and the Swedish Covenant Churches

are born out of revivals. Both are keen to live up to that heritage. Forms for evangelistic work have changed but the zeal is still there. When with this background you enter into the wider ecumenical fellowship, you do so with certain suspicions—suspicions of liturgical churches, folk churches with their often wide nominal membership, institutionalized churches, churches more interested in the purity of doctrine than of making people alive in Christ. Certainly, these elements exist. But as the dialogue develops you realize that evangelism is one of the main concerns of all churches, and the accents differ depending upon the environment in which they live.

There are some, in Muslim or in communist countries, who are not allowed to evangelize, either because of legal restrictions or aggressive social pressure. But most churches are very much concerned and struggle as we do with the task of making the gospel known to others, both adults and the younger generation.

In a document adopted by the Central Committee of the WCC in 1982 entitled, "Mission and Evangelism—An Ecumenical Affirmation," we read:

> The Church proclaims Jesus, risen from the dead. Through the resurrection, God vindicates Jesus, and opens up a new period of missionary obedience until he comes again. The proclamation of the Gospel includes an invitation to recognize and accept in a personal decision the saving lordship of Christ. It is the announcement of a personal encounter, mediated by the Holy Spirit, with the living Christ, receiving his forgiveness and making a personal acceptance of the call to discipleship and a life of service. Many of those who are attracted to Christ are put off by what they see in the life of the churches as well as in individual Christians. In some countries there is pressure to limit religion to the private life of the believer—to assert that freedom to believe should be enough. The Christian faith challenges that assumption. The Church claims the right to exist publicly—visibly—and to address itself openly to issues of human concern. The planting of the Church in different cultures demands a positive attitude

towards inculturation of the Gospel. This growing
cultural diversity could create some difficulties. In
our attempt to express the catholicity of the Church
we may lose the sense of its unity, but the unity we
look for is not uniformity but the multiple expression of a common faith and a common mission.

Today's renewals of mission and evangelism are just additional illustrations of the fact that the churches have learned
very much indeed from each other during the short time of
intensified contacts. Only "together with all the saints. . . ."

In Paul's writings to the young, inexperienced, small
Christian churches that were influenced and frustrated by the
religious and philosophical pluralism of those days, one of his
most urgent themes is that of Christian unity as he pours out
his heart in his pleas to proclaim Christ in the vast empire.
He writes of members in the one body, stones in the one temple, members of God's household. In his letter to the Ephesians (2:18) he prays, "that you, being rooted and grounded
in love, may have power to comprehend with all the saints
what is the breadth and length and height and depth, and to
know the love of Christ which surpasses all knowledge, that
you may be filled with all the fullness of God."

This is true today. Only together with all the saints, with
all God's people, shall we understand the richness of God's
love, revealed in Christ. All churches are tempted to become
self-sufficient and self-centered, considering themselves to be
the normal, not to say normative, church.

Today the Church of Christ in different parts of the world
lives in a variety of conditions with a variety of experiences
that are almost inexhaustible. Today we have the means of
learning from each other, which were not available for the
early Christians, who had as their means of communication
the paved roads of the Romans and the Mediterranean. We
have the "Mediterranean of the mass media," the flights, the
privileges of personal encounters. We in the churches of the
West could profit immensely by listening more closely to the
churches in the East and in the Third World.

It is only in close contact with the churches in other parts
of the world that we in an extremely complicated and agonizing time can become the instruments of God's love, to bring

individuals to see his glory and become instruments for justice and peace and a more fair distribution of the resources to all children in God's world. The ecumenical movement of our century, grown out of the missionary enterprise, is God's challenge to our churches to break out of our self-centeredness, to widen our horizons and thus equip us for the task of being bearers of hope in a world of disruption and despair.

We in the Swedish Mission Covenant have found it to be a blessing to be a member of the wide fellowship of churches in all parts of the world, not polemicizing at a distance against things we do not like or accept, but making our voice heard in the midst of that joyous and agonizing fellowship.

Endnotes

[1] The literature about the ecumenical movement and the WCC and its documents are probably well known to the readers of this *Festschrift*. The following might be considered as basic books and documents: Ruth Rouse and Stephen Neill, eds., *A History of the Ecumenical Movement 1517-1948* (Philadelphia: Westminster Press, 1954); Harold E. Fey, *A History of the Ecumenical Movement, Vol. 2, 1948-1968* (Philadelphia: Westminster Press, 1970); W. A. Visser't Hooft, *Memoirs* (London: SCM Press, 1973); the official reports of the WCC assemblies:

1. *The Amsterdam Report* (London: SCM Press, 1949).
2. *The Evanston Report* (London: SCM Press, 1955).
3. *The New Delhi Report* (London: SCM Press, 1962).
4. *The Uppsala Report* (Geneva: WCC, 1968).
5. *Breaking Barriers, Nairobi Assembly, 1975* (WCC/Eerdmans, 1976).
6. *Gathered for Life, Vancouver Assembly, 1983* (WCC/Eerdmans, 1983).

The printed minutes from all Central Committee meetings, Faith and Order conferences, and conferences arranged by the other sub-units of the council; e.g., Baptism, Eucharist, and Ministry, WCC, 1982; Guidelines for Dialogue with People of Living Faiths and Ideologies, WCC, 1982; Arnold Bittinger, ed., *The Church Is Charismatic,* (WCC, 1982); B. Sjollema, *Isolating Apartheid* (WCC, 1982); Abrecht/Koshy, *Before It Is Too Late (The Challenge of Nuclear Disarmament)* (WCC, 1983).

[2] See John Mbiti, ed., *Confessing Christ in Different Cultures* (WCC, 1977).

[3] See the WCC Central Committee declaration in Toronto, 1950, on "The Church, the Churches, and the World Council of Churches."

[4] *Baptism, Eucharist, and Ministry, Faith and Order Paper 111* (WCC, 1982).

[5] See Central Committee minutes with their resolutions on racism, disarmament, human rights, technology and the future, and so on.

Ecumenism in The Evangelical Covenant Church

Milton B. Engebretson

The purpose of this essay is to trace the responses, attitudes, and actions of Covenant people to ecumenical emphases and trends during the past thirty years. It therefore becomes necessary to take a quick glance at predisposing events in the Church at large that influenced the Covenant and other denominations in their interchurch actions. In 1948 in Amsterdam, the World Council of Churches (WCC) made its bid to unify the Church by holding its first worldwide General Assembly with the very appropriate theme, "Man's Disorder/God's Design." Representation by delegations from denominations pretty well covered the whole Christian Church. Whether or not its general secretary, Willem Visser't Hooft, and his staff were successful in communicating to conservative evangelicals that this meeting was indeed the central corps of the Church of Jesus Christ is immaterial. What this assembly did do without question was awaken all church bodies everywhere to a fact that could no longer be ignored: the Church was in reality one body and alive globally, and it was finally giving public recognition that a united witness and work were essential to being the Church in the world. That assembly also forced (indirectly) all denominations to ponder questions of conciliar alignments and affiliation. Whether steps were taken toward affiliation or toward the creation of more acceptable new federations, mattered little. What mattered was that an awareness of the "oneness of the body of Christ" had penetrated the consciousness of church leaders everywhere, thereby demanding some kind of response.

Amsterdam was followed by Evanston '54, New Delhi '60, Uppsala '68, Nairobi '75, and Vancouver '83. These assemblies grew in influence and acceptance as Uppsala saw the first vocal and articulate en masse delegations from Third World countries; and Nairobi witnessed, refreshingly, the domination of the scene by delegates from Third World countries whose questions on almost any proposed action or legislation were, "What does the Bible teach on this issue?" or, "What would Jesus do were he making this decision?" Vancouver seemed to reintroduce the importance of Bible study to the assembly.

On the American scene, the National Association of Evangelicals (NAE) was organized in 1942, followed by the National Council of Churches (NCC) in 1950 (successor to the Federal Council of Churches, founded in 1908). Among other global ecumenical ventures that followed, though not billed as such, was the first International Congress on Evangelism held in the famed Congresse Halle in West Berlin in 1966. Representation came from some 137 countries. The purpose of the meeting was to inspire, inform, and share methods of training Christians everywhere to win the unchurched of the world to Christ through evangelization. An undeniable fringe benefit of the congress was the significant stride it made in fanning the flames of ecumenism, more than could be imagined or admitted. The fact that Billy Graham was open "to all those who are ready to hear his message and support his effort, regardless of denominational affiliation or theological brandname"[1] brought representation to this congress from everywhere. To stand with this vast audience on the opening evening and sing, "To God be the glory, great things he hath done," was a spiritual, emotional, and ecumenical experience defying expression.

The Lausanne Congress that followed in 1974 probably did more to set the stage and the agenda for the General Assembly of the 1975 WCC meeting in Nairobi than almost any other world event, with the possible exception of the elevation of the status of women. Though the agendas, programs, emphases, objectives, and conclusions experienced by the congresses and the assemblies were very different from one another, many of the same people were present at both. Christians from a wide variety of backgrounds (political, economic, and ecclesiastical) began working together to carry out the mandate of communicating, living, and obeying the gospel, suggesting a real expression of the unity of the body of Christ, perhaps not experienced since the first century.

The postwar period nurtured thoughts about merger possibilities between similar church bodies, and some not so similar. The result was a series of attempted mergers, some successful and others not. Among the new churches were The American Lutheran Church, Lutheran Church in America, United Church of Christ, and The Evangelical Free Church of America. Though the Covenant has on occasion discussed merger possibilities, it has chosen to retain its historic identity. For several years, merger was contemplated with the Swedish Free Church, culminating in 1921 when the Covenant approved a referendum to send the question to the churches for vote, while the Free Church chose to end the discussion.

The Covenant Church, however, was caught up in the flow when attitudes thickened about national and international councils and affiliations, and it too began to analyze its posture and initiated explorations. The Annual Meeting of 1956 heard the report of the Comity Commission. The commission saw that its assignment included pointing the denomination in the direction of some form of action on the "growing concern for oneness within the body of Christ."[2] It presented a resolution on the issue to the 1956 Annual Meeting. The Annual Meeting of 1963 reaffirmed the 1956 report in its attempt to adopt a resolution from the Commission on Interchurch Relations, giving particular attention to the following:

> That the Covenant's elected administrators may enter into discussions looking toward closer cooperation and possible merger with other denominations whose theological orientation and whose concept of the nature and mission of the church are similar to our own; That the administrators shall inform the Executive Board of all such consultations, and, should such consultations appear favorable, that the Executive Board shall advise our constituency accordingly and bring appropriate recommendations to the Annual Meeting.[3]

The meeting also took a major stride toward action by expanding the Interchurch Relations Commission. A special committee was formed composed of the existing Commission on Interchurch Relations, the Council of Administrators, and two additional members—Earl C. Dahlstrom and Wesley W. Nelson. Its assignment was to study the whole matter of Covenant interchurch relations and to report its findings and recommendations, if any, to the Covenant Executive Board, which in turn would make recommendations to the Covenant Annual Meeting.[4]

The special committee did its work during 1963-64 and, through the Executive Board, presented a resolution to the Annual Meeting to replace the 1956 resolution. It embodied a statement of Covenant identity and a specific resolution on merger, requesting the Annual Meeting for authorization "to proceed with investigations and conversations, looking toward closer co-operation and possible mergers with one or more church bodies." It also contained a specific paragraph on affiliation with interchurch bodies. Again authorization was requested for the special committee to "be responsible for providing information designed to stimulate dialogue on personal, local, and regional levels in preparation for the decisions of the Annual Meeting in 1966."[5] The recommendation with its resolutions failed to pass by a tie vote. The tie vote was broken as the moderator cast the deciding vote to defeat the motion. The very next action proposed to the 1964 assembly was by Karl A. Olsson, president of North Park College and Theological Seminary and a member of the special committee. His proposal was for a substitute motion as follows:

> That we herewith instruct the Special Committee on Interchurch Relations to prepare a simple referendum for our local churches on the question of affiliation with interchurch organizations of national and international scope and that the results of this referendum be made known to the next Annual Meeting (1965), that such a referendum is to be conducted at an officially constituted meeting of each congregation, and that the report of each church show how the vote was taken.[6]

It was clarified that the action was not intended to be a binding vote, but rather a straw vote as a guide.

The substitute motion found the support of the Annual Meeting and was conducted during the ensuing year. The results were as follows: 400 churches (more than two-thirds) participated in the referendum. Nearly 25,000 Covenanters (about 40 percent) voted in the referendum.[7]

Vote I

For the WCC	4,752 (19%)
Against the WCC	15,021 (61%)
Undecided	4,215 (17%)
No information (spoiled votes, etc.)	850 (3%)

Vote II

For the NAE	6,149 (25%)
For NCC	2,819 (11%)
For American Council	868 (3%)
For none of these	9,221 (37%)
Undecided	4,881 (20%)
No information	900 (4%)

The convincing nature of the straw vote put the matter of conciliar arrangements to rest, though a careful study of the results might cause one to conclude that the issue could resurface before much more time passes. Since younger Covenanters tended to be more interested in affiliation than older, if a progressive conservatism is not a phenomenon of the aging process, a renewed interest could emerge.

A previous move was also noteworthy. In 1962 the entire Midwinter Conference centered on conciliar bodies—their scope, work, and justification for being. The underlying agenda was the focus of the Covenant Church and the ecumenical posture it ought to be assuming. Featured speakers were Paul S. Rees (past president) and Harold Ockenga (then president) of the National Association of Evangelicals, and Edwin Dahlberg, president of the NCC. It is my considered opinion that this conference came as close to a clear denominational confrontation about the probability of conciliar affiliations as has ever been experienced. Some 275 Covenant pastors attended the conference.

Between 1964 and 1966 discussions were pursued with denominations concerning the potential for merger with the Covenant. Visits were arranged with the Moravian Church in America, Church of the Brethren, Church of God (Anderson, Indiana), Mennonite Church (Newton, Kansas), and The American Lutheran Church. Nothing much resulted beyond initial conversations. A few years later in 1969, with the concurrence of the Interchurch Relations Commission (the special committee was now disbanded), the president of the Covenant hosted a meeting at North Park College and Theological Seminary with the leadership of several denominations. Included were the Baptist General Conference, Conservative Congregational Christian Conference, Church of the Lutheran Brethren of America, North American Baptist Conference, Moravian Church, Church of God (Anderson, Indiana), Mennonite Church, and Church of the Mennonite Brethren. The purpose was to discuss areas of commonality in theology and ecclesiology, and also to attempt to uncover areas where duplicate efforts were being experienced, particularly on fields of world mission. This gathering did muster up a bit of excitement, but only as long as it was hosted and sponsored by The Evangelical Covenant Church. Realizing that interest in merger was in decline, even on the national scene in mainline churches, further scheduling of meetings fell off by 1972, signaling the end of all discussions about merger possibilities to date.

Changes began to occur in several areas. The NAE picked up momentum and in a sense enjoyed riding the crest of the wave of neo-evangelicalism through the nationwide and almost worldwide emphasis on "born-again Christianity." The NCC, however, appeared to be losing ground. The discontinuance of general assemblies is probably the most telling indication; the last general assembly was held in Dallas in 1971.

It should be noted that the Covenant Church always availed itself of the privilege extended by the NAE, the NCC, and the WCC to send delegate-observers to their general assemblies. Merger emphasis slipped to the back burner of most denominational agendas with the exception of the Lutheran bodies and the Presbyterians, which have recently entered respectively into major mergers. The United Church of Christ and the Disciples (The Christian Church) efforts have been slowed considerably.

The Covenant Church, however, has continued to become more involved nationally and internationally. Nationally, a group which called themselves the Malone College Consultation had met annually for about a decade. The purpose of this consultation was to develop an ongoing dialogue between leadership of church bodies within the NCC and those not so affiliated. The group met annually at Malone College in Akron, Ohio, until 1970 when a decision was made that it had about run its course and should be disbanded. The founders of this group were Ralph P. Hanson and Paul S. Rees (Covenant); John H. Yoder (Mennonite); Eugene Smith (Methodist), general secretary of the NCC; John Coventry Smith (Presbyterian); Carl F. H. Henry (Fuller Theological Seminary); and others.

Also in 1970 Eugene Smith, John Coventry Smith, William Thompson, and myself, together with Frederick Schiotz and Robert Marshall (Lutheran), concluded that it was time for a new venture in ecumenicity within the United States. A meeting was set at the O'Hare Inn, Chicago (with broader representation than is named above), early in 1971 to attempt to call for a meeting including the titular heads (i.e., archbishops, bishops, presidents, general secretaries, et. al.) of the WCC, NCC, NAE, and nonaffiliate church bodies to meet annually to discuss the mission of the church, focusing on some specific phase of that mission. Invited were the leaders from all Protestant denominations in the U.S., all Orthodox church bodies, as well as representation from the Roman Catholic Church (preferably the presiding bishop from the National Conference of Catholic Bishops), the president of the NAE, the president of Church Women United, and the president and general secretary of the NCC. The meeting would be held with open and free discussions without the presence of the press or the media, either religious or secular.

The first meeting was held in St. Louis, Missouri, at the Statler Hilton Hotel in 1972 with some sixty leaders participating. The steering committee chairperson was Frederick Schiotz, retired president of The American Lutheran Church, and Milton Engebretson, president of The Evangelical Covenant Church, was the convening chairperson. A year later Engebretson became the steering committee chairperson and remained so for the next fifteen years. The group took the name, the Meeting of U.S. Churchmen, later revising it to the Meeting of U.S. Church Leaders. The framework for this meeting was as follows:

1) An organization much like the NCC will continue, retaining its "advocacy" function.
2) Most nonmember churches will probably not take out membership in such a continuing council. Selective participation will continue in units of the NCC for nonmember churches.

3) There will be more fluctuations in interchurch relations and organization in years ahead than in prior years. "KEY 1973" will probably be influential in those changes.
4) One of the places where the Holy Spirit does his work is in such gatherings of Christians, seeking his guidance for the Christian task.

Pursuant to these assumptions, Robert Marshall of the Lutheran Church in America asked, "Is there value in an annual conference of church leaders?" He specifically did not refer to representatives of churches, but to persons who are in titular or executive leadership of their own communions. Marshall expressed his own desire to meet with people who "sit where I sit" and discuss with them the role of the church in the world at this time. All present concurred that an annual, or at least biennial, conference of church leaders did have much to offer. It has since become an annual event.

It has become an important meeting for Christian unity, far more so than ever anticipated. It is the only mix that unites for open discussion leadership from the broad spectrum of the church in the U.S. In fact it was seen by Bishop David Preus of the ALC and others as the possible base for a new conciliar expression in the U.S.[8] It remains the forum it was intended to be from its beginning. It continues to be an enriching experience for all who attend. Involvement does have its rewards, as rare moments of historical significance do occur. At the meeting in Cincinnati, Ohio, in 1973, William Cardinal Baum of the Catholic Archdiocese of Washington, D.C. referred to a survey recently conducted to determine the biblical literacy and knowledge among young people. In his words, "the findings left him somewhat appalled." In the moment of silence that followed he turned and looked squarely at the faces of the leaders of four of the Lutheran church bodies in America, who happened to be seated next to each other, and questioned in effect, "Whatever happened to the basic principle propounded by your founding father, Martin Luther, 'Salvation by grace through faith in Jesus Christ with nothing beside'? That is what my young people and the world need to hear again today with conviction and vigor." One could have expected such a spontaneous outburst from a relatively little known parish priest, but not at that point in history from a cardinal.

Such moments are not the be-all, end-all basis upon which the unity of Christ's body gets resolved, but they are examples of the power of Christ and the penetration of his ways in the affairs of humankind when the risk is taken to sit down together to try to understand more about Christ.

A rather impressive slate of speakers have addressed the assembly over the years.[9] The group continues, now led by Harold Bennett of the Southern Baptist Convention, and it appears that it will have a long life. The current steering committee is composed of Harold Bennett (Southern Baptist), Milton B. Engebretson (Covenant), David Preus (Lutheran), Warren Magnuson (Baptist General Conference), Joseph Cardinal Bernardin (Catholic), and Kara Cole (Friends). Suggestions have been made to expand the meeting to become more inclusive and move it from ad hoc to organized. The fellowship afforded by the meeting's free nature, composition, and style continues to be appreciated. How long will it last? God only knows. But that it has served a real function in building a bridge of understanding between leaders from a variety of persuasions on the ever-changing scale from conservative to liberal theologically, and from the NAE to the WCC organizationally, is unquestionable. Its purpose remains to prepare a base for fellowship and cooperation in the future within the body of Christ, and the value of that leaves little or no need for discussion.

Internationally, interest heightened in the International Federation of Free Evangelical Churches, an organization in which the Covenant Church was a charter member dating back to its organization in Bern, Switzerland, in 1948. The organization consists of nineteen denominations, fifteen on the continent, two American, and two in Canada. The European denominations are ''Free'' or ''Covenant'' churches, depending on who is doing the reporting (free means nonstate). They are from Greece, France, Spain, Czechoslovakia, East Germany, West Germany, The Netherlands, Finland (Finnish as well as Swedish-speaking), Norway, Switzerland, Sweden (Covenant and Missionary Alliance), Denmark, and Belgium. In addition, nonmember churches attend from Rumania, Bulgaria, Poland, and England. The Evangelical Covenant Church and The Evangelical Free Church of America, from the USA, and the same two bodies from Canada make a total of twenty-three church bodies numbering more than 350,000 Christians. Paul E. Larsen, president of the Covenant, currently serves as a member of the federation's executive board.

Increased involvement by the Covenant Church came when it invited The Evangelical Free Church of America to co-host a theological conference on the campuses of Trinity Evangelical Divinity School and North Park Theological Seminary in August 1971. Plans for this conference were developed by Karl A. Olsson, Milton Engebretson, Arnold T. Olson, president of The Evangelical Free Church of America, and Harry Evans, president of Trinity College. In my opinion, this was a conference that changed the nature of the federation's meetings, scheduling such theological conferences every four years. All have been well-attended. In 1978 the president of The Evangelical Covenant Church was the first non-European to be elected president of the federation and served for the constitutionally allotted two four-year terms.

The larger denominations of the federation have through their world relief grants been of extremely significant help to the smaller churches, especially those in the eastern bloc, Greece, and Spain. The federation has also served to strengthen ties between the evangelical churches in Europe and those in North America. The sharing of ecclesiological dynamics, especially in the area of church growth, has given stimulus to new ventures in growth by some European bodies. Its theological conferences have through open sharing created forums of freedom with renewed bases for understanding and cooperation. The future sees newer denominations that have been created as a result of member church mission work as potential members of the federation. Should this occur, the federation would include denominations that now exist in India, Japan, Taiwan, Thailand, Ecuador, Colombia, Mexico, Zaire, and People's Republic of the Congo, to name a few. It has already seen cooperation between member bodies in world mission work and programs of student and faculty exchange in education. The potential for the future in both fields is encouraging.

In summary, the Covenant Church has played an important role in international and particularly national ecumenical ventures. It has done so by maintaining its position of nonaffiliation with any conciliar body. The past thirty years have seen this body involved far beyond its size. Its ecumenical involvement and leadership was overtly carried out by administration. The influence for the unity of the body of Christ was, however, possible only because of a denominational constituency that set administration free to act on its behalf. It is somewhat ironic that when organizational pressures that tended to coerce conciliar alignments relaxed, conciliar action increased and the Covenant has been privileged both to share and lead in uniting Christian leadership in America and the world.

If there is a future of strength for the Church in the world (and I bet my life on the fact that there is), it can only be realized if every effort is made by Christians to join with others regardless of persuasion to be the Church in the world. The words of Christ still stand: "Holy Father, protect them by the power of your name—the name you gave me—*so that they may be one as we are one.* . . . Father, just as you are in me and I am in you. May they also be *in us so that the world may believe that you have sent me*" (John 17:11,21, NIV, emphasis mine).

If there is anything that I have learned through the privilege of serving and leading, it is simply this, that if you truly represent the people you serve, their experience and their enthusiasm for Christ, and are willing to take the risks and really work, the opportunities to serve and lead are absolutely unlimited. The influence for what is good and right at such levels are proportionate to one's commitment to what his or her constituents believe. Belief systems such as the Covenant are solid; the security of one's ground gives a leader a strong place on which to stand and from which to launch out.

The very first brush I had with the NCC was in St. Louis, Missouri, in December 1963. I was assigned to a group for discussions on inner-city ministries. The star of the group was a pastor who waxed eloquently about his work. Most of those present were mesmerized. The man was doing a commendable piece of work. I listened and listened for some word about Christ, salvation, redemption, or something to help the poor and underprivileged people he spoke of, so that after being given temporary food and shelter, they could have a solid base upon which to build new lives. My questions were perhaps less than sophisticated, but my persistence finally drove the man to explode with, "What are you talking about, salvation or something? If you're talking about the *living* Christ, man, I have never met him." I responded with, "Thank you sir, that is what I thought you were implying. Now that we have that issue clarified we can talk." A good interchange followed right there in the group. On the last day of the conference when I was checking out, I saw that person clear across the lobby of the hotel. When he spotted me, he came swiftly across the entire distance and said, "Milton, I'm glad to have been with you. You have really got me thinking. I am going home, and you better believe that I'm going to make my search for the *living Christ.*"

Being in a bridge position between conciliar bodies has been important, and some strides have been made. The Covenant cannot, however, be neutral forever. It is not the best for its inner well-being. It has been given too much. It needs to share its interpretation of the freedom that comes from new life in Jesus Christ uncompromisingly with the rest of the Church throughout the world. I for one hope that the issue of conciliar alignments resurfaces and gets a good response from Covenanters. Planet earth is a big place. Christ's body is also vastly expanded beyond our imaginings or comprehension. There are Christians out there who quite crucially need us as we need them for the fulfillment of Christ's prayer, "that they may be one," and for our well-being as a church in the world.

Endnotes

[1] Karl A. Olsson, *Into One Body . . . By the Cross* (Chicago: Covenant Press, 1985, 1986), p. 386.
[2] *Covenant Yearbook,* 1963, pp. 221-223.
[3] *Ibid.,* p. 223.
[4] *Ibid.,* p. 224.
[5] *Covenant Yearbook,* 1964, pp. 201-203.
[6] *Ibid.,* p. 203.
[7] *Report of the Special Committee on Interchurch Relations.* Inter-Church Referendum Results, p. 2
Interchurch Relations Referendum Voting Results
1) Four hundred churches—more than two out of three—participated in the referendum. Nearly 25,000 Covenanters—about two out of five—voted in the referendum.
2) About three out of five Covenanters opposed affiliation by the

denomination with an international ecumenical body, and two out of five opposed affiliation with any national ecumenical body. About one out of five was undecided about affiliation with either.

3) One out of five favored joining the World Council of Churches. One out of four favored joining the National Association of Evangelicals. One out of nine favored joining the National Council of Churches. One out of thirty-three favored joining the American Council of Churches.

4) Generally speaking, Covenanters tended to differ in their views of affiliation with interchurch bodies depending on where they lived, their age, and their sex.

a) Those living in the western two-thirds of the country tended to favor the NAE and oppose the WCC. Those living in the eastern one-third of the country showed a slight preference for the NCC and favored the WCC.

b) Those living in large urban centers tended to be more interested in affiliation with interchurch bodies than those living in rural areas or in small towns.

c) Young people tended to be more interested in affiliation with interchurch bodies than older people.

d) Men tended to be more interested in affiliation with interchurch bodies than women.

[8] Milton B. Engebretson, "The Meeting of U.S. Church Leaders (A History)," p. 3. It was at the fifth meeting that Bishop David Preus first presented a paper on *A New Conciliar Expression.* The seventh meeting was held in Minneapolis, Minnesota, and dealt with the theme: *The Mission of the Church/The Unity of Christ's Body.* Billy Graham, Archbishop James Roach of St. Paul, and Roy Harrisville of Luther Theological Seminary were the featured speakers. Billy Graham, however, canceled due to illness and sent John Akers in his place. It was at this meeting that Preus's paper, *A New Conciliar Expression* was resubmitted and discussed at length. Though the paper called for broader involvements, its intentions were blown completely out of proportion by the media in its efforts to create the impression to the public that the Meeting of U.S. Church Leaders was being called behind closed doors to plan an alternative conciliar organization to meet the demands of an American church dissatisfied with councils. This erroneous presupposition by the media resulted from a recent CBS "60 Minutes" program that had attacked the World and National Council of Churches. A meeting with reporters following the sessions by William Thompson and myself gave the public a more accurate account of the intentions of Preus's paper and the continuing purpose of the Meeting of U.S. Church Leaders.

[9] *Ibid.,* pp. 3-4.

Archbishop Iakovis, Greek Orthodox Church

Lloyd Ogilvie, First Presbyterian Church, Hollywood, California

Paul S. Rees, World Vision International and The Evangelical Covenant Church

Karl A. Olsson, Faith at Work and The Evangelical Covenant Church

Elton Trueblood, Earlham College, Richmond, Indiana

Members of Congress John B. Anderson and Paul Simon
David Hubbard, Fuller Theological Seminary, Pasadena, California
Alvin Rogness, Luther Theological Seminary, St. Paul, Minnesota
Joseph Cardinal Bernardin, Chicago, Illinois
William Cardinal Baum, Washington, D.C.
Archbishop John Roach, St. Paul, Minnesota
George Gallup, Jr., Princeton, New Jersey
Krister Stendahl, Harvard Divinity School, Cambridge, Massachusetts
Dale Moody, Southern Baptist Theological Seminary, Louisville, Kentucky
William Hull, Southern Baptist Theological Seminary, Louisville, Kentucky
James I. McCord, Princeton Theological Seminary, Princeton, New Jersey
Sandra R. Brown, Princeton Theological Seminary, Princeton, New Jersey
Granger E. Westberg, Downers Grove, Illinois
Donald Senior, Catholic Theological Union, Chicago, Illinois

It is a special privilege and an honor to cover the area of the interchurch relations of the Covenant Church in this volume of tribute to Karl A. Olsson. Not many people on earth have had a more profound influence on my life and ministry than Karl. He is endowed with an abundance of innate talent which, to his everlasting credit, he continually develops. We all benefit. His contributions to the ecumenical life of the Covenant are remarkable. Not only is his name a household word, so to speak, among the membership within many North American denominations because of his speaking and writing, but he is also highly respected and esteemed in church leadership on the international scene. He was one of the featured lecturers at the Meeting of U.S. Church Leaders in 1973. He has also lectured at several theological conferences of the International Federation of Free Evangelical Churches. He is revered as a reputable scholar, theologian, and church historian by the leadership of the federation. Few among us have done more to extend the influence, mystique, and mission of the Covenant Church to the church bodies of the world than Karl A. Olsson.

Peace and the Christian Citizen*

Conrad Bergendoff

"Peace is the will of God." Whence do we derive this truth? From the Bible, you say. Does not the prophet Isaiah promise that the Lord "shall judge between the nations, and shall decide for many peoples; and they shall beat their swords into plowshares, and their spears into pruning hooks; nation shall not lift up sword against nation, neither shall they learn war any more"? (2:4).

These words are in the future tense, "They *shall* not learn war any more." But what of the past? Have you not, in reading the Old Testament, sometimes wondered about the will of God? Its books are filled with war. One of the psalms sums up some of the many chapters of warfare in the words, "He it was who smote the first-born in Egypt . . . who smote many nations and slew mighty kings, Sihon, king of the Amorites, and Og, king of Bashan, and all the kingdoms of Canaan, and gave their land as a heritage, a heritage to his people Israel" (135:8,10-12). And this was only the beginning. Once settled, the tribes engaged in constant strife, even civil war. Saul, David, Solomon were warriors. Their descendants were embroiled with the great powers of the day—Egypt, Babylon, Assyria—and the result was defeat, exile, and captivity.

It was against such a background that the prophet declared: "For every boot of the tramping warrior in battle tumult and every garment rolled in blood will be burned as fuel for the fire. For to us a child is born, to us a son is given; and the government will be upon his shoulder, and his name will be called 'Wonderful Counselor, Mighty God, Everlasting Father, Prince of Peace' " (Isaiah 9:5-6).

*This paper was presented at a Peace Seminar of the Illinois Synod of the Lutheran Church in America in Moline, Illinois, September 15, 1984.

What can we say of "the will of God" in the Old Testament? In reality we have to say that throughout there was violence, aggression, warfare. Was it the will of God that the Promised Land should be obtained by bloodshed? Looking back at the few victories Israel won over other cities it was natural for the chronicler to attribute the outcome to the will of God. So Americans saw the victories won against native Americans as we possessed this land. But listen to Jeremiah's interpretation of Israel's history: "From their earliest days Israel and Judah have been doing what is wrong in my eyes" (32:30, NEB). "I brought you into a fruitful land to enjoy its fruit and the goodness of it; but when you entered upon it you defiled it and made the home I gave you loathsome" (2:7, NEB). "They came and took possession of it, but did not obey thee or follow thy law, they disobeyed all thy commands" (32:35, NEB). Coming into the Promised Land, Israel soon worshiped false gods, and the result was not peace but captivity and exile. The Old Testament does not justify war. It reveals that despite the sins of Israel, God reveals his purpose of bringing a different kind of kingdom into the world.

To the Christian the coming of Christ is the beginning of a new age. The risen Christ is a power different from the dominions of the world. They rely on force. Jesus calls for voluntary obedience. He could command legions of angels; he refuses them. When a disciple drew a sword, he forbade him, saying, "He who takes to the sword will perish with the sword." When Pilate asked, "Where is your kingdom?" Jesus answered, "Everyone who is of the truth hears my voice" (John 18:37). Earlier in Galilee he had described members of the kingdom, "the poor in spirit, those who mourn, the meek, those who hunger and thirst for righteousness, the merciful, the pure in heart, the peacemakers, those persecuted for righteousness' sake" (Matthew 5). His ministry was a demonstration of that kind of a kingdom. His death was the response of humankind to such a gospel. His resurrection and presence in his people was the revelation of a power that cannot be quenched by hatred and unbelief. His Spirit is still powerful in the world.

It was that Spirit that upheld the disciples as they carried his message over the Mediterranean world, enabling Paul to witness even in imperial Rome. They knew that military might

would not abdicate to Christ, but they also remembered that
they could be a salt in corruption and a leaven in the social
body. They knew, too, that governments could be instruments
of God, necessary to preserve order and make life possible
where conflict threatened anarchy. They themselves had inherited a Mosaic law that gave government the right to enforce
a behavior that reflected the will of God. They realized that
this would create a problem in a kind of dual citizenship. They
taught, "let every person be subject to the governing authorities" (Romans 13), but when Peter was questioned by the
council in Jerusalem, he answered, "We must obey God rather
than men." In writing to the Philippians Paul declared, "Our
citizenship is in heaven" (3:20, NEB). Interestingly it was in
Philippi, where Paul and Silas had been put in prison, that Paul
made the magistrates afraid when he told them that he was
a Roman citizen and they had broken the law of the city, which
was a Roman colony, by imprisoning him without trial. In this
city Paul was a citizen of Rome and a citizen of heaven.

The tension grew greater after Christianity became the
religion embraced by the Empire. The story is too long to
review here. Was the emperor or the pope to decide the place
of the church in the state? For centuries that was the challenge.
We can briefly state that in the matter of war the state dominated. Not only did the papacy bless the policies of the government but the popes themselves declared and even led wars,
as against the Muslims in the Crusades. Realizing the incongru-
ity of witnessing to the cross by wielding or consecrating the
sword, the medieval church did its best to mitigate wherever
possible the evil effects by trying to set up criteria for "just
wars." The reformers did not go much beyond this position,
and the result seems to be that in Christian history there is
not much difference from the war-studded pages of the Old
Testament.

Not that the Prince of Peace was left without witness altogether in the church after Constantine. In a sense the monastic
movement was a retreat into a world without war. But witness
to an unarmed Christ was left to small groups such as the Men-
nonites and the Quakers. A concession was made to individuals who refused to conform—the principle of conscientious
objection was allowed. Meanwhile, leaders of thought who
might not necessarily acknowledge Christ as their inspiration

began to write against the folly of war. Erasmus, also, used much of the vocabulary of the horrors of war in describing its barbarism. And every century produced elaborate ideas of some universal council or organization by which nations would avoid recourse to conflict. Once it was thought that war was made by monarchs or the aristocratic class and that a change of form of government would give the people the right to veto war. But time revealed that even democracies could fight, more savagely and needlessly than ever before. The formidable leagues by which nations were to resolve differences were swept away one after another by the waves of militarism. It was found that no nation would accept an authority above its own sovereignty. The formula that superseded any superior power, human or divine, was "national interests." This justified any secret diplomacy, any international contract, any covert action within a nation or beyond its borders. Needless to say, this is the situation today. If anything, the Church has less influence now to stay the course of international development. The will of God is without meaning except as each nation, including Muslim states, claims to be his interpreter while one of the superpowers eliminates God from its vocabulary altogether.

So much for the past. Today there is something new. The age of the nuclear bomb is upon us. That has aroused the Church to think anew about its duty. The Catholic Church has led the way through the pastoral letter of the National Conference of Catholic Bishops in May 1983. The letter quotes from the *Pastoral Constitution,* one of the documents of the second Vatican council in 1962: "It is necessary to undertake a completely fresh appraisal of war." The atomic bomb has shattered all the old views of war. The Catholic Church has had its concept of a "just war" to justify its attitude. Two of the criteria demanded 1) that there be a proportionality between the costs and the results of war, and 2) that there be a discrimination between the combatants and the noncombatants. It is impossible in nuclear war to meet those requirements. Hence there can be no justification of war with these weapons. The bishops reject any policy that contemplates the use of nuclear bombs, and they question the moral grounds of building arsenals as a deterrent to an enemy. They entitle their letter "The Challenge of Peace," and address their people as to what their response as Christians should be in these perilous times.

In this situation what has been the theological significance of "A Proposed Social Statement of the Lutheran Church in America"? Despite its repeated references to "politics of peace," I have questioned its *political* importance. Have the numerous authorities to whom it was sent asked whom it represents? All Lutherans in the U.S.? No, less than a third when it was presented. Will its most critical point—nuclear arsenals as deterrent—be the voice of the new Evangelical Lutheran Church of America? It was not in the LCA where the vote was 354 to 319. Which way? It really doesn't matter. Then what does matter?

The truth is that Lutherans are no different from others on the question of war. A Catholic priest and former member of Congress, Robert Drinan, concludes as to his own church that "probably the actual state of things today is that as a matter of practice Catholics have not any views of war different from non-Catholics or non-Christians."[1] In their reaction to Vietnam, Lutherans did not distinguish themselves as pioneers of peace. In 1970 *Public Opinion Quarterly* published the results of a poll of Protestant clergy taken in 1968. While an increasing protest against the war was rising, 82 percent of the Southern Baptists, 50 percent of the Missouri Synod Lutherans, 39 percent of the ALC Lutherans, and 28 percent of the LCA Lutherans called for *increasing the military effort.*[2] As a rule these pastors said their congregations were more hawkish than themselves. Is there much difference between Lutherans and non-Christians on the question of war and peace?

What has the Church to say today that is new? Here I find the statement of the Catholic bishops helpful. They clearly assert that in the face of the threat of nuclear war all the old arguments justifying war are obsolete. "In the words of our Holy Father, we need a 'moral about-face.' The whole world must summon the moral courage and technical means to say 'no' to nuclear conflict; 'no' to weapons of mass destruction; 'no' to an arms race which robs the poor and the vulnerable; and 'no' to the moral danger of a nuclear age which places before humankind indefensible choices of constant terror or surrender."[3]

Helpful, too, is the clear distinction between those

addressed. The letter speaks both to American citizens in general and to Catholics specifically. It is a distinction to be borne in mind in our Lutheran discussions. We are Christian church members, we are also American citizens. I am a little doubtful about our Lutheran statement's constant reference to "politics of peace." The Church is not a political party. As citizens we are members of political parties. The two are distinguished in Lutheran theology. As citizens we are responsible for the policies of our government and the Lutheran church member cannot escape responsibility for participation in the political process. It is the state, not the church, that chooses war. Less obvious are the duties of the Christian church member in the making of peace and war. I would like to stress what I consider some of those duties.

The New Testament opens with the birth of John who was to prepare the way of Jesus "when the day shall dawn upon us from on high to give light to those who sit in darkness and in shadow of death, to guide our feet into the way of peace" (Luke 1:78-79). The Old Testament prophets declared peace in the midst of the horror of war. It is the mission of the Church to announce that there is a kingdom of peace and righteousness in Christ no matter what the nations do. Indeed, this is the only source of hope for humankind, which seems bent on destroying itself. At the same time it is a judgment on these nations that have perfected the instruments of warfare but have yet to learn the way of peace. Their teacher is not the Prince of Peace but Machiavelli's prince. And when they draw back from the brink of world disaster, they begin again to put their trust in "conventional warfare," the kind that left fifty million of America's best youth on the battlefields of five continents. Only the Church dares assert this is the will of humankind, not of God. Only the Church knows of another kind of wisdom and power and justice.

It is the mission of the Church to obey the command of Christ, "Love your enemies." Yes, you may smile—some even laugh out loud. Is this not naive? The psychology of war teaches us to hate our enemies. Not only the military, the *whole nation* is to be whipped up into a frenzy of hatred. Then you are ready to fight. I speak with memories of two world wars, Korea, and Vietnam. But psychology can also teach us that fear and hatred blind us, so that we see some distortion of our enemy. Truth is the first casualty of war. We may not expect our nation to love our enemies, but we can seek to understand why they are enemies. We may find that they are human. If the CIA pictures them as monsters, why should we negotiate? If they are not to be trusted, is there any other solution than to annihilate them? We have need of a Christian Intelligence Agency dedicated to reconciliation. The Christian knows that we as Americans are not blameless. We were the first—and the only one—to use the bomb. Have we not been provocative in the arms race?

If the Church has any relevance in this crisis it is to seek and follow the truth—the whole truth and nothing but the truth. A Christian response to an enemy is to hope that we can and will learn to live together on this small earth. Our enemy also is a creature of God. Why do we limit patriotism to death in war? Is it not patriotic to try to avoid war and its human sacrifice? To call those who work for peace "soft on communism" is not only unpatriotic, it is untrue. "Where there is no vision, the people perish." All of us perish when we lose the vision of a world where peoples can live together. The Church is crippled if within its own membership there is no difference from non-Christians in regard to the inevitability of war, even nuclear war.

These are two contributions of the Church to our troubled world—in proclaiming that peace, not war, is the destiny of humanity, and to treat enemies as fellow creatures of God. A third is equally peculiar to the Christian, and a test of our sincerity as members of the Church of Christ—prayer. "The end of all things," St. Peter wrote to fellow Christians, "is at hand; be ye therefore sober, and calm, so that you can pray." Not controlled by the passions of the day, but in self-control and equanimity we turn to a Power greater than atomic arsenals. We pray, as Jesus himself prayed in a supreme crisis, not for our wills but that God's will might be done—and in prayer we may discern the difference. God is not a power to be summoned to consecrate our ambitions. His altar is the throne from which we see his way for our life. In the fellowship of the Prince of Peace we can go forth to our participation in the affairs of society and state, hoping to witness to him even where his will is not done.

Endnotes

[1] Robert F. Drinan, *Vietnam and Armageddon: Peace, War and the Christian Conscience* (New York: Sheed and Ward, 1970), p. 29.

[2] *Public Opinion Quarterly,* 34 (1970), 43-52.

[3] *The Challenge of Peace: God's Promise and Our Response* (Washington, D.C.: United States Catholic Conference, 1983), pp. 101f.

Acculturation or Inculturation?

A Contemporary Evangelical Theology of the Atonement

Robert K. Johnston

James Davison Hunter's study of American evangelicalism's turn from objective to subjective categories of thought leads him to label this phenomenon "Accommodation: The Domestication of Belief."[1] His thesis is that evangelicalism, as a result of its interaction with modernity, has undergone subtle but real change. There has been concession and compromise. In documenting this conclusion Hunter analyzes the titles of evangelical literature published in 1980 from eight leading houses. Although the omission of Eerdmans, Inter-Varsity, and Baker (presses with more traditional academic interest) skews his findings, it is nonetheless telling that 12.3 percent of all the titles surveyed were oriented toward "understanding the emotional complexities of human experience from an evangelical perspective."[2]

With other Americans, evangelicals are asking, "Who am I?" Of the books Hunter examined that focused on the human, a third dealt with one's emotional and psychological maturity, with self-actualization. (One might understand Karl Olsson's book *Find Yourself in the Bible* [1974] as an early example of this.) A slightly smaller percentage emphasized the need both to understand and to solve emotional problems (pressure, fear, loneliness, etc.). And another 28 percent were oriented toward "Christian" forms of narcissism and hedonism. Hunter's examples include books such as *Dare to Live Now, Life without Limits,* and *Living the Adventure.* (Again, Karl Olsson's book *Come to the Party: An Invitation to a Freer Lifestyle* [1972] would seem an earlier example.) To be sure, such "hedonism" expressed within an evangelical worldview did not have the same quality as that found in secular literature. Self-infatuation and vanity were not the foci. Nevertheless,

Hunter found in this literature "the conviction that human experience should be characterized by unfathomable inner joy and happiness and the unquenchable expectancy of good things."[3]

In his most recent book, *Evangelicalism: The Coming Generation,* Hunter provides a second illustration of this "accommodation" to modernity, quoting from Robert Schuller's book, *Self-Esteem: The New Reformation* (1983). In this book which was sent free of charge to a quarter of a million religious leaders across America, Schuller criticizes reformational theology for not being a "well-rounded, full-orbed, honestly-interrelated theology system." Traditional Protestant theology, thinks Schuller, has wrongly centered its definition of sin on "rebellion against God." Such a notion for Schuller is not incorrect as much as it is shallow and insulting to the human being. The core of sin is in reality "a lack of self-esteem." In this light, salvation means:

> . . . to be permanently lifted from sin (psychological self-abuse with all its consequences as seen above) and shame to self-esteem and its God glorifying human need-meeting, constructive and creative consequences. . . . To be saved is to know that Christ forgives me and now I dare to believe that I am somebody and I can do something for God and for my fellow human beings.[4]

We must not risk further assault on the person, argues Schuller, by continuing to teach humankind's lack of worth in God's sight.

Schuller provides Hunter his paradigm. How has the traditional judgmental aspects of evangelicalism's soteriology found acceptance in a socially and religiously tolerant society such as America? "How is it that so exclusivistic a group can experience such broadly based social acceptance in any modern society?" There has been, thinks Hunter, "a softening and polishing of the more hardline and barbed elements of the orthodox Protestant world view." The doctrinal core has remained unchanged, but it has been culturally edited for the sake of civility. In the words of Hunter:

> The civilizing process entails a deemphasis of evan-

gelicalism's more offensive aspects: the notions of
inherent evil, sinful conduct and lifestyles, the wrath
of a righteous and jealous god, and eternal agony
and death in hell. The deemphasis has been more
quantitative than qualitative. The offensive elements
are, in the main, neither substantively devalued nor
glossed over as unimportant. They are simply not
referred to as much as they have been in the past.
These elements have not lost their doctrinal centrality, but have lost a stylistic centrality once taken for
granted in the preaching and teaching in this tradition.[5]

Here, then, is a thesis concerning American evangelicalism.
Acculturation has taken place under the press of modernity.
Efforts at cooperation have inevitably necessitated concession.
Like most other Christian movements that have dared to open
themselves to engage the world, evangelicalism finds itself civ-
ilized, and yet compromised.[6]

I. Acculturation or Inculturation?

Is Hunter correct? Is the subjectivism that he chronicles the
sociologically inevitable compromise that has resulted from
neofundamentalism's encounter with modernity? Examples
can surely be given where this is the case. Schuller's redefinition of sin would seem to be one, although his background
is not fundamentalism. A theology of prosperity that equates
Christianity with success would be another. But could not
evangelicalism's recent recasting of Christianity in terms of
the human subject have a more complex basis as well? Rather
than being rooted in civil religion, could it not be based prax-
iologically in the dialogue between Scripture and society, God's
story and our own? Rather than judging our turn toward the
human as simple acculturation with its resultant blurring of
the apostolic faith, could not evangelicalism's positive focus
upon humankind represent initial, largely intuitive efforts at
inculturation, the contextualizing of the gospel? (Certainly this
has been the case for Karl Olsson as his writing has taken on
a relational character.)

When John Piper's *Desiring God: Meditations of a Christian Hedonist* appeared (1986), it created controversy. Pub-

lished by the conservative Multnomah Press, the book would seem to illustrate Hunter's thesis. Piper, a General Conference Baptist minister who has taught at Bethel College, states his intention as offering an interpretation of the catechism, namely: "The chief end of man is to glorify God *by* enjoying him forever." Our motive for Christian service and church-going should be, he thinks, our desire for happiness or pleasure. Since Piper understands happiness to be a basic human need, there is no moral judgment attached to such an observation. If anything the problem facing humankind is not "in the intensity of our desire for happiness, but in the weakness of it."[7] To be sure, Piper warns against making a god out of pleasure or of viewing God instrumentally as a means of worldly pleasure. Rather, humankind's highest joy is found only in the worship of God and our happiness in sharing with others his love. It is not our seeking after happiness but the object of that happiness that is the central problem for humankind today.

Piper's book is shaped around a meditation on Scripture. It owes much to the thought of Jonathan Edwards, who is Piper's constant theological companion. Yet when asked why he has picked up and made central those traditional, biblical themes of happiness and joy, Piper turns not to Scripture or tradition, but to an assessment of contemporary life. When asked why he adopts the controversial terminology of "Christian hedonism" rather than repeating the straightforward biblical command, "Believe in the Lord Jesus and you will be saved," Piper says it is because belief in Jesus has become an empty phrase in America. "Millions of unconverted people . . . say they believe in Jesus."[8] In order to communicate the gospel effectively, Piper argues for a biblical focus on Christian hedonism. In serving God you will find your true happiness.

Piper's focus on happiness/hedonism attempts to be responsive both to Scripture and to our contemporary age. If the gospel is to mean anything, it must connect with the lives of its hearers. One can question whether the term "Christian hedonism" has meaning beyond its shock value. Negative connotations intrude. But Piper has recognized that the topic "glorifying God" can best be addressed today from the viewpoint of its subject and not its object, from a discussion of our desire for God. Whereas ontologically, glorifying God has pri-

ority for Piper, epistemologically he believes happiness to be
the central concern. Hunter might think this a compromise,
a simple example of civil religion, of cultural accommodation.
But *Desiring God's* attempted cultural translation of biblical
truth is more complex.

Where Hunter's critique of books like Piper's provides
more insight is in his observation that evangelical literature
dealing with contemporary human sensitivities remains at the
doctrinal level largely immutable. That is, a larger, rational
theological structure is maintained, even if it is not emphasized. For Piper this finds expression in his discussion of the
cross. Although Piper's exploration of Christian happiness leads
him to discuss that topic from "below," from the standpoint
of humankind, no parallel presentation of the atonement is
provided. Rather than selecting those biblical images concerning the cross that speak of humankind (e.g., we are *received*
into the family of God, we are *freed* from slavery, our relationship with God is *restored,* etc.), Piper remains traditionally
"objective" in his analysis: "The death of Christ is the wisdom
of God by which the love *of God* saves sinners from the wrath
of God, and all the while upholds and demonstrates the righteousness *of God.*"[9] The atonement as God's righteous act
remains the theological focus for Piper, even while his desire
to foster a living faith in his readers causes him elsewhere to
stress the importance of human happiness. Understanding the
cross as primarily God's transaction, Piper largely ignores its
implications for his topic, Christian happiness.

A more successful attempt at developing a contextualized
understanding of the gospel that includes the cross has been
made by William Dyrness. Like Piper, his concern is with communicating and extending the Christian faith. In fact the title
of his most recent manuscript is *How Does America Hear the
Gospel?* Theology, particularly in North America, has become
professionalized, abstracted from life. As a result it is too often
reduced to reflection on previous thinking. For Dyrness American evangelical theology has lost its essential nature as a biblically informed reflection on life.

Dyrness desires his theology to be "both biblical and
American." Recognizing that American culture is diverse, he
nonetheless concentrates his thinking initially on certain core
values of white, middle-class America, allowing other voices

into the conversation as critics and foils. He isolates three complexes of values: "Americans' materialist bias, their tempermental optimism and their individualism." He then asks "how these values enhance or impede our understanding of the Gospel." Only by knowing how we hear God's word today can we become more effective in our mission and more vital in our theology.[10]

Because Americans have come to believe that the good life is their right, the gospel must be presented first in those terms, thinks Dyrness. Moreover, there is in America "the dominant feeling that things are going to turn out all right. This surely must be dealt with . . . this cultural optimism." One approach that Dyrness rejects is to insist that people be made to know first that they are sinners, so that they then can believe in salvation. No, awareness of sin will be for many Americans a result and not the precondition for encountering God's love in Jesus Christ. If effective communication is our goal, then Christians will need to make the love and goodness of God their entrance to the gospel.

Ultimately, suffering will need to be seen; sin exposed. And it will. Dyrness believes that the gospel will challenge many of our fundamental values. God's holiness and justice will be understood as complementing his love. There is not only an ethos of privilege but an ethos of need. We are not only individuals, but part of a community. This movement in repentance towards Christian maturity, however, will be for most Americans in the direction from love toward justice, from privilege to need, not vice versa. Dryness summarizes the options: "The one begins with enmity and hears the challenge of Christ's death as reconciliation; the other begins with individual fulfillment and hears the Gospel as a fellowship of suffering."[11]

II. A Contemporary Evangelical Theology of the Atonement

The observations of Dyrness are preliminary but point in the right direction. In a class at New College, Berkeley, which I jointly taught with him in 1986 and in three subsequent class situations at North Park Theological Seminary, students responded to the question, "Do you expect your world to be good and pleasant or evil and difficult?'' by saying it was supposed to be good. Although they might experience a variety of frustration along the way, they expected to succeed. This is surely not the only answer one could have given. Think how different such an ethos is than that found in most Negro spirituals, for example. But it is consistent with what we have been led to expect by such analyses of the American character as Daniel Yankelovitch's *New Rules* and Robert Bellah's *Habits of the Heart.*

When these same students were asked what Americans consider their primary goal to be, self-fulfillment was the answer. Our heroes are those like Abraham Lincoln who overcame a nervous breakdown, failure in business, and repeated defeat in public elections only to become the president of the United States. Such perseverance continues to be given popular expression in box-office hits such as the play *Starlight Express* where the old reliable steam engine overcomes adversity and setbacks to defeat both the electric (modernity!) and the diesel (the devil!) engines in the big race. While success is admired, most hope it will come with a minimum of pain. Like Horatio Alger, or Benjamin Franklin's Poor Richard, we desire a more consistent course from rags to riches than Lincoln had. In fact, the Lincoln "myth" must compete in the American mind with another: Superman. We would have our success presented to us as a given and expressed through power, not death. Consider Rambo.

When asked what Americans consider "evil," the answers my students gave centered on anything that stands in the way of one's personal fulfillment. Thus, as an American society today, we often believe that divorce will save us. As Christians we regularly shop for another church where "I'll be ministered to." It is difficult to think of the common good apart from that which will make my own life better the majority of times. It is such a mindset that caused Piper in our discussion above to describe glorifying God in terms of Christian hedonism. It is not the language of accountability that resonates with the American ethos, but that of fulfillment.

What has this to do with a theology of the atonement? Since the beginnings of the church, Christians have declared that "Christ died for our sins in accordance with the Scriptures" (1 Corinthians 15:3; cf., Philippians 2:7-8). But these early confessions and hymns were not meant to provide theories of the atonement so much as testimonies to its reality and to the new life that believers had experienced in Christ.[12] Under the Spirit's continued inspiration, a variety of images were used to explain the meaning of the cross. None of these descriptions was meant to explain fully the mystery of the atonement they had experienced, but all were faithful to its reality.

The biblical writers turned for their language concerning the cross both to the Old Testament and to their contemporary experience.[13] As in their *temple worship,* Jesus was portrayed as a high priest, offering himself as a sacrifice, once for all, to accomplish our redemption. The Epistle to the Hebrews, in particular, developed this understanding of Christ's death (Hebrews 2:17; 9:12-14, 26; cf., Mark 10:45). Behind such imagery is Jesus' own acceptance of his identification with the suffering servant of Isaiah 53: "Behold, the Lamb of God, who takes away the sin of the world!" (John 1:29). Complementing this description was another taken not only from the Old Testament but from *contemporary commerce.* We have been ransomed as slaves from the auction block "with the precious blood of Christ" (1 Peter 1:18-19). We have been "bought with a price." As such, we are not again to "become slaves of men" (1 Corinthians 7:23).

The Apostle Paul was particularly fond of turning to the *law courts* for his metaphors concerning the meaning of the cross. We are "justified by his blood" (Romans 5:6-11). "Christ redeemed us from the curse of the law" (Galatians 3:13). Although the necessary penalty for our sin is death, the free gift of God in Christ Jesus our Lord is eternal life (Romans 6:23). If such language suggests images of God as judge, other biblical metaphors focus instead on Christ as a mighty warrior. On the *battlefield,* Christ entered into conflict with the devil and triumphed (Hebrews 2:14). Reflecting Jesus' own definition of his ministry in terms of a battle against evil powers, the New Testament writers saw the cross and resurrection of Jesus as the decisive victory.

Elsewhere in the New Testament, the cross is understood as accomplishing reconciliation, the restoration of relationships both with God and between people. "All this is from God, who through Christ reconciled us to himself and gave us the ministry of reconciliation" (2 Corinthians 5:18). Draw-

ing its meaning in part from *family life,* this image finds in
love the power to heal. As John expresses it, "We love, because
he first loved us" (1 John 4:19). Driver points out that the word
reconciliation means literally to "re-concile," to bring people into council again.[14] The image is at times *political.*
Through the cross, a new humanity has been formed from all
nations (Ephesians 2:16). "For in him all the fullness of God
was pleased to dwell, and through him to reconcile to himself
all things, whether on earth or in heaven, making peace by
the blood of his cross" (Colossians 1:19-20).

When speaking of the cross, the context of family life
proved helpful to the New Testament writers in still another
way. The metaphor of *adoption* was used to describe how
we have been brought into God's family. Just as Jesus addressed
God the Father as "Abba," so can we through the cross:
" . . . God sent forth his Son . . . to redeem those who were
under the law, so that we might receive adoption as sons. And
because you are sons, God has sent the Spirit of his Son into
our hearts, crying 'Abba! Father!' " (Galatians 4:4-6). With
these and other word pictures, the New Testament writers have
spoken to us of God's act of salvation. Neither redemption
nor ransom, justification nor triumph, reconciliation nor adoption tells the full story of the cross. John Driver is correct:
"The plurality of images used to understand the work of Christ
is essential. The apostolic community allowed all to stand in
a complementary relationship rather than attempting to reduce
them to a single theory or dogmatic statement."[15] Often the
images overlap, as in the fourth chapter of Galatians where
Paul combines our redemption from slavery with our adoption as children (Galatians 4:1-7). Sometimes several will come
near to being conflated (cf., 1 Peter 1:18-19). But the crux of
the gospel cannot be reduced to one image. There remains an
overflow of meaning.

Evangelicals have often been uncomfortable with this plurality of meaning. In particular, the images having to do with
the law court and the vocabulary of justification have been
made to dominate. Typical perhaps is J. I. Packer's Tyndale
Lecture in 1973, "What Did the Cross Achieve? The Logic of
Penal Substitution."[16] In itself a model of both scholarship and
faith, the lecture can nevertheless be questioned. Packer states
his task to be that of explicating a belief that is "a distinguish-

ing mark of the world-wide evangelical fraternity: namely, the belief that Christ's death on the cross had the character of *penal substitution,* and that it was in virtue of this fact that it brought salvation to mankind." Packer understands his viewpoint to be similar to the reformers, a redefinition of Anselm's notion of Christ's *satisfactio* (satisfaction). Packer admits that there are a variety of other biblical images and models used to describe the work of Christ. Moreover, mystery will remain in any discussion of the atonement.

Nonetheless, Packer argues that penal substitution be understood as the central theological model for the cross. He wants to avoid caricature. His model is meant to convey the meaning of the cross, not its mechanics. It might best be viewed, in fact, as a dramatic idea:

> The notion which the phrase "penal substitution" expresses is that Jesus Christ our Lord, moved by a love that was determined to do everything necessary to save us, endured and exhausted the destructive divine judgment for which we were otherwise inescapably destined, and so won us forgiveness, adoption and glory.[17]

One notes that other models have, in fact, been combined by Packer with that of the law court. "Love," "forgiveness," "adoption," and "glory" all suggest other primary word pictures. It is the law court that provides the integration, however.

For Packer, the word "penal" is there not to create questions about guilt. It is not meant to imply an impersonal, external God responding to the law. It is certainly not intended to describe the means by which the punishment for humankind's sins was transferred to Jesus. Rather it is meant for Packer to evoke awareness that Jesus bore the judgment I deserved because he loved me. Although the term "penal" is extra-biblical, Packer believes it communicates biblical truth.

The question must be asked, however: does "penal" vocabulary continue to highlight for modern Americans the character of Christ's redeeming love? Does it communicate biblical truth today? If it does not, then Packer himself says it "stands self-condemned."[18] While Packer would have us believe that traditional Christian language can still communicate effectively to contemporary humanity if it is adequately explained and qualified, the preceding discussion would cause one to question this. Dietrich Bonhoeffer suggested from his prison cell during World War II that our theological language of redemption has lost something of its force and meaningfulness within contemporary society. Bonhoeffer even believed that in a post-Christian age the Church might for a time be reduced in its witness simply to prayer and righteous action.[19] This judgment has proved hyperbolic but its insight retains validity. Christians today are being called to demonstrate through renewed worship and service that their faith is real. In addition, Christians are exploring the use of other less traditional theological vocabulary including other biblical models of the atonement. The church needs to speak in a language more atune to where modern women and men live. If mission is our goal, communication must begin where people are.

Could it be that many secular Americans are rejecting the message of the cross today because they lack any strong cultural model for understanding it? If I am correct that it is not the language of accountability but that of fulfillment that most easily resonates with the American ethos, then should we not shape our communication of the gospel accordingly? There are other biblical images of the cross that can communicate to moderns in ways more understandable and convincing than that of the law court.

Our most effective evangelism has recognized intuitively the need to present the gospel in the context of images of human fulfillment. For example, Bill Bright's "Four Spiritual Laws" begins, "God loves you and has a wonderful plan for your life." Similarly, when evangelical collegians and seminarians were asked by James Hunter how they would try to persuade someone to become a Christian, 67 percent said they would first talk to a nonbeliever about either "the sense of meaning and purpose in life" that comes from being a Christian or the fact that "God has made a difference in my life." Only one in ten said they would speak first of the wrath of God.[20]

Some will object that such "subjective" interpretations of the gospel represent a danger. John Stott in his excellent book *The Cross of Christ* (1986) states that it is his intention to make clear once again for our generation the distinction between an "objective" and "subjective" understanding of the atonement. The meaning of the atonement is found "in what *God* did when in Christ on the cross he took our place and bore our sin."[21] This is surely the case. Criticism of subjectivist theories of the atonement has validity if such models deny the objective meaning of the cross as God's action on our behalf. The love of God enfleshed in Jesus Christ is more than an example of sacrificial love to be imitated by the Christian. It is the objective basis for the "ransom" that has been paid, the "sacrifice" that has been accomplished, the "victory" that has been won, and the "relationship" that has been secured. "We love, because *he first loved us*" (1 John 4:19). But it is also the case that "*we love.*" One need not juxtapose objective and subjective understandings of the cross. The cross reflects both. Criticism of subjectivist theories go back as far as Bernard of Clairvaux who charged Peter Abelard with teaching that Christ lived and died *only* to point out the limits that our love should go. If such was indeed his position, Abelard deserves criticism for understanding the cross in sub-biblical terms. The atonement accomplished more than providing a compelling example of the love of God. But scholarship today recognizes that even in Abelard, his soteriology centering on our responsive act of love went beyond the mere arousal of love for God within humankind. There was an objective, theocentric side of Abelard that his critics have chosen to overlook.[22] Abelard is not to be criticized for failing to understand reconciliation as ontologically God's action towards us, but for denying the validity of such other biblical models as "propitiation" and "justification." Recognizing a tendency toward legalism and abstraction in the dominate theological discussions of the atonement in his day, he wrongly reduced the multiple descriptions of the cross to one. The language of righteousness in Romans, for example, was transposed as reconciliation.

What is questionable about the explications of the meaning of the cross that Packer and Stott provide is not their objective doctrine, but their language and emphases. Both theologians are reacting to abuses perceived within subjectivist interpretations of the atonement. As such, their constructive statements remain somewhat disconnected from the dominant subjective American ethos. Their biblical exegesis has the same high standards that we have come to expect from their other writings. But despite their best intentions, their focus upon legal metaphor, upon divine satisfaction, causes a distancing from the modern reader. The discussion remains somehow abstracted and intellectualized.

As in the nineteenth century when revivals swept through Sweden, there is the need in evangelical discussion of the cross "for a new *picture* with its own distinctive feeling tone."[23] Evangelical theology today risks communicating with regard to the cross a sterile orthodoxy. Many of its readers understand God to be standing over against sinful humanity in righteous wrath needing his holiness to be satisfied in order that relationship can be restored. This is the case, protestations of caricature not withstanding, for contemporary Americans have heard the cross discussed through ears atuned to images of fulfillment. If the gospel is again to evoke faithful response, we need to help modern men and women see the cross as revealing the extent to which God our heavenly Father has expressed his love so that we might be reconciled to him and to his world. It is the imagery of family life, of restored relationship, that holds the greatest initial promise for effective communication today. Only as this biblical model is grasped will others (including that of the law court) take on new relevance and possibility. As William Dyrness recognizes, "communication takes place from the known to the unknown." [24]

In his summary of the origins of The Evangelical Covenant Church, Donald Frisk reminds us that the favorite text of these revival people was the parable of the prodigal son. What they heard in this story was the amazing reality of the father's love. (Again, one finds in Karl Olsson's repeated use of the prodigal son a similar focus.) Salvation for them became "a joyous and life-changing entrance into personal relationship with God."[25] When Paul Peter Waldenström attempted to express this fact theologically, Covenanters argued about whether such a subjective view of the atonement as his was correct. (And they still do!) There is no doubt that a stress on the atonement as "for our benefit" such as Waldenström suggested can cause one to lose sight of the fact that it is accomplished by God through the death of Jesus Christ. But Waldenström could not have been clearer that this was not his intention. Waldenström was attempting to confront those who would reduce the atonement to a transaction that God had accomplished which we could then ignore. His mission was nothing less than the revival of his church. If a like mission is to continue to characterize both the Covenant and the wider evangelical church, might we not need to take again today a similar risk?

Endnotes

[1] The title of chapter six, James Davison Hunter, *American Evangelicalism: Conservative Religion and the Boundary of Modernity* (New Brunswick, N.J.: Rutgers University Press, 1983).

[2] *Ibid.*, p. 41.

[3] *Ibid.*, p. 45.

[4] Robert Schuller, *Self-Esteem: The New Reformation,* pp. 145-146, 65, 98-99, quoted in James Davison Hunter, *Evangelicalism: The Coming Generation* (Chicago: University of Chicago Press, 1987), p. 70.

[5] Hunter, *American Evangelicalism,* p. 87.

[6] For a similar analysis of the history of Fuller Theological Seminary, see Terry Muck, "Waiting for the Second Coming," review of *Reforming Fundamentalism* by George Marsden (Grand Rapids: Eerdmans, 1987), *New York Times Review of Books,* January 24, 1988.

[7] John Piper, *Desiring God: Meditations of a Christian Hedonist* (Portland: Multnomah Press, 1986), pp. 14-16.

[8] *Ibid.*, p. 42.

[9] *Ibid.* (italics added).

[10] William A. Dyrness, *How Does America Hear the Gospel?* Unpublished manuscript, nonpaginated.

[11] *Ibid.*

[12] Cf. John Driver, *Understanding the Atonement for the Mission of the Church* (Scottdale, PA: Herald Press, 1986).

[13] An excellent summary is provided by Donald C. Frisk, *Covenant Affirmations: This We Believe* (Chicago: Covenant Press, 1981), pp. 92-96.

[14] Cf. Driver, *Understanding the Atonement,* p. 26.

[15] *Ibid.*, pp. 15-19.

[16] J. I. Packer, "What Did the Cross Achieve? The Logic of Penal Substitution," *Tyndale Bulletin,* 25 (1974), 3-45.

[17] *Ibid.*, 25.

[18] *Ibid.*, 42.

[19] Dietrich Bonhoeffer, *Letters and Papers From Prison,* Eberhard Bethge, ed. (New York: Macmillan, 1955), pp. 151, 190-191.

[20] Hunter, *Evangelicalism: The Coming Generation,* pp. 39-40.

[21] John Stott, *The Cross of Christ* (Downers Grove, IL: Inter-Varsity Press, 1988), p. 9.

[22] Cf. Allister McGrath, "The Moral Theory of the Atonement: An Historical, and Theological Critique," *Scottish Journal of Theology,* 38 (1985), 207.

[23] Frisk, *Covenant Affirmations,* p. 99.
[24] Dyrness, *How Does America Hear the Gospel?* nonpaginated.
[25] Frisk, *Covenant Affirmations,* p. 100.

Bibliography
The Published and Unpublished Writings of Karl A. Olsson

Compiled by Timothy J. Johnson

1931

"En Kristens Segersång," *Förbundets Veckotidning* 20 (1) January 6, 1931: 1.

" 'Tis Yule Tonight!" *Our Covenant: An Illustrated Annual of the Swedish Evangelical Mission Covenant of America, A Review of the Year 1930,* v. 5. Edited by G. F. Hedstrand and E. Gustav Johnson. Chicago: Covenant Book Concern, 1931.

1932

Poem, "The Lyric Aim," written under the pen name "Carolavi," *Pegasus* [literary magazine published by The Pegasus Club, North Park College, Chicago], v. 3, May 1932: 2.

Poem, "Gray Days_____," *Pegasus,* v. 3, May 1932: 9.

Poem, "Gloucester Road," *Pegasus,* v. 3, May 1932: 10-11.

Poem, "May," *Pegasus,* v. 3, May 1932: 12.

Poem, "Eastertide," *Pegasus,* v. 3, May 1983: 25.

1933

"The Villager," *Our Covenant: An Illustrated Annual of the Swedish Evangelical Mission Covenant of America, A Record for the Year 1932,* v. 7: 72. Edited by G. F. Hedstrand. Chicago: Covenant Book Concern, 1933.

Poem, "To David Nyvall on His 70th Birthday, January 19, '33," *North Park College News* January 25, 1933: 3.

Poem, "Crucified," *North Park College News* March 22, 1933: 1.

Poem, "Out of the Winds," written under the pen name "Carolavi," *Pegasus,* v. 4, May 1933: 9.

Poem, "Corpus Juvenis," *Pegasus,* v. 4, May 1933: 15. [Also published in *The Hills Are Ready for Climbing: A Collection of Poems by Undergraduates of American Colleges and Universities.* New York: E. P. Dutton, 1934. See also *Pegasus* v. 10, 1939.]

Poem, "Success," *Pegasus,* v. 4, May 1933: 23.

Poem, "The Passing," *Pegasus,* v. 4, May 1933: 28.

Poem, "Release," *Pegasus,* v. 4, May 1933: 30.

1934

"The Weekly Pulpit—Lent," *Veckobladet,* March 13, 1934: 8.

"From Our Book Stall" [reviews of *The Winding Road* by Walter Lindberg, and *Mary of Nazareth* by Mary Borden], *Veckobladet,* March 13, 1934: 8.

"From Our Book Stall" [reviews of *What about Church Suppers* by J. Hoifjeld, *The Pocket Bible Handbook* by Henry Hampton Halley, and *Evangelism in the New Age* by Austen Kennedy de Blois], *Veckobladet,* March 20, 1934: 8.

"From Our Book Stall" [reviews of *Russia Challenges Religion* by George Mecklenburg, *Frozen Assets and Other Sermons* by William Edwards Blederwolf, *The Partiality of Jesus* by E. C. Comfort, and *Notable Confessions* by Theodore Walz], *Veckobladet,* March 27, 1934: 8.

"From Our Book Stall" [reviews of *His Right to Die* by Norman B. Harrison, *Palestine and the Jew Today in the Light of Prophecy* by Milton B. Lindberg, and *The Conflict of the Ages* by Arno C. Gaebelein], *Veckobladet,* April 10, 1934: 8.

"From Our Book Stall" [reviews of *Is It Possible* and *The Credentials of Jesus* both by Hjalmar Sundquist, and *He Is Here* by Charles M. Sheldon], *Veckobladet,* April 17, 1934: 8.

"From Our Book Stall" [reviews of *Mästarens Väg* and *Guds folk och Människosonens dagar* both by Frank Mangs, *The Sermon on the Mount* by Clovis G. Chappell, and *Sermons from the Parables* also by Chappell], *Veckobladet,* April 24, 1934: 8.

"From Our Book Stall" [reviews of *St. Mark* by W. Graham Scroggie, *Mooring Masts of Revelation* by Melvin Grove Kyle, and *Sermons from Life* by Clarence Macartney], *Veckobladet,* May 1, 1934: 8.

"From Our Book Stall" [review of *Kagawa* by Willaim Axling], *Veckobladet,* May 8, 1934: 9.

"From Our Book Stall" [reviews of *Pilgrims's Progress* by John Bunyan and *Paradise Lost* by John Milton], *Veckobladet,* May 15, 1934: 8.

"From Our Book Stall" [reviews of *The World's Best Loved Poems* and *The Best Loved Religious Poems* both edited by James Gilchrist Lawson], *Veckobladet,* May 22, 1934: 8.

"From Our Book Stall" [commentary on the joy of browsing], *Veckobladet,* May 29, 1934: 8.

Poem, "Welcome," *Pegasus,* v. 5, May 1934: 5.

Poem, "Friendship," *Pegasus,* v. 5, May 1934: 8.

Poem, "Independent Courage," *Pegasus,* v. 5, May 1934: 11.

Poem, "The New Solomon," *Pegasus,* v. 5, May 1934: 29.

Poem, "Equinox," *Pegasus,* v. 5, May 1934: 30.

Poem, "Epilogue," *Pegasus,* v. 5, May 1934: 32.

Poem, "Saga," *The Gateway* [publication of the Ken Rune Chapter, English Dept., Macalester College], June, 1934.

Poem, "The Victors," *North Park College News* June 5, 1934: 2.

"From Our Book Stall" [KAO's personal credo in the choice of good literature], *Veckobladet,* June 12, 1934: 8.

"From Our Book Stall" [reviews of *The Golden Jubilee* (Evangelical Free Church fiftieth anniversary) and *Pegasus* (North

Park College literary magazine)], *Veckobladet,* June 19, 1934: 10.

"From Our Book Stall" [commentary on knowing authors, Edwin Arlington Robinson as example], *Veckobladet,* July 3, 1934: 8.

"From Our Book Stall" [review of *Our China Mission* by Peter Matson], *Veckobladet,* July 10, 1934: 8.

"From Our Book Stall" [review of *The Christian Message for the World Today* published by Rount Table Press], *Veckobladet,* July 24, 1934: 8.

"From Our Book Stall" [commentary on the Bible and on Nils W. Lund] *Veckobladet,* July 31, 1934: 8.

"From Our Book Stall" [commentary on David Nyvall's "Via" books, and on *Christ and Japan* by Toyohiko Kagawa, translated by William Axling], *Veckobladet,* August 7, 1934: 8.

"From Our Book Stall" [commentary on plans for a Covenant ministerial quarterly], *Veckobladet,* August 21, 1934: 8.

"From Our Book Stall" [review of *Problems of Young Christians* by Martin Hegland], *Veckobladet,* August 28, 1934: 8.

"From Our Book Stall" [review of *Our Daily Bread* by Gösta Larson], *Veckobladet,* September 4, 1934: 8.

"From Our Book Stall" [further review of Kagawa's *Christ and Japan* and commentary on Swedish language], *Veckobladet,* September 18, 1934: 8.

"From Our Book Stall" [commentary on reading and books], *Veckobladet,* September 25, 1934: 8.

"From Our Book Stall" [review of *Is the Bible True* by F. C. Atkinson], *Veckobladet,* October 16, 1934: 11.

"From Our Book Stall" [review of *A Man and His Conscience* by Jarl Hemmer], *Veckobladet,* December 4, 1934: 4.

"From Our Book Stall" [commentary and reviews on books for Christmas, including *C. A. Björk, Levnadsteckning* by C. V. Bowman; *Our Covenant 1935; The Discovery and Re-Discovery of America* by Thomas Peter Christensen; and *His*

Book, or Structure in Scripture by Norman B. Harrison],
Veckobladet, December 18, 1934: 5.

"From Our Book Stall" [commentary on the history of print-
ing, review of *The Christian Life* by Hallesby], *Veckobladet,*
December 25, 1934: 6.

1935

"From Our Book Stall" [commentary on Frostenson's poems],
Veckobladet, January 1, 1935: 5.

[Untitled] *The North Parker* 1 (1) January 1935: 1,3 + .

"From Our Book Stall" [review of *Owls to Athens* by Herman
Wildenvey, translated by Joseph Auslander], *Veckobladet,*
February 5, 1935: 5.

"Keep Coals Glowing," *The North Parker* 1 (3) March 1935:
1,4.

Poem, "Heroics," *Pegasus,* v. 6, May 1935: 5.

Poem, "Holy City," *Pegasus,* v. 6, May 1935: 15.

Poem, "To Timothy," *Covenant Weekly* 24 (32) August 6,
1935: 2.

"Latest Writing of Prof. N. W. Lund Is Published," *North Park
College News* October 28, 1935: 1.

"Sabbatsvilan," *Covenant Weekly* 24 (47) November 19, 1935:
2.

"A Munition Maker Goes to Tea with His Wife and Daughters,"
North Park College News December 16, 1935: 2.

1936

[Guest Editorial] *The North Parker* 2 (11) March 1936: 2.

Poem, "Ointment of the Apothecary," *Pegasus,* v. 7, May
1936: 6-7.

Poem, "To a Victorious Friend, N. W. Lund," *Pegasus,* v. 7,
May 1936: 15.

Poem, "Charles Wilson Speaks," *The North Parker* 3 (17)

December 1936: 1.

1937

"As You Pause for the Ferry," *Our Covenant: An Illustrated Annual of the Swedish Evangelical Mission Covenant of America,* v. 11: 73. Edited by G. F. Hedstrand. Chicago: Covenant Book Concern, 1937.

"A City Grows Old," *Covenant Weekly* 26 (7) February 16, 1937: 8.

"The Old Pulpit," *Covenant Weekly* 26 (22) June 1, 1937: 1-2.

"The Old Pulpit (cont.)," *Covenant Weekly* 26 (23) June 8, 1937: 5.

Poem, " 'We All Do Fade as a Leaf,' " *Covenant Weekly* 26 (43) October 26, 1937: 1.

"After Six Decades," *Covenant Weekly* 26 (44) November 2, 1937: 8.

"Celebrate 60th Anniversary," *Covenant Weekly* 26 (48) November 30, 1937: 8.

1938

Poem, "To David Nyvall (on the occasion of his 75th birthday)," *The North Parker* 4 (27) January 1938: 3.

"Has Oxford a Word for the Covenant?" *Covenant Weekly* 27 (10) March 8, 1938: 5.

"Studies in Amos," *Covenant Weekly* 27 (40) October 4, 1938: 6.

"The Message of Amos," *Covenant Weekly* 27 (41) October 11, 1938: 6.

"Amos' Importance for Our Day," *Covenant Weekly* 27 (42) October 18, 1938: 6.

Poem, "Incarnation," *Covenant Weekly* 27 (51) December 20, 1938: 4. [Also published in *The North Parker* 5 (3) December 1938: 1]

1939

"Blodets Under: Radiopredikan hållen i Rockfords Missions-tabernakel den 29 januari 1939," *Covenant Weekly* 28 (9) February 28, 1939: 1.

Poem, "Corpus Juvenis," *Pegasus,* v. 10, May 1939: 18.

Poem, "Holy City," *Pegasus,* v. 10, May 1939: 28.

Poem, "Holy Sonnets I: Incarnation," *Pegasus,* v. 10, May 1939: 44.

Poem, "Holy Sonnets II: Redemption," *Pegasus,* v. 10, May 1939: 44.

"Democracy and Criticism," *Covenant Weekly* 28 (34) August 29, 1939: 2.

1940

"A. Samuel Wallgren," *Our Covenant 1940: An Illustrated Annual of the Evangelical Mission Covenant Church of America,* v. 15: 81-83. Edited by G. F. Hedstrand. Chicago: Covenant Book Concern, 1940.

1941

"The Church and the Social Order," *Covenant Quarterly* 1: 12-19.

"A. Samuel Wallgren, 1885-1940: For a Decade the Devoted Friend of Pegasus," *Pegasus,* v. 12, May 1941: 20-21.

"Christian Nobility," *Covenant Home Altar* 3 (2) May 5, 1941: 39.

"Christian Resoluteness," *Covenant Home Altar* 3 (2) May 6, 1941: 40.

"Be Not Hasty to Be Angry," *Covenant Home Altar* 3 (2) May 7, 1941: 41.

"Christ's Fellowship Shortens the Way," *Covenant Home Altar* 3 (2) May 8, 1941: 42.

"The Apostles' Commission," *Covenant Home Altar* 3 (2) May 9, 1941: 43.

"Wisdom in Life," *Covenant Home Altar* 3 (2) May 10, 1941: 44.

"The Blessedness of Being Needed," *Covenant Home Altar* 3 (2) May 11, 1941: 45.

"Welcome to North Park," *Covenant Weekly* 30 (21) May 23, 1941: 7.

"Security of the Upright," *Covenant Home Altar* 3 (3) August 4, 1941: 39.

"The Heath in the Desert," *Covenant Home Altar* 3 (3) August 5, 1941: 40.

The Green Tree," *Covenant Home Altar* 3 (3) August 6, 1941: 41.

"More than Conquerors," *Covenant Home Altar* 3 (3) August 7, 1941: 42.

"God's Finality," *Covenant Home Altar* 3 (3) August 8, 1941: 43.

"Search Me, O God," *Covenant Home Altar* 3 (3) August 9, 1941: 44.

"Who Then Is Faithful?" *Covenant Home Altar* 3 (3) August 10, 1941: 45.

"The Banner of Sovereignty," *Covenant Home Altar* 3 (4) November 3, 1941: 38.

"The Meaning of Suffering," *Covenant Home Altar* 3 (4) November 4, 1941: 39.

"Personal Discipline," *Covenant Home Altar* 3 (4) November 5, 1941: 40.

"The Power to Endure," *Covenant Home Altar* 3 (4) November 6, 1941: 41.

"The Lord of Seasons," *Covenant Home Altar* 3 (4) November 7, 1941: 42.

"Bless Ye God," *Covenant Home Altar* 3 (4) November 8, 1941: 43.

"The Christian Offensive," *Covenant Home Altar* 3 (4) November 9, 1941: 44.

1942

"Christian Conception of Man," *Covenant Quarterly* 2: 26-32.

1944

"Mission of the Chaplain," *Covenant Quarterly* 4: 40-45.

"The Faithfulness of God," *Covenant Weekly* 33 (30) July 28, 1944: 2.

1947

"The Service of the Church School," *Covenant Weekly* 36 (37) September 12, 1947: 8.

1948

Theology and Rhetoric in the Writings of Thomas Shepard. Thesis—University of Chicago, 1948. Microfilm of typescript. Chicago: University of Chicago Library, Dept. of Photographic Reproduction, 1976.

"The Church and the Advancement of Learning," *Covenant Quarterly* 8: 195-202.

"The New Orthodoxy and the Old," *Covenant Quarterly* 8: 67-79.

1949

"Beginnings of Congregational Church Polity," *Covenant Quarterly* 9: 3-10.

1950

"The State and Education," *Covenant Quarterly* 10: 67-76.

1951

"Understanding Our Church: Covenant Church Polity," *Covenant Weekly* 40 (31) August 3, 1951: 3-4.

"Fredrika Bremer and Ralph Waldo Emerson," *Swedish Pioneer Historical Quarterly* 2 (2) 1951: 39-52.

1953

"The Evangelical Mission Covenant Church and the Free Churches of Swedish Background," in *The American Church of the Protestant Heritage* pp. 249-276. Edited by Vergilius Ture Anselm Ferm. New York: Philosophical Library, 1953.

"Covenant Beginnings: Mystical," *Covenant Quarterly* 13: 40-54.

"Covenant Beginnings: Communal," *Covenant Quarterly* 13: 67-82.

"Covenant Beginnings: Doctrinal," *Covenant Quarterly* 13: 99-114.

"The Tragedy of Unbelief," *Covenant Home Altar* 15 (3) September 16, 1953.

1954

According to Thy Word: A Confirmation Study of Bible History, Church History, and the Christian Faith. Clifford W. Bjorklund, Harry J. Ekstam, Karl A. Olsson, Donald C. Frisk. Chicago: Covenant Press, 1954.

The Evangelical Covenant Church: The Covenant Comes of Age. Chicago: Covenant Press, 1954. [Jointly authored with David Nyvall, who wrote the section entitled *The Swedish Covenanters.*]

"The Disciple's Orientation—Six Lectures," in *Committed, United in Christ—to Discipleship: A Resume of Lectures, Sermons, and Events of the Sixth Quadrennial Convention of Covenant Youth of America, August 9-15, 1954,* 65-101. Edited by Erick I. Gustafson. Chicago: Covenant Youth of America, 1954.
"Narrow or Broad: The Search for a Christian Method."
"Focus or Diffusion: The Meaning of Worship."
"Citizen or Stranger: The Function of the Christian Community."

"Good or Bad Wisdom: Does the Christian Faith Make Sense?"

"Freedom or Law: Must a Christian Be Told What to Do?"

"Commitment or Escape: How Is the Christian Hope Relevant Today?"

"Evangelism and Covenant History," *Covenant Quarterly* 14: 80-95.

"Svenskhet, kultur och kristendom," *Covenant Weekly* 43 (11) March 12, 1954: 2.

1955

"Our Changing World," *Covenant Weekly* July 15, 1955: 5.

"The Leveling Process," *Covenant Weekly* July 22, 1955: 5.

"Eugene Solie, Milwaukee Pastor, Dies in California," *Covenant Weekly* 44 (50) July 29, 1955: 1.

"The Shriners Visit Chicago," *Covenant Weekly* July 29, 1955: 5.

"Fences," *Covenant Weekly* August 5, 1955: 5.

"Myth and Fact," *Covenant Weekly* August 12, 1955: 5.

"Psychiatry and Faith," *Covenant Weekly* August 19, 1955: 5.

"The Enriching Detour," *Covenant Weekly* August 26, 1955: 5.

"The Secular and the Sacred,"*Covenant Weekly* September 2, 1955: 5.

"The Compleat Angler," *Covenant Weekly* September 9, 1955: 5.

"The Mysterious North," *Covenant Weekly* September 16, 1955: 5.

"The Golden Fleece," *Covenant Weekly* September 23, 1955: 5.

"Serpents and Doves," *Covenant Weekly* September 30, 1955: 5.

"Triple Brass," *Covenant Weekly* October 7, 1955: 5.

"The Lynching of Justice" *Covenant Weekly* October 14, 1955: 5.

"Brass Tacks," *Covenant Weekly* October 21, 1955: 5.

"The Blessed Virgin Mary," *Covenant Weekly* October 28, 1955: 5.

"The Laying of a Ghost," *Covenant Weekly* November 4, 1955: 7.

"The Church and the Chestnut Tree," *Covenant Weekly* November 11, 1955: 5.

"Unhappily Ever After," *Covenant Weekly* November 18, 1955: 5.

"Robin Hood and His Merry In-laws," *Covenant Weekly* November 25, 1955: 5.

"The Delphic Oracle," *Covenant Weekly* December 2, 1955: 5.

"The Line of Least Resistance," *Covenant Weekly* December 9, 1955: 5.

"Gray Squirrel, Gray Squirrel," *Covenant Weekly* December 16, 1955: 5.

"The House of Christmas," *Covenant Weekly* December 23, 1955: 5.

"The Moving Finger Writes," *Covenant Weekly* December 30, 1955: 5.

1956

"A Detective Story without an Ending," *Our Covenant, 1956: An Illustrated Annual of the Evangelical Mission Covenant Church of America,* v. 31: 29-36. Edited by Carl Philip Anderson. Chicago: Covenant Press, 1956.

"The Golden Horn," *Covenant Weekly* January 6, 1956: 5.

"The Glass of Fashion," *Covenant Weekly* January 13, 1956: 5.

"The Slaughter of the Innocents," *Covenant Weekly* January 20, 1956: 5.

"The Cotter's Saturday Morning," *Covenant Weekly* January 27, 1956: 5.

"The Power of the Positive," *Covenant Weekly* February 3, 1956: 5.

"The World in Our Pockets," *Covenant Weekly* February 10, 1956: 5.

"The Homecoming of Randy Eckman," *Covenant Weekly* February 17, 1956: 5.

"When We Were Very Young," *Covenant Weekly* February 24, 1956: 5.

"The Mail Bag," *Covenant Weekly* March 2, 1956: 7.

"Manana," *Covenant Weekly* March 9, 1956: 5.

"Vitamins and the Way of Life," *Covenant Weekly* March 16, 1956: 5.

"The Bitter Pleasure," *Covenant Weekly* March 23, 1956: 5.

"The Integration of Islam," *Covenant Weekly* March 30, 1956: 5.

"Shallow Deeps," *Covenant Weekly* April 6, 1956: 5.

"The Little Foxes," *Covenant Weekly* April 13, 1956: 5.

"Hot Foot," *Covenant Weekly* April 20, 1956: 5.

"Politics Without Protocol," *Covenant Weekly* April 27, 1956: 5.

Review of *Pass för Amerika* by Erland Sundström, *Swedish Pioneer Historical Quarterly* 7 (2) 1956: 78-79.

"It Is the Thing to Do," *Covenant Weekly* May 4, 1956: 5.

"One Hundred Candles," *Covenant Weekly* May 11, 1956: 5.

"The Rising Tide," *Covenant Weekly* May 18, 1956: 5.

"Down You Go," *Covenant Weekly* May 25, 1956: 5.

"Fervent Heat," *Covenant Weekly* June 1, 1956: 5.

"Forgiveness," *Covenant Weekly* June 8, 1956: 5.

"Grass," *Covenant Weekly* June 15, 1956: 5.

"The King's Evil," *Covenant Weekly* June 22, 1956: 5.

"I Got a Robe," *Covenant Weekly* June 29, 1956: 5.

"Relax!" *Covenant Weekly* July 6, 1956: 5.

"Boors at the Ball Park," *Covenant Weekly* July 13, 1956: 5.

"Fate," *Covenant Weekly* July 20, 1956: 7.

"Mama," *Covenant Weekly* July 27, 1956: 5.

"The Phony Claim," *Covenant Weekly* August 3, 1956: 5.

"Customs," *Covenant Weekly* August 10, 1956: 5.

"Separate Vacations," *Covenant Weekly* August 17, 1956: 5.

"Look Homeward, Angel!" *Covenant Weekly* August 24, 1956: 5.

"Lac La Ronge," *Covenant Weekly* August 31, 1956: 5.

Review of *The Development of Modern Christianity* by Frederick A. Norwood, *The Chaplain* 13 (4) 1956: 37-38.

"There was an old woman . . . " *Covenant Weekly* September 7, 1956: 5.

"Small Expectations," *Covenant Weekly* September 14, 1956: 5.

"Practical Poppycock," *Covenant Weekly* September 21, 1956: 5.

"On Travel," *Covenant Weekly* September 28, 1956: 5.

"On the Gilding of Lilies," *Covenant Weekly* October 5, 1956: 5.

"The Swan," *Covenant Weekly* October 12, 1956: 5.

"Happy Birthday!" *Covenant Weekly* October 19, 1956: 5.

"Live Fast, Die Young," *Covenant Weekly* October 26, 1956: 5.

"The Hard and Gemlike Flame," *Covenant Weekly* November 2, 1956: 5.

"Time and the Timeless," *Covenant Weekly* November 9, 1956: 5.

"Size, Speed, and Cost," *Covenant Weekly* November 16, 1956: 5.

"Melvin," *Covenant Weekly* November 23, 1956: 5.

"Richard Larson Called Home at Age of 56," *Covenant Weekly* 45 (48) November 30, 1956: 1.

"Warm Hearts and Cold Feet," *Covenant Weekly* November 30, 1956: 5.

"Sessions of Sweet Silent Thought," *Covenant Weekly* December 7, 1956: 5.

"Nils Holgersson and Dante Alighieri," *Covenant Weekly* December 14, 1956: 5.

"It Pays to Advertise," *Covenant Weekly* December 21, 1956: 5.

"A Right Jolly Old Elf," *Covenant Weekly* December 28, 1956: 5.

1957

"The Covenant Pastor as Leader and Servant," unpublished typescript [1957?] Covenant Archives: Karl A. Olsson Papers.

"Blessings from Bofors," *Covenant Weekly* January 4, 1957: 5.

"Justice in a Christmas Card," *Covenant Weekly* January 11, 1957: 5.

"Mush," *Covenant Weekly* January 18, 1957: 5.

"On Images," *Covenant Weekly* January 25, 1957: 5.

"The Day Burning Like an Oven," *Covenant Weekly* February 1, 1957: 5.

"The Wicket Gate," *Covenant Weekly* February 8, 1957: 5.

"Evangelists and Bishops," *Covenant Weekly* February 15, 1957: 5.

"On the Value of Courtesy," *Covenant Weekly* February 22, 1957: 5.

Review of *The Theology of Reinhold Niebuhr* by Hans Hofmann, *The Chaplain* 14 (1) 1957: 39-41.

"Life in a Goldfish Bowl," *Covenant Weekly* March 1, 1957: 5.

"Food Plus," *Covenant Weekly* March 7, 1957: 7,11.

"Tennyson Reconsidered," *Covenant Weekly* March 15, 1957: 5.

"Rock 'n Roll Is Here to Stay," *Covenant Weekly* March 22, 1957: 7,9.

"Time's Winged Chariot," *Covenant Weekly* March 29, 1957: 5.

"Sons and Daughters of . . . " *Covenant Weekly* April 5, 1957: 5.

"On a Level with Baffin Land," *Covenant Weekly* April 12, 1957: 5.

"An Inheritance Incorruptible," *Covenant Weekly* April 19, 1957: 5.

" 'And They Cast Lots . . . ' " *Covenant Weekly* April 26, 1957: 5.

" 'This Is My Body . . . ' " *Covenant Weekly* May 3, 1957: 5.

"The Growth of the Zucchetto," *Covenant Weekly* May 10, 1957: 5.

"The Recurrent and the Unique," *Covenant Weekly* May 17, 1957: 5.

"Mr. Benson," *Covenant Weekly* May 24, 1957: 5.

"Saying It with Flowers," *Covenant Weekly* May 31, 1957: 5.

"Journal of a May Sunday," *Covenant Weekly* June 7, 1957: 5.

" 'He who digs a pit . . . ' " *Covenant Weekly* June 14, 1957: 5.

"The Feudal Mind," *Covenant Weekly* June 21, 1957: 5.

"It Made America Great," *Covenant Weekly* June 28, 1957: 5.

"De Senectute (On Old Age)," *Covenant Weekly* July 5, 1957: 5.

"Content in Fire," *Covenant Weekly* July 12, 1957: 5.

"Ode to the Simple," *Covenant Weekly* July 19, 1957: 5.

"Nature and Culture," *Covenant Weekly* July 26, 1957: 5.

"Summer Scapegoat," *Covenant Weekly* August 2, 1957: 5.

"Dark Pharisee," *Covenant Weekly* August 9, 1957: 5.

"The Silent Woman," *Covenant Weekly* August 16, 1957: 5.

"Brideshead Revisited," *Covenant Weekly* August 23, 1957: 5.

"Reinhold Niebuhr and Billy Graham," *Covenant Weekly* August 30, 1957: 5.

"I Wish They'd Stop Smiling," *Covenant Weekly* September 6, 1957: 5.

"The Hatred of Theologians," *Covenant Weekly* September 13, 1957: 5.

"The Battle of Tail Feathers," *Covenant Weekly* September 20, 1957: 5.

"Agreeable Albert," *Covenant Weekly* September 27, 1957: 5.

" 'To Thine Own Self Be True,' " *Covenant Weekly* October 4, 1957: 5.

"No Parking," *Covenant Weekly* October 11, 1957: 5.

"Fantasian Flu," *Covenant Weekly* October 18, 1957: 5.

"Pusey Among the Lions," *Covenant Weekly* October 25, 1957: 5.

"Failure Is Failure," *Covenant Weekly* November 1, 1957: 5.

"And No Nonsense," *Covenant Weekly* November 8, 1957: 5.

"Signs of the Times," *Covenant Weekly* November 15, 1957: 5.

"On Dragging Your Feet," *Covenant Weekly* November 22, 1957: 5.

"Some Trust in Horses," *Covenant Weekly* November 29, 1957: 5.

"Go, Go, Go!" *Covenant Weekly* December 6, 1957: 5.

"The Torch of Smoky Pine," *Covenant Weekly* December 13, 1957: 5.

"Wishing upon a Star," *Covenant Weekly* December 27, 1957: 5.

1958

"Covenant Higher Education: Its History," *Covenant Quarterly* 18: 3-23.

"The Christmas Story Dramatized," *Covenant Weekly* January 3, 1958: 5.

"If It Weren't for Pressfield Hatch," *Covenant Weekly* January 10, 1958: 5.

"The Grammarian's Funeral," *Covenant Weekly* January 17, 1958: 5.

"The Soap Bubble," *Covenant Weekly* January 24, 1958: 7.

"Canossa," *Covenant Weekly* January 31, 1958: 5.

" 'The woman thou gavest me . . . ' " *Covenant Weekly* February 7, 1958: 5.

"The Pure and Simple Mind," *Covenant Weekly* February 14, 1958: 7.

"Behavioral Science," *Covenant Weekly* February 21, 1958: 5.

"Quit Ye Like Men," *Covenant Weekly* February 28, 1958: 7.

"Food Plus," *Covenant Weekly* March 7, 1958: 7.

"Chicago and the Curia," *Covenant Weekly* March 14, 1958: 7.

"Rock 'n Roll Is Here to Stay," *Covenant Weekly* March 21, 1958: 7.

"Time's Winged Chariot," *Covenant Weekly* March 28, 1958: 7.

"The Happy Eggs," *Covenant Weekly* April 4, 1958: 7.

"Graded Washbowls," *Covenant Weekly* April 11, 1958: 7.

"Woodman, Spare That Tree!" *Covenant Weekly* April 18, 1958: 7.

"Dear Diary," *Covenant Weekly* April 25, 1958: 7.

"On Washing Dishes," *Covenant Weekly* May 2, 1958: 7.

"On Being a Real Man," *Covenant Weekly* May 9, 1958: 7.

"Bruised Idealist," *Covenant Weekly* May 16, 1958: 7.

"The Conversion of the Jews," *Covenant Weekly* May 23, 1958: 7.

"Prescription for a Wrinkled Neck," *Covenant Weekly* May 30, 1958: 7.

"Developing a Christian Family in Today's World," *The Link* 16 (5) 1958: 52-55.

"The Unity We Seek," *Covenant Weekly* June 6, 1958: 7.

"Hints on How to Maintain Family Togetherness," *Covenant Weekly* 47 (24) June 13, 1958: 3, 12.

"Molly and Me," *Covenant Weekly* June 13, 1958: 7.

"Sermons in Stones," *Covenant Weekly* June 20, 1958: 7.

"The Gift without the Giver," *Covenant Weekly* June 27, 1958: 7.

"The Old Oaken Bucket," *Covenant Weekly* July 4, 1958: 7.

"Crisis in Private Education," *Covenant Weekly* July 11, 1958: 7.

"New Low in Sales Patter," *Covenant Weekly* July 18, 1958: 7.

"Zorro!" *Covenant Weekly* July 25, 1958: 7.

" 'Tenting Tonight,' " *Covenant Weekly* August 1, 1958: 7.

"Children Are Good for Bireley's," *Covenant Weekly* August 8, 1958: 7.

"The Far Off and Divine Event," *Covenant Weekly* August 15, 1958: 7.

" 'Adults may sit in the gallery . . . ' " *Covenant Weekly* August 22, 1958: 7.

"Simple Needs Create Covenant Architecture," *Covenant Weekly* 47 (35) August 29, 1958: 1,10.

"My Feet Are Killing Me," *Covenant Weekly* August 29, 1958: 7.

"Space Mentality," *Covenant Weekly* September 5, 1958: 9.

"Sticks and Stones," *Covenant Weekly* September 12, 1958: 7.

"Idle Tears," *Covenant Weekly* September 19, 1958: 7.

"Toys," *Covenant Weekly* September 26, 1958: 7.

"When Death Strikes," *The Link* 16 (9) 1958: 48-50, 58.

"Indispensables," *Covenant Weekly* October 3, 1958: 7.

"Creed, Canticle, and Battle Cry," *Covenant Weekly* October 10, 1958: 7.

"Fresh," *Covenant Weekly* October 17, 1958: 7.

"The Again-Bite of Conscience," *Covenant Weekly* October 24, 1958: 7.

"On This Rock?" *Covenant Weekly* October 31, 1958: 7.

Review of *Resa till Amerika 1864 med emigrantskeppet Ernst Merck* by Måns Hultin, *Swedish Pioneer Historical Quarterly* 9 (4) 1958: 141-143.

"In Bed We Sleep," *Covenant Weekly* November 7, 1958: 7.

"Bigotry at Benning?" *Covenant Weekly* November 14, 1958: 7.

"Sin in Sweden," *Covenant Weekly* November 21, 1958: 7.

"Gossip and Guilt," *Covenant Weekly* November 28, 1958: 7.

"Great Books and your Pocketbook," *Covenant Weekly* December 5, 1958: 7.

"What Is It?" *Covenant Weekly* December 12, 1958: 7.

"Discarded Idols," *Covenant Weekly* December 19, 1958: 7.

"The Trickster Tricked," *Covenant Weekly* December 26, 1958: 7.

1959

Christian and Lawyer. John Mulder and Karl Olsson. Norman, Oklahoma: University of Oklahoma Press, 1959. [Reprinted from the *Oklahoma Law Review.*]

Things Common and Preferred: Christian Perspectives. Minneapolis: Augsburg Publishing House, 1959.

"Old Stuff," *Covenant Companion* January 2, 1959: 12.

"Immortality in Steel," *Covenant Companion* January 9, 1959: 12.

"Mouth of the Gift Horse," *Covenant Companion* January 16, 1959: 12.

"Hey, You!" *Covenant Companion* January 23, 1959: 12.

"The Story of Our Freedoms," *Covenant Companion* January 30, 1959: 4-6,19.

"Dimensions," *Covenant Companion* January 30, 1959: 12.

"Revolt of the Amateur," *Covenant Companion* February 6, 1959: 12.

"Dark Night of the Soul," *Covenant Companion* February 13, 1959: 12.

"Houses of Cedarwood," *Covenant Companion* February 20, 1959: 12.

"The World Looks at the Church," *Covenant Companion* February 27, 1959: 12.

"Innocents Abroad," *Covenant Companion* March 6, 1959: 12.

"House of Toothpicks," *Covenant Companion* March 13, 1959: 12.

"The Last Enemy," *Covenant Companion* March 20, 1959: 12.

"Laughter in Athens," *Covenant Companion* March 27, 1959: 12.

"To Make Excuses," *Covenant Companion* April 3, 1959: 12.

"The Bower of Bliss," *Covenant Companion* April 10, 1959: 12.

"Wise Custom," *Covenant Companion* April 17, 1959: 12.

"The Deadly Sins," *Covenant Companion* April 24, 1959: 12.

Review of *Reflections on the Psalms* by C. S. Lewis, *The Chaplain* 16 (2) 1959: 59-60.

"The Deadly Sins: Pride," *Covenant Companion* May 1, 1959: 12.

"The Deadly Sins: Pride (cont.)," *Covenant Companion* May 8, 1959: 12.

"The Deadly Sins: Pride (concluded)," *Covenant Companion* May 15, 1959: 12.

"Theological Education—Why?" *Covenant Companion* May 22, 1959: 4-5, 19.

"The Deadly Sins: Envy," *Covenant Companion* May 22, 1959: 12.

"A Salute to Our Chaplains," *Covenant Companion* May 29, 1959: 4-5.

"The Deadly Sins: Envy and Its Brother," *Covenant Companion* May 29, 1959: 12.

"Are You Willing to Pay the Price?" *The Link* 17 (5) 1959: 48-50.

"The Deadly Sins: Anatomy of Envy," *Covenant Companion* June 5, 1959: 12.

"The Deadly Sins: Anger," *Covenant Companion* June 12, 1959: 12.

"The Deadly Sins: Anger (cont.)," *Covenant Companion* June 19, 1959: 12.

"The Deadly Sins: Anger as Disturbance," *Covenant Companion* June 26, 1959: 12.

"The Deadly Sins: Acadia (Sloth)," *Covenant Companion* July 3, 1959: 12.

"The Deadly Sins: On Sloth and Boredom," *Covenant Companion* July 10, 1959: 12.

"The Deadly Sins: Sloth and Its Remedy," *Covenant Companion* July 17, 1959: 12.

"The Deadly Sins: Avarice," *Covenant Companion* July 24, 1959: 12.

"The Deadly Sins: Getting and Spending," *Covenant Companion* July 31, 1959: 12.

"Are You Willing to Pay the Price?" *Covenant Companion* August 7, 1959: 6,7.

"The Deadly Sins: Greed and Money," *Covenant Companion* August 7, 1959: 12.

"The Deadly Sins: Gluttony," *Covenant Companion* August 14, 1959: 12.

"The Deadly Sins: Gluttony (cont.)," *Covenant Companion* August 21, 1959: 12.

"The Deadly Sins: Gluttony (cont.)," *Covenant Companion* August 28, 1959: 12.

Review of *The Reality of the Church* by Claude Welch, *The Chaplain* 16 (4) 1959: 34-35.

"North Park Opens Its Doors with . . . the Sound of Hammers," *Covenant Companion* September 4, 1959: 8-11.

"The Deadly Sins: Gluttony and Conviviality," *Covenant Companion* September 4, 1959: 12.

"On North Park Sunday: 'Give with Glad, Generous Hearts,' Says Karl Olsson," *Covenant Companion* September 11, 1959: 3.

"The Seven Deadly Sins: Lust," *Covenant Companion* September 11, 1959: 12.

"The Seven Deadly Sins: Lust," *Covenant Companion* September 18, 1959: 12.

"The Deadly Sins: Lust," *Covenant Companion* September 25, 1959: 12.

"Prexy's Open Letter," *North Park College Academy News* 1 (1) September 25, 1959: 2.

"The Idea of a Christian School: An Address . . . to the Faculty Conference of North Park College and Theological Seminary, September 25, 1959 . . . " Covenant Archives: Karl A. Olsson Papers.

"Memo," *North Park College News* 39 (1) September 30, 1959: 2.

"The Deadly Sins: Lust," *Covenant Companion* October 2, 1959: 12.

"The God of Abraham," *Covenant Companion* October 9, 1959: 12.

"The Game," *Covenant Companion* October 16, 1959: 12.

"Horn and Hammer," *Covenant Companion* October 23, 1959: 12.

"In Loving Memory," *Covenant Companion* October 30, 1959: 12.

"Memo," *North Park College News* 39 (3) November 4, 1959: 2.

"Above Idealism," *Covenant Companion* November 6, 1959: 12.

"Divine Foolishness and Human Learning (Address delivered by KAO at his inauguration as fifth president of North Park College last week)," *Covenant Companion* November 13, 1959: 4-6. [Reprinted in booklet form by Al Norberg, who also printed KAO's lyrics which appeared on the Olsson's yearly Christmas card.]

"Mojave Revisited," *Covenant Companion* November 13, 1959: 12.

"End of an Era," *Covenant Companion* November 20, 1959: 12.

"Wanted: Something to Wait For," *Covenant Companion* November 27, 1959: 12.

"Christmas All the Year," *Covenant Companion* December 4, 1959: 12.

"Memo," *North Park College News* 40 (5) December 9, 1959: 2.

"Laundromat Unlimited," *Covenant Companion* December 11, 1959: 12.

"Simples," *Covenant Companion* December 18, 1959: 12.

"Space and Sanctity," *Covenant Companion* December 25, 1959: 12.

1960

"Report of Board of Directors of North Park College and Theological Seminary," *1960 Yearbook of the Evangelical Covenant Church of America*: 150-158. Chicago: Evangelical Covenant Church of America, 1960.

"Another Year Is Dawning," *Covenant Companion* January 1, 1960: 12.

"The Vanishing American," *Covenant Companion* January 8, 1960: 12.

" 'Rhythm of Blessedness,' " *Covenant Companion* January 15, 1960: 12.

"Finegan and Francis," *Covenant Companion* January 22, 1960: 12.

"Homer Nods," *North Park College News* 40 (7) January 27, 1960: 2.

"Crowds," *Covenant Companion* January 29, 1960: 12.

"Homesickness," *Covenant Companion* February 5, 1960: 12.

"The Future of Man," *Covenant Companion* February 12, 1960: 12.

"You Are There at . . . the Founding Conference," *Covenant Companion* February 19, 1960: 3-5.

"You Are There When . . . the Mission Friends Talk about Education," *Covenant Companion* February 19, 1960: 10-11.

"The Devil Was Sick," *Covenant Companion* February 19, 1960: 12.

"Snow," *Covenant Companion* February 26, 1960: 12.

"Divine Foolishness and Human Learning," *The Chaplain* 17 (1) 1960: 17-24. [See entry for November 13, 1959.]

"Hail and Farewell," *Covenant Companion* March 4, 1960: 12.

"Farewell to Sven Lidman (concluded)," *Covenant Companion* March 11, 1960: 12.

"Lullabye with Trumpets," *Covenant Companion* March 18, 1960: 12.

"Go Go and the Welfare Board," *Covenant Companion* March 25, 1960: 12.

"School, Church Carry on Conversation," *Covenant Companion* March 25, 1960: 14-15.

"Valley of Decision," *Covenant Companion* April 1, 1960: 12.

"Mailer among the Moralists," *Covenant Companion* April 8, 1960: 12.

"Paradise Regained," *Covenant Companion* April 15, 1960: 12.

"Decrepit Ethics," *Covenant Companion* April 22, 1960: 12.

"This Nettle, Danger," *Covenant Companion* April 29, 1960: 12.

"The Camera's Eye," *Covenant Companion* May 6, 1960: 12.

"Guilt and Innocence," *Covenant Companion* May 13, 1960: 12.

"Big Brother," *Covenant Companion* May 20, 1960: 12.

"Monumental Mother," *Covenant Companion* May 27, 1960: 12.

"The Big Deal," *Covenant Companion* June 3, 1960: 12.

"Glory in the Garret," *Covenant Companion* June 10, 1960: 12.

"We Shall Be Changed," *Covenant Companion* June 17, 1960: 12.

"The Poison of Asps," *Covenant Companion* June 24, 1960: 12.

"Cholesterol," *Covenant Companion* July 1, 1960: 12.

"Waters of Babylon," *Covenant Companion* July 8, 1960: 12.

"An Angry God," *Covenant Companion* July 15, 1960: 8.

"Drives," *Covenant Companion* July 22, 1960: 8.

"Ill at Ease in Zion," *Covenant Companion* July 29, 1960: 8.

"To the Stars," *Covenant Companion* August 5, 1960: 8.

"Black and White," *Covenant Companion* August 12, 1960: 8.

"Bigotry with Candor," *Covenant Companion* August 19, 1960: 8.

"The Book about Life," *Covenant Companion* August 26, 1960: 8.

"The Tragedy of Francis Powers," *Covenant Companion* September 2, 1960: 8.

"Presenting . . . the Teacher: Heart of the School," *Covenant Companion* September 9, 1960: 3.

"The Decarnation of the Word," *Covenant Companion* September 9, 1960: 12.

"Impedimenta," *Covenant Companion* September 16, 1960: 12.

"Fictions," *Covenant Companion* September 23, 1960: 12.

"Apples and Radishes," *North Park College News* 41 (2) September 30, 1960: 2.

"Danger in the Afternoon," *Covenant Companion* September 30, 1960: 12.

"No Continuing City," *Covenant Companion* October 7, 1960: 12.

"President's Welcome," *North Park Academy News* 2 (2) October 7, 1960: 2.

"Ode to Duty," *Covenant Companion* October 14, 1960: 12.

"The New Birth," *Covenant Companion* October 21, 1960: 12.

"The Embarrassment of Equality," *Covenant Companion* October 28, 1960: 12.

Reviews of *American Catholics: A Protestant-Jewish View,* edited by Philip Scharper and *A Message to Catholics and Protestants* by Oscar Cullmann, *The Chaplain* 17 (5) 1960: 55-56.

"To Go on Pilgrimages," *Covenant Companion* November 4, 1960: 12.

"Left to Myself," *Covenant Companion* November 11, 1960: 12.

"Panic and Passion," *Covenant Companion* November 18, 1960: 12.

"Good Morning, Mr. Troutfeather," *North Park Academy News* 2 (5) November 18, 1960: 2.

"The Winter of Our Discontent," *Covenant Companion* November 25, 1960: 12.

"Winter of Happiness," *Covenant Companion* December 2, 1960: 12.

"The Mirror of Life," *Covenant Companion* December 9, 1960: 12.

"Christmas—The Derived, the Original," *North Park College News* 41 (10) December 16, 1960: 2.

"The Heresy of Luck," *Covenant Companion* December 16, 1960: 12.

"Nativity," *Covenant Companion* December 23, 1960: 12.

"The Great Church," *Covenant Companion* December 30, 1960: 12.

1961

Quality of Mercy: Swedish Covenant Hospital and Covenant Home, Seventy-fifth Anniversary 1886-1961. Chicago: s.n., 1961.

"Report of the Board of Directors of North Park College and Theological Seminary," *1961 Yearbook of the Evangelical Covenant Church of America*: 146-159. Chicago: Evangelical Covenant Church of America, 1961.

"Händel," *Covenant Companion* January 6, 1961: 12.

"Morning Becomes," *Covenant Companion* January 13, 1961: 12.

"When We Dead Waken," *Covenant Companion* January 20, 1961: 12.

"Elephants," *Covenant Companion* January 27, 1961: 12.

"Dream of Splendor" [Address delivered at reception of their Royal Highnesses Princesses Birgitta and Desiree of Sweden at North Park College, Chicago, November 13, 1960], *Swedish Pioneer Historical Quarterly* 12 (1) 1961: 3-9. [Reprinted in booklet form under the title *God Jul: A Christmas Greeting* and distributed by Gunnar Jarring, Ambassador of Sweden.]

"Except a Corn of Wheat," *Covenant Companion* February 3, 1961: 12.

"All Flesh Is Grass," *Covenant Companion* February 10, 1961: 12.

"The Mystique of Authority," *Covenant Companion* February 17, 1961: 12.

"On Being a Cosmopolitan," *Covenant Companion* February 24, 1961: 12.

"Gray," *Covenant Companion* March 3, 1961: 12.

"Buffon," *Covenant Companion* March 10, 1961: 12.

"Airy Nothing," *Covenant Companion* March 17, 1961: 12.

"Under the Sun," *Covenant Companion* March 24, 1961: 12.

"Implications of Accreditation, History: Decades of Dreams," *North Park College News* 41 (19) March 30, 1961: 2.

"Bi-focals," *Covenant Companion* March 31, 1961: 12.

"Good-bye, Mr. Chips?" *Covenant Companion* April 7, 1961: 12.

"Sulks," *Covenant Companion* April 14, 1961: 12.

"The Organization Man," *Covenant Companion* April 21, 1961: 12.

"The Chemistry of Time," *Covenant Companion* April 28, 1961: 12.

"Annuit Coeptis," *Covenant Companion* May 5, 1961: 12.

"Infirmary of Grace," *Covenant Companion* May 12, 1961: 12.

"Saints and Sinners," *Covenant Companion* May 19, 1961: 12.

"More about Saints," *Covenant Companion* May 26, 1961: 12.

"All This Juice and Joy," *Covenant Companion* June 2, 1961: 12.

"FY," *Covenant Companion* June 9, 1961: 12.

"In the Sign of the Crab," *Covenant Companion* June 16, 1961: 12.

"Miss Porcupine," *Covenant Companion* June 23, 1961: 12.

"In the Beginning Was the Word . . . " *Covenant Companion* June 30, 1961: 12.

" 'Divine Mercy and Human . . . ' " *Covenant Companion* July 7, 1961: 6.

"Bleak House," *Covenant Companion* July 7, 1961: 12.

"Wondrous Pitiful," *Covenant Companion* July 14, 1961: 8.

"Rebuttal," *Covenant Companion* July 21, 1961: 8.

"The Apple Orchard," *Covenant Companion* July 28, 1961: 8.

"The Well-tempered Clavichord," *Covenant Companion* August 4, 1961: 8.

"Sand Box Farewell!" *North Park College News* 42 (1) August 10, 1961: 2.

"We Cannot Escape History," *Covenant Companion* August 11, 1961: 8.

"I Was in Prison," *Covenant Companion* August 18, 1961: 8.

"Silence in Heaven," *Covenant Companion* August 25, 1961: 8.

"The Inner Links," *Covenant Companion* September 1, 1961: 8.

"Silence on Earth," *Covenant Companion* September 8, 1961: 8.

"Megatons and Sparrows," *Covenant Companion* September 15, 1961: 12.

"Nothing of Value Comes Free," *North Park College News* 42 (1) September 22, 1961: 2.

"Sniper," *Covenant Companion* September 22, 1961: 12.

" 'Not that we would be unclothed . . . ' " *Covenant Companion* September 29, 1961: 12.

"Who Would These Fardels Bear?" *Covenant Companion* October 6, 1961: 12.

"Arms and the Man I Sing," *Covenant Companion* October 13, 1961: 12.

"Too Much Joy?" *Covenant Companion* October 20, 1961: 12.

"Land That I Love," *Covenant Companion* October 27, 1961: 12.

"The Rat and the Pellet," *Covenant Companion* November 3, 1961: 12.

"Pynchnose," *Covenant Companion* November 10, 1961: 12.

"Service," *Covenant Companion* November 17, 1961: 12.

"From the President . . . " *North Park Academy News* 3 (5) November 17, 1961: 2.

"Canker on the Ivy," *Covenant Companion* November 24, 1961: 12.

"We Won," *Covenant Companion* December 1, 1961: 12.

"To Thine Own Self Be True," *Covenant Companion* December 8, 1961: 12.

"A Time for Christmas," *North Park College News* 42 (10) December 15, 1961: 2.

"Christmas Counterpoint," *Covenant Companion* December 15, 1961: 12.

"Christmas Fast," *Covenant Companion* December 22, 1961: 12.

"Vigilance and Vigilantes," *Covenant Companion* December 29, 1961: 12.

1962

By One Spirit. Chicago: Covenant Press, 1962.

Seven Sins and Seven Virtues. New York: Harper & Brothers, 1962. London: Hodder & Stoughton, 1962.

"Report of the Board of Directors of North Park College and Theological Seminary" *1962 Yearbook of the Evangelical Covenant Church of America*: 141-148. Chicago: Evangelical Covenant Church of America, 1962.

"The Pride of Mediocrity," *Covenant Companion* January 5, 1962: 12.

"Two Kinds of Merriment," *Covenant Companion* January 12, 1962: 12.

"Survival," *Covenant Companion* January 19, 1962: 12.

"Shoe Polish," *Covenant Companion* January 26, 1962: 12.

"The Black Christ," *Covenant Companion* February 2, 1962: 12.

"In Journeyings Often . . . " *Covenant Companion* February 9, 1962: 12.

"End of a Pilgrimage," *Covenant Companion* February 16, 1962: 12.

"Oxology," *Covenant Companion* February 23, 1962: 12.

"Tensile Strength," *Covenant Companion* March 2, 1962: 12.

"Cat and Mouse," *Covenant Companion* March 9, 1962: 12.

"Let George Do It," *Covenant Companion* March 16, 1962: 12.

"Arrow from the Other Side," *Covenant Companion* March 23, 1962: 12.

"Vertigo," *Covenant Companion* March 30, 1962: 12.

"Lenten Delicacies," *Covenant Companion* April 6, 1962: 12.

"Short Day's Journey into Night," *Covenant Companion* April 13, 1962: 12.

"Sinners in the Hands of a Timid Man," *Covenant Companion* April 20, 1962: 12.

"You Can't Win," *Covenant Companion* April 27, 1962: 12.

"The Habitual and the Holy," *The Chaplain* 19 (2) 1962: 1-5.

"The Church Is Face to Face," *Covenant Companion* May 4, 1962: 12.

"The Good Woman," *Covenant Companion* May 11, 1962: 12.

" 'Very Conservative,' " *Covenant Companion* May 18, 1962: 12.

"The Fast and the Flimsy," *Covenant Companion* May 25, 1962: 12.

"Welfare and Gratitude," *Covenant Companion* June 1, 1962: 12.

"Cricket in Our Prayers," *Covenant Companion* June 8, 1962: 12.

"Just When We're Safest," *Covenant Companion* June 15, 1962: 12.

"Treasures," *Covenant Companion* June 22, 1962: 12.

"Eyes to the Hills," *Covenant Companion* June 29, 1962: 12.

"Christian Witness," *Covenant Companion* July 6, 1962: 12.

"Implied Atheism," *Covenant Companion* July 13, 1962: 12.

"The Big and the Small," *Covenant Companion* July 20, 1962: 8.

"The Body Electric," *Covenant Companion* July 27, 1962: 8.

"Swedish Pioneer Historical Society . . . Constitution," *Swedish Pioneer Historical Quarterly* 13 (3) 1962: 128-133. [Constitution Committee consisted of C. George Ericson, chair; Karl A. Olsson, B. W. Selin, E. Gustav Johnson.]

"Good Housekeeping . . . " *Covenant Companion* August 3, 1962: 8.

"Tenting Tonight," *Covenant Companion* August 10, 1962: 8.

"The Great Gulf," *Covenant Companion* August 17, 1962: 8.

"Locked Garden," *Covenant Companion* August 24, 1962: 8.

"Quotables," *Covenant Companion* August 31, 1962: 8.

"Frozen Grief," *Covenant Companion* September 7, 1962: 8.

"Olsson Discusses 'God's Purpose,' " *Covenant Companion* September 14, 1962: 8-9.

"Blood and Fire," *Covenant Companion* September 14, 1962: 12.

"Carnage," *Covenant Companion* September 21, 1962: 12.

"Lady Poverty," *Covenant Companion* September 28, 1962: 12.

"Babel Re-enacted," *Covenant Companion* October 5, 1962: 12.

"Innocent Abroad," *Covenant Companion* October 12, 1962: 12.

"$12,000," *Covenant Companion* October 19, 1962: 12.

"Built-in Obsolescence," *Covenant Companion* October 26, 1962: 12.

"Art and History," *Covenant Companion* November 2, 1962: 12.

"K.O. Explains 'Four Lads' Policy," *North Park College News* 43 (5) November 9, 1962: 2.

"Perspective," *Covenant Companion* November 9, 1962: 12.

"Smoke," *Covenant Companion* November 16, 1962: 12.

"Indigestion," *Covenant Companion* November 23, 1962: 12.

"The Monster," *Covenant Companion* November 30, 1962: 12.

"Surprise Party," *Covenant Companion* December 7, 1962: 12.

"Eternal Moment," *Covenant Companion* December 14, 1962: 12.

"The Vision of God," *Covenant Companion* December 21, 1962: 12.

"Breach of Promise," *Covenant Companion* December 28, 1962: 12.

1963

Passion. New York: Harper & Row, 1963.

Holy Masquerade. By Olov Hartman. Translated by Karl A. Olsson. Grand Rapids, Mich.: Eerdmans, 1963. Ann Arbor,

Mich.: University Microfilms International, 1980. [Translation of *Helig Maskerad*.]

"Paul Peter Waldenström and Augustana," in *The Swedish Immigrant Community in Transition: Essays in Honor of Dr. Conrad Bergendoff:* 107-120. Edited by J. Iverne Dowie and Ernest M. Espelie. Rock Island, Ill.: Augustana Historical Society, 1963.

"Report of the Board of Directors of North Park College and Theological Seminary," *1963 Yearbook of the Evangelical Covenant Church of America*: 160-167. Chicago: Evangelical Covenant Church of America, 1963.

"A Voice in Ramah," *Covenant Companion* January 4, 1963: 12.

"Sparta," *Covenant Companion* January 11, 1962: 12.

"Redeeming the Time," *Covenant Companion* January 18, 1963: 12.

"De-icer," *Covenant Companion* January 25, 1963: 12.

"The Crisis of Cost in Higher Education," *Covenant Companion* February 1, 1963: 10-11.

"The Cracked Bell," *Covenant Companion* February 1, 1963: 12.

"File 13," *Covenant Companion* February 8, 1963: 12.

"What Paul Could Not Have Written," *Covenant Companion* February 15, 1963: 12.

"The God Game," *Covenant Companion* February 22, 1963: 12.

"Outside the Camp: Excerpt from *Passion*," *Christian Century* 80 February 27, 1963: 264-267.

"Keys," *Covenant Companion* March 1, 1963: 12.

"Old Hat," *Covenant Companion* March 8, 1963: 12.

"Hell," *Covenant Companion* March 15, 1963: 12.

"The Flesh Becomes Words," *Covenant Companion* March 22, 1963: 12.

"I Show You a Mystery," *Covenant Companion* March 29, 1963: 12.

"Blessed Are the Sober," *Covenant Companion* April 5, 1963: 12.

"Village among the High Rise," *Covenant Companion* April 12, 1963: 12.

"The Untouchables," *Covenant Companion* April 19, 1963: 12.

"The Wreck of the Thresher," *Covenant Companion* April 26, 1963: 12.

Review of *Utvandrarnas Kyrka: En bok om Augustana* by Sam Rönnegard. *Swedish Pioneer Historical Quarterly* 14 (2) 1963: 92-93.

"Age," *Covenant Companion* May 3, 1963: 12.

"Style," *Covenant Companion* May 10, 1963: 12.

"One Day," *Covenant Companion* May 17, 1963: 12.

"Showers," *Covenant Companion* May 24, 1963: 12.

"The Hour Blue," *Covenant Companion* May 31, 1963: 12.

"The Form of a Servant," *Covenant Companion* June 7, 1963: 8-9.

"Brick Layers," *Covenant Companion* June 7, 1963: 12.

"All Flags Flying," *Covenant Companion* June 14, 1963: 12.

"On Being Fifty," *Covenant Companion* June 21, 1963: 12.

"The Triumph of Atheism," *Covenant Companion* June 28, 1963: 12.

"Squoosh!" *Covenant Companion* July 5, 1963: 12.

"The Mills of the Gods," *Covenant Companion* July 12, 1963: 8.

"Pots and Kettles," *Covenant Companion* July 19, 1963: 8.

"Eight Years," *Covenant Companion* July 26, 1963: 8.

" 'Praise Him with Strings,' " *Covenant Companion* August 2, 1963: 8.

"Tourists Not Allowed," *Covenant Companion* August 9, 1963: 8.

"Braces," *Covenant Companion* August 16, 1963: 8.

"Laughing Ostrich," *Covenant Companion* August 23, 1963: 8.

"Skeletons in the Meadow," *Covenant Companion* August 30, 1963: 8.

" 'Brave as a charwoman,' " *Covenant Companion* September 6, 1963: 8.

"The Volcanic Campus," *Covenant Companion* Septemer 13, 1963: 12.

"Baseball and God," *Covenant Companion* September 20, 1963: 12.

"President Discusses College Journalism," *North Park College News* 44 (1) September 25, 1963: 2-3.

"The Horns of Elfland," *Covenant Companion* September 27, 1963: 12.

" 'When we did away with God . . . ' " *Covenant Companion* October 4, 1963: 12.

"Dreadful Freedom," *Covenant Companion* October 11, 1963: 12.

"People on the Pan," *Covenant Companion* October 12, 1963: 12.

"The Old Surveyor," *Covenant Companion* October 25, 1963: 12.

"The Mercy of Limits," *Covenant Companion* November 1, 1963: 12.

"The God Who Saves," *Covenant Companion* November 8, 1963: 12.

The Nature of Our Struggle [Address given at the Annual Banquet of the Minnehaha Fellowship, November 9, 1963], Minneapolis: Minnehaha Academy, 1963.

"The Highest," *Covenant Companion* November 15, 1963: 12.

"Godding," *Covenant Companion* November 22, 1963: 12.

"Sprightly Spoofery," *Christian Century* 80 November 27, 1963: 1469.

"Nut-Cracker Suite," *Covenant Companion* November 29, 1963: 12.

"With Wings Like Eagles," *Covenant Companion* December 6, 1963: 12.

"Heresy of Aloneness," *Covenant Companion* December 13, 1963: 12.

"Poor," *Covenant Companion* December 20, 1963: 12.

" 'What's in a Name?' " *Covenant Companion* December 27, 1963: 12.

1964

"Report of the Board of Directors of North Park College and Theological Seminary," *1964 Yearbook of the Evangelical Covenant Church of America*: 123-129. Chicago: Evangelical Covenant Church of America, 1964.

"No Other Name," *Covenant Companion* January 3, 1964: 12.

"Blue Laws and Blue Noses," *Covenant Companion* January 10, 1964: 12.

"Clutter," *Covenant Companion* January 17, 1964: 12.

"Sabbath Rest," *Covenant Companion* January 24, 1964: 12.

" 'I brought you into the world . . . ' " *Covenant Companion* January 31, 1964: 12.

"Program for a Revolutionary," *Covenant Companion* February 7, 1964: 12.

" 'Foul and unnatural murder,' " *Covenant Companion* February 14, 1964: 12.

"The Meaning of Murder," *Covenant Companion* February 21, 1964: 12.

"Murder Minor," *Covenant Companion* February 28, 1964: 12.

"The Scarlet Letter," *Covenant Companion* March 6, 1964: 12.

" 'Do Not Sin Again,' " *Covenant Companion* March 13, 1964: 12.

"Of Missions and Men," *Covenant Companion* March 20, 1964: 12.

"Happy Ending," *Covenant Companion* March 27, 1964: 12.

"The Covenant Church and Merger," *Covenant Companion* April 3, 1964: 4-6.

"Stealth," *Covenant Companion* April 3, 1964: 12.

"Balance and Imbalance," *Covenant Companion* April 10, 1964: 12.

"Peanuts," *Covenant Companion* April 17, 1964: 12.

"Community of Song," *Covenant Companion* April 24, 1964: 6,7.

"Botticelli and the Fly," *Covenant Companion* April 24, 1964: 12.

"Peculiar Witness," *Covenant Companion* May 1, 1964: 12.

"The Tall Tale," *Covenant Companion* May 8, 1964: 12.

"The Altar of Perfume," *Covenant Companion* May 15, 1964: 12.

"The Haunted House," *Covenant Companion* May 22, 1964: 12.

"Heart's Desire," *Covenant Companion* May 29, 1964: 12.

"The Midas Touch," *Covenant Companion* June 5, 1964: 12.

"Cheap, Cheap," *Covenant Companion* June 12, 1964: 12.

"I'm Sick of 'Freedom,' " *Covenant Companion* June 19, 1964: 12.

"Sad Hatter," *Covenant Companion* June 26, 1964: 12.

"Few to Praise," *Covenant Companion* July 3, 1964: 12.

"Place Names," *Covenant Companion* July 17, 1964: 12.

"The Noise of Your Solemn Critics," *Covenant Companion* July 31, 1964: 12.

"The Little Woman," *Covenant Companion* August 14, 1964: 12.

"The Little Woman Again," *Covenant Companion* August 28, 1964: 12.

" . . . And Gladly Teach," *Covenant Companion* September 11, 1964: 2-3.

"Reasons," *Covenant Companion* September 11, 1964: 12.

"Canonized Rebel," *Covenant Companion* September 18, 1964: 12.

"The Church without 'Her,' " *Covenant Companion* September 25, 1964: 12.

"Moracles," *Covenant Companion* October 2, 1964: 12.

"People," *Covenant Companion* October 9, 1964: 12.

"I'll Go Where You Want Me to Go," *Covenant Companion* October 16, 1964: 12.

"Dubuque," *Covenant Companion* October 23, 1964: 12.

"The Catastrophe of Silence," *Covenant Companion* October 30, 1964: 12.

"Ashamed of the Gospel?" *Covenant Companion* November 6, 1964: 12.

"Expert," *Covenant Companion* November 20, 1964: 12.

"Hour Blue," *Covenant Companion* December 4, 1964: 16.

"Green Christmas," *Covenant Companion* December 18, 1964: 16.

1965

"Paul Carlson . . . Student," *There Was a Man, His Name: Paul Carlson.* Chicago: Covenant Press, 1965: 54-62.

"Report of the Board of Directors of North Park College and Theological Seminary," *Covenant Yearbook for 1965*: 134-142. Chicago: Evangelical Covenant Church of America, 1965.

"His Master's Voice," *Covenant Companion* January 1, 1965: 16.

"On Second Thought," *Covenant Companion* January 15, 1965: 16.

"Cult of Despair," *Covenant Companion* January 29, 1965: 16.

"Problems," *Covenant Companion* February 12, 1965: 16.

"Terror to Crime," *Covenant Companion* February 26, 1965: 16.

"Untrue Bounce," *Covenant Companion* March 12, 1965: 16.

"People," *Covenant Companion* March 26, 1965: 16.

"My Brother's Keeper," *Covenant Companion* April 9, 1965: 16.

"Unholy Simplicity," *Covenant Companion* April 23, 1965: 16.

"The Restrainer," *Covenant Companion* May 7, 1965: 16.

"Seven Great Minutes of Sharing," *Covenant Companion* May 21, 1965: 16.

"Operation Protest," *North Park College News* 45 (24) June 4, 1965: 2.

"Long Live the King," *Covenant Companion* June 4, 1965: 16.

"Hot Potato," *Covenant Companion* June 18, 1965: 16.

"The Theological Posture of the Seminary and Covenant Faith: An Address to the Covenant Ministerium, Chicago, Illinois. June 21, 1965," Chicago: North Park Theological Seminary, 1965. [Held in Mellander Library, North Park Theological Seminary.]

"I Love Her under God," *Covenant Companion* July 2, 1965: 3-5. [See entry for *The Chaplain*, August 1965.]

"Happy Returns?" *Covenant Companion* July 2, 1965: 16.

"George MacDonald and the Upper Peninsula," *Covenant Companion* July 16, 1965: 16.

"Reflections on a Cinder," *Covenant Companion* July 30, 1965: 12.

"Black Sheep," *Covenant Companion* August 13, 1965: 12.

"Summer Sunday Evening Series, 1965." Sponsored by the Covenant Churches of the Northside of Chicago. Chicago, 1965. [Taped sermon, August 15, 1965]

"Your Humble Obedient Servant," *Covenant Companion* August 27, 1965: 12.

"I Love Her under God," *The Chaplain* 22 (4) August 1965: 14-20. [Reprinted in booklet form, Chicago: North Park College and Theological Seminary, n.d.]

"The Son Come to Himself," *Covenant Companion* September 10, 1965: 8-9,24.

"Continuing Education," *Covenant Companion* September 10, 1965: 16.

"The Influence of Pietism on Social Action," *Moravian Theological Seminary Bulletin.* Fall 1965: 45-56.

"Pietism and Its Relevance to the Modern World," *Moravian Theological Seminary Bulletin.* Fall 1965: 32-44.

"Optics," *Covenant Companion* September 24, 1965: 16.

"The Secular Theology of Mary Poppins," *Covenant Companion* October 8, 1965: 16.

"Denatured," *Covenant Companion* October 22, 1965: 16.

"Yes and No," *Covenant Companion* November 5, 1965: 16.

"All Souls," *Covenant Companion* November 19, 1965: 16.

"That Heavenly Half Hour," *Covenant Companion* December 3, 1965: 16.

"Oh, to Live in a Time with Clear Colors, When the Ministers Believed," by Olav Hartman. [Reprint of excerpt.] Translated by Karl A. Olsson. *Christianity Today* 10 December 3, 1965: 5-7.

"The Joyous Vision," *Covenant Companion* December 17, 1965: 16.

"Great Gulf," *Covenant Companion* December 31, 1965: 16.

1966

"Report of the Board of Directors of North Park College and Theological Seminary," *Covenant Yearbook 1966*: 112-118. Chicago: Evangelical Covenant Church of America, 1966.

"Controversy on Inspiration in the Covenant of Sweden," *Covenant Quarterly* 24 (1) 1966: 3-17.

"Något om självkritiken: de amerikanska kyrkorna," *Tro och Liv* (1) 1966: 4-9.

"Sweetness and Light: Carl Hanson as Teacher," *Covenant Quarterly* 24 (2) 1966: 13-18.

"Simple and Foolish: 1," *Covenant Companion* January 14, 1966: 16.

"Simple and Foolish: 2," *Covenant Companion* January 28, 1966: 16.

"Bones," *Covenant Companion* February 11, 1966: 16.

"Speed Kills," *Covenant Companion* February 25, 1966: 16.

"The Old Morality and the New." Tape recording of paper delivered at the Conference on Christian Higher Education, March 4, 1966. Recording held in Covenant Archives: Audio-Visual Collection.

"Acoustic Perfume," *Covenant Companion* March 11, 1966: 16.

"Education's Challenge," *The Viking Voice* 7 (11) March 18, 1966: 3.

"Honest . . . " *Covenant Companion* March 25, 1966: 16.

"Give Us Victories," *Covenant Companion* April 8, 1966: 16.

"Vision of Consequence," *Covenant Companion* April 22, 1966: 16.

"Hell's Suburbs," *Covenant Companion* May 6, 1966: 16.

"The Ferry," *Covenant Companion* May 20, 1966: 16.

"Limbo," *Covenant Companion* June 3, 1966: 16.

"Worm's-eye view," *Covenant Companion* June 17, 1966: 16.

"The Immoralists: 1," *Covenant Companion* July 1, 1966: 16.

"The Immoralists: 2," *Covenant Companion* July 15, 1966: 16.

"The Immoralists: 3," *Covenant Companion* July 29, 1966: 12.

"The Gluttonous," *Covenant Companion* August 12, 1966: 12.

"To Keep and to Squander," *Covenant Companion* August 26, 1966: 12.

"Our Fears and Hopes," *Covenant Companion* September 9, 1966: 4-5.

"Rage and Outrage," *Covenant Companion* September 9, 1966: 16.

"Defiance," *Covenant Companion* September 23, 1966: 16.

"Hot Blood," *Covenant Companion* October 7, 1966: 16.

"Maimed Rites," *Covenant Companion* October 21, 1966: 16.

"Waste of Shame," *Covenant Companion* November 4, 1966: 16.

"A Regenerate Church: Is It a Necessity Today?" *Covenant Companion* November 18, 1966: 8-10.

"Letter from Spain: 1," *Covenant Companion* November 18, 1966: 16.

"Letter from Spain: 2," *Covenant Companion* December 2, 1966: 16.

"Letter from Spain: 3," *Covenant Companion* December 16, 1966: 16.

"Perhaps," *Covenant Companion* December 30, 1966: 16.

1967

Pietismen. Stockholm: Gummessons, 1967.

"Report of the Board of Directors of North Park College and Theological Seminary," *Covenant Yearbook 1967*: 124-134. Chicago: Evangelical Covenant Church of America, 1967.

"Letter from Italy," *Covenant Companion* January 13, 1967: 16.

"Letter in General," *Covenant Companion* January 27, 1967: 16.

"Letter from Italy: 2," *Covenant Companion* February 10, 1967: 16.

"Letter from Sweden: 1," *Covenant Companion* February 24, 1967: 16.

"Letter from Sweden: 2," *Covenant Companion* March 10, 1967: 16.

"Letter from Sweden: 3," *Covenant Companion* March 24, 1967: 16.

"Letter from 'Die Maur' (The Wall)," *Covenant Companion* April 7, 1967: 30-31.

"Crisis in Mission Identity," *Covenant Companion* April 21, 1967: 4-6.

"Letter from Turkey," *Covenant Companion* April 21, 1967: 30-31.

"The Muted Church," *Covenant Companion* May 5, 1967: 30-31.

"Flies," *Covenant Companion* May 19, 1967: 30-31.

"The Cult of Ann Landers," *Covenant Companion* June 2, 1967: 30-31.

"Do the Boys Carry It Away?" *Covenant Companion* June 16, 1967: 30-31.

" 'Then I don't feel so bad,' " *Covenant Companion* June 30, 1967: 30-31.

"What Good People Need," *Covenant Companion* July 14, 1967: 30-31.

"The Oil of Gladness," *Covenant Companion* July 28, 1967: 22-23.

"The Booze Culture," *Covenant Companion* August 11, 1967: 22-23.

"The Tailor Re-tailored," *Covenant Companion* August 25, 1967: 22-23.

"Ways and Means of Money," *Covenant Companion* September 8, 1967: 4-7.

"Be Angry and Sin Not," *Covenant Companion* September 8, 1967: 30-31.

"On Being a Greek in the Forest," *Covenant Companion* September 22, 1967: 30-31.

"Prayer at Washington Cathedral," *The Chaplain* 24 (5) 1967: Back Cover.

"Feedback," *Covenant Companion* October 6, 1967: 30-31.

"Pike's Peak," *Covenant Companion* October 20, 1967: 28-29.

"Alcohol Problems," *Covenant Companion* November 3, 1967: 30-31.

"The Football Game," *Covenant Companion* November 17, 1967: 28-29.

"Reflections on the Chaplaincy," *The Chaplain* 24 (6) 1967: 3-6.

"Only One Door," *Covenant Companion* December 1, 1967: 30-31.

"The Theologian at Christmas," *Covenant Companion* December 15, 1967: 30-31.

"New Wine," *Covenant Companion* December 29, 1967: 6-7.

"If Thou Be Near . . . " *Covenant Companion* December 29, 1967: 30-31.

1968

The God Game. Cleveland: World Publishing Co., 1968.

Sju Laster och Sju Dygder. [Translation of *Seven Sins and Seven Virtues*], Karl A. Olsson. Translated by Birgitta Nelson. Stockholm: Gummessons, 1968.

"Report of the Board of Directors of North Park College and Theological Seminary," *Covenant Yearbook 1968*: 105-114. Chicago: Evangelical Covenant Church of America, 1968.

"The Tortured Planet," *Covenant Companion* January 12, 1968: 30-31.

"Splendor," *Covenant Companion* January 26, 1968: 30-31.

"The Cougar's Bite," *Covenant Companion* February 9, 1968: 30-31.

"Anatomy of a Faith," *Covenant Companion* February 23, 1968: 30-31.

"The End of the Ages," *Covenant Companion* March 8, 1968: 30-31.

"A Little While," *Covenant Companion* March 22, 1968: 30-31.

"Plain and Fancy," *Covenant Companion* April 5, 1968: 30-31.

"Pen in Hand," *Covenant Companion* April 19, 1968: 30-31.

"Guess Who's Coming to Stay with Us," *Covenant Companion* May 3, 1968: 30-31.

"I Wander Lonely," *Covenant Companion* May 17, 1968: 30-31.

"Overheard," *Covenant Companion* May 31, 1968: 30-31.

" 'Blessed Are You Poor,' " *Covenant Companion* June 14, 1968: 30-31.

"Good Night, Sweet Prince," *Covenant Companion* July 1, 1968: 22-23.

"The Big Simple," *Covenant Companion* July 15, 1968: 30-31.

"Brave Men—Living and Dead," *The Chaplain* 25 (4) 1968: 3-6.

"Bare Minimum," *Covenant Companion* August 1, 1968: 22-23.

"Those Friends Thou Hast . . . " *Covenant Companion* August 15, 1968: 22-23.

" 'Learn of Me': the Challenge of Change," *Covenant Companion* September 1, 1968: 13-15.

"Despair under the Elms," *Covenant Companion* September 1, 1968: 30-31.

"Collision Course," *Covenant Companion* September 15, 1968: 30-31.

"Words without Moorings," *Covenant Companion* October 1, 1968: 30-31.

"Unworthy Servants," *Covenant Companion* October 15, 1968: 30-31.

"Installation of Glenn Paul Anderson (Prayer), October 20, 1968." Covenant Archives: Karl A. Olsson Papers.

"Blowing Bubbles," *Covenant Companion* November 1, 1968: 30-31.

"Time Bomb," *Covenant Companion* November 15, 1968: 30-31.

"Security," *Covenant Companion* December 1, 1968: 30-31.

"The Extravagant Claim," *Covenant Companion* December 15, 1968: 30-31.

1969

"Report of the Board of Directors of North Park College and Theological Seminary," *Covenant Yearbook 1969*: 90-96. Chicago: Evangelical Covenant Church of America, 1969.

"Damascus," *Covenant Companion* January 1, 1969: 30-31.

"The Wall," *Covenant Companion* January 15, 1969: 30-31.

"Hem till Guds Jerusalem," music/lyrics by J. P. Gronhamn, translated by KAO for the North Park College Choir, January 15, 1969. Covenant Archives: Karl A. Olsson Papers.

"Jesus från Nasaret går här fram," lyrics by A. Frostenson, translated by KAO for the North Park College Choir, January 15, 1969. Covenant Archives: Karl A. Olsson Papers.

"Telephone Time," *Covenant Companion* February 1, 1969: 30-31.

"The Hand That Made Us," *Covenant Companion* February 15, 1969: 30-31.

"Deadly Serious," *Covenant Companion* March 1, 1969: 30-31.

"North Park College Academy: Position Paper." Covenant Archives: Karl A. Olsson Papers.

"Academy Traditions End—Memories Live On" [portion of position paper prepared by KAO], *North Park College News* 49 (16) March 14, 1969: 1,3.

"Uncle Wiggly," *Covenant Companion* March 15, 1969: 30-31.

"Knight of the Woeful Figure," *Covenant Companion* April 1, 1969: 30-31.

"Scape Goat," *Covenant Companion* April 15, 1969: 30-31.

"The Joy of Irrelevance," *Covenant Companion* May 1, 1969: 30-31.

"Se, Jesus burit all vår synd," lyrics by Selma Sundelius-Lagerström, translated by KAO for the North Park College Choir, May 5, 1969. Covenant Archives: Karl A. Olsson Papers.

"Det givs en tid för andra tider," lyrics by Lina Sandell, translated by KAO for the North Park College Choir, May 5, 1969. Covenant Archives: Karl A. Olsson Papers.

"Brave Men—Living and Dead," *Covenant Companion* May 15, 1969: 10-11.

"The Curse of Being Unblessed," *Covenant Companion* May 15, 1969: 30-31.

"Prayer for the Graduates (North Park Commencement 1969)." Covenant Archives: Karl A. Olsson Papers.

"Charge to the Graduates (North Park Commencement 1969)." Covenant Archives: Karl A. Olsson Papers.

"Self-Reliance in Spring," *Covenant Companion* June 1, 1969: 30-31.

" 'They're Going for the Big Ones,' " *Covenant Companion* June 15, 1969: 30-31.

"Statement on the Closing of North Park College Academy." Covenant Archives: Karl A. Olsson Papers.

"For All the Saints . . . " *Covenant Companion* July 1, 1969: 22-23.

"Manifesto," *Covenant Companion* July 15, 1969: 22-23.

"I Love Thy Church O Lord," *Covenant Companion* August 1, 1969: 22-23.

"Disposables," *Covenant Companion* August 15, 1969: 22-23.

"One Cubit to His Stature," *Covenant Companion* September 1, 1969: 30-31.

"Being & Becoming: the Matter of Integrity," *Covenant Companion* September 15, 1969: 3-5.

"Mowing," *Covenant Companion* September 15, 1969: 30-31.

"Ichabod and the Packers," *Covenant Companion* October 1, 1969: 30-31.

"Wow!" *Covenant Companion* October 15, 1969: 30-31.

"Pouch People," *Covenant Companion* November 1, 1969: 30-31.

"The Hatter Revisited," *Covenant Companion* November 15, 1969: 30-31.

"Ugly, Ugly," *Covenant Companion* December 1, 1969: 30-31.

"Pearl Gray," *Covenant Companion* December 15, 1969: 30-31.

1970

Att Leka Gud. [Translation of *The God Game*] Stockholm: Gummessons, 1970.

"Report of the Board of Directors of North Park College and Theological Seminary," *Covenant Yearbook 1970*: 101-107. Chicago: Evangelical Covenant Church of America, 1970.

"The Shape of the Future for the Church College," *Centennial Review* 14 (1) 1970: 57-70.

"What Was Pietism?" *Covenant Quarterly* 28 (1): 3-14.

"The Gift," *Covenant Companion* January 1, 1970: 30-31.

"Demonic Advent," *Covenant Companion* January 15, 1970: 30-31.

"Dirge for a Decade," *Covenant Companion* February 1, 1970: 30-31.

"Congo Letter," *Covenant Companion* February 15, 1970: 30-31.

"Congo Letter: II," *Covenant Companion* March 1, 1970: 30-31.

"Karl A. Olsson Resigns North Park Presidency" [Text of letter of resignation], *Covenant Companion* March 15, 1970: 17.

"Congo Letter III: The Lost Corner," *Covenant Companion* March 15, 1970: 30-31.

"Congo Letter IV: Black Christ," *Covenant Companion* April 1, 1970: 30-31.

"I Want to Go Home Again," *Covenant Companion* April 15, 1970: 30-31.

"King," *Covenant Companion* May 1, 1970: 30-31.

Letter to Pastors and Church Chairmen regarding events on the North Park campus relating to Kent State and Cambodia, May 11, 1970. Covenant Archives: Karl A. Olsson Papers.

"The Two Faces of Adam," *Covenant Companion* May 15, 1970: 30-31.

"The Charge to the Class of 1970," Covenant Archives: Karl A. Olsson Papers.

"A Nice Day," *Covenant Companion* June 1, 1970: 30-31.

"Bilge on Its Way Up," *Covenant Companion* June 15, 1970: 30-31.

" 'Offenses Must Needs Come,' " *Covenant Companion* July 1, 1970: 22-23.

"Check and Balance," *Covenant Companion* July 15, 1970: 22-23.

"Crime in Arcadia," *Covenant Companion* August 1, 1970: 22-23.

"Carpenter," *Covenant Companion* August 15, 1970: 22-23.

"Reforming the Reformation," *U.S. Catholic and Jubliee* 35 August 1970: 42-43.

"Pilgrimage," *Covenant Companion* September 1, 1970: 30-31.

"Pilgrimage: Ephesus," *Covenant Companion* September 15, 1970: 30-31.

"Profile of a Servant," *The Chaplain* 27 (5) 1970: 3-8.

"Pilgrimage: Athens," *Covenant Companion* October 1, 1970: 30-31.

"Pilgrimage: Istanbul," *Covenant Companion* October 15, 1970: 30-31.

"Pilgrimage: Corinth," *Covenant Companion* November 1, 1970: 30-31.

"Pilgrimage: Rome," *Covenant Companion* November 15, 1970: 30-31.

"Pilgrimage: Florence," *Covenant Companion* December 1, 1970: 30-31.

"Pilgrimage: Geneva," *Covenant Companion* December 15, 1970: 30-31.

1971

"Pilgrimage: Wittenberg," *Covenant Companion* January 1, 1970: 30-31.

"Pilgrimage: Aldersgate," *Covenant Companion* January 15, 1971: 30-31.

"Leviathan Unleashed," *Covenant Companion* February 1, 1971: 30-31.

"Analysis and the Last Judgment," *Covenant Companion* February 15, 1971: 30-31.

"Our Earthly House of This Tabernacle . . . " *Covenant Companion* March 1, 1971: 30-31.

"The Turn to Jesus," *Covenant Companion* March 15, 1971: 30-31.

"The Cooling of Pretension," *Covenant Companion* April 1, 1971: 30-31.

"Trust," *Covenant Companion* April 15, 1971: 30-31.

"It's All Right To Be Merely Human," *Faith At Work* 84 (2) 1971: 22-23.

"I Am Curious (Red, White, and Blue)," *Covenant Companion* May 1, 1971: 30-31.

"Engineer and Artist," *Covenant Companion* May 15, 1971: 30-31.

"The Giant Killer," *Covenant Companion* June 1, 1971: 30-31.

"Cerebus in Paradise," *Covenant Companion* June 15, 1971: 30-31.

"A Future to Hope In," *Faith At Work* 84 (3) 1971: 28-29.

"I Didn't Do It," *Covenant Companion* July 1, 1971: 22-23.

"Critics and Criticism," *Covenant Companion* July 15, 1971: 22-23.

"The Path of the Just," *Covenant Companion* August 1, 1971: 22-23.

"What We Are All About," *Covenant Companion* August 15, 1971: 22-23.

"Similarities and Differences in the Churches of the Federation—America," paper delivered at The International Federation of Free Evangelical Churches Theological Conference, August 29—September 4, 1971. [Held in Mellander Library, North Park Theological Seminary.]

"Righteous Empire," *Covenant Companion* September 1, 1971: 3-5.

"A Touch of Madness," *Covenant Companion* September 1, 1971: 30-31.

"Buttons for Little People . . . " *Covenant Companion* September 15, 1971: 30-31.

"Bittersweet," *Covenant Companion* October 1, 1971: 30-31.

"Get Up and Do It Again," *Covenant Companion* October 15, 1971: 30-31.

"The Snake Is My Brother," *Faith At Work* 84 (5) 1971: 24-25.

"The Jesus People in the Long Stretch," *Covenant Companion* November 1, 1971: 28-29.

"On Age," *Covenant Companion* November 15, 1971: 30-31.

"Recollections of . . . Childhood," *Covenant Companion* December 1, 1971: 30-31.

"Justice in a Christmas Card," *Covenant Companion* December 15, 1971: 30-31.

1972

Come to the Party: An Invitation to a Freer Life Style. Waco, Texas: Word Books, 1972.

"Come, Let Us Praise Him," hymn by Lina Sandell, translated by KAO, *Hymns of Scandinavian Heritage*. Chicago: Covenant Press, 1972. No. 1.

"When All the World Is Sleeping," hymn by Lina Sandell, translated by KAO, *Hymns of Scandinavian Heritage*. Chicago: Covenant Press, 1972. No. 5.

"O Let Your Soul Now Be Filled with Gladness," hymn by Peter Jonsson Aschan, translated by KAO, *Hymns of Scandinavian Heritage*. Chicago: Covenant Press, 1972. No. 11.

"Jesus, Jesus, Name Most Precious," hymn by Carl Boberg, translated by KAO, *Hymns of Scandinavian Heritage*. Chicago: Covenant Press, 1972. No. 12.

"In the Springtime Fair," hymn by Lina Sandell, translated by KAO, *Hymns of Scandinavian Heritage*. Chicago: Covenant Press, 1972. No. 13.

"Now Shine a Thousand Candles Bright," hymn by Emmy Kohler, translated by KAO, *Hymns of Scandinavian Heritage*. Chicago: Covenant Press, 1972. No. 22.

"The Groaning of America," *Covenant Companion* January 1, 1972: 30-31.

"What Is Man?" *Covenant Companion* January 15, 1972: 30-31.

"Moral Disarmament," *Covenant Companion* February 1, 1972: 30-31.

"The Decline of Lutfisk," *Covenant Companion* February 15, 1972: 30-31.

"Posture of Perfection," *Faith At Work* 85 (1) 1972: 32-33.

" 'The Endless Games . . . ' " *Covenant Companion* March 1, 1972: 30-31.

"Jesus and Institutions," *Covenant Companion* March 15, 1972: 30-31.

"When Honor's at the Stake," *Covenant Companion* April 1, 1972: 30-31.

"Present Shock," *Covenant Companion* April 15, 1972: 30-31.

"The Party Is for You," *Faith At Work* 85 (2) 1972: 34,35.

"The Computers," *Covenant Companion* May 1, 1972: 30-31.

"all those capitals," *Covenant Companion* May 15, 1972: 30-31.

"Foreign Objects," *Covenant Companion* June 1, 1972: 30-31.

"Meat and Poison," *Covenant Companion* June 15, 1972: 30-31.

"What Is Man?" *Faith At Work* 85 (3) 1972: 36-37.

"Imitation," *Covenant Companion* July 1, 1972: 22-23.

"The Inverted Pyramid," *Covenant Companion* July 15, 1972: 22-23.

"The Well of the Past," *Covenant Companion* August 1, 1972: 22-23.

"The Hitchhikers," *Covenant Companion* August 15, 1972: 22-23.

"Requiem for a Dead Father," *Covenant Companion* September 1, 1972: 30-31.

"No Fault," *Covenant Companion* September 15, 1972: 30-31.

"On Being a Grandfather," *Covenant Companion* October 1, 1972: 30-31.

"All Is Discovered," *Covenant Companion* October 15, 1972: 30-31.

"The Castle of Indolence," *Covenant Companion* November 1, 1972: 30-31.

"Taxes and Death," *Covenant Companion* November 15, 1972: 30-31.

"Dialogues with Myself: My Body," *Covenant Companion* December 1, 1972: 30-31.

"Dialogues with Myself: My Body (cont.)," *Covenant Companion* December 15, 1972: 30-31.

1973

"When All the World Is Sleeping," hymn by Lina Sandell, translated by KAO, *The Covenant Hymnal.* Chicago: Covenant Press, 1973. No. 48.

"Now Shine a Thousand Candles Bright," hymn by Emmy Kohler, translated by J. Irving Erickson and KAO, *The Covenant Hymnal.* Chicago, Covenant Press, 1973. No. 145.

"Come, Let Us Praise Him," hymn by Lina Sandell, translated by KAO, *The Covenant Hymnal.* Chicago: Covenant Press, 1973. No. 244.

"Jesus, Jesus, Name Most Precious," hymn by Carl Boberg, translated by KAO, *The Covenant Hymnal.* Chicago: Covenant Press, 1973. No. 252.

"In the Springtime Fair," hymn by Lina Sandell, translated by KAO, *The Covenant Hymnal.* Chicago: Covenant Press, 1973. No. 298.

"O Let Your Soul Now Be Filled with Gladness," hymn by Peter Jönsson Aschan, translated by KAO, *The Covenant Hymnal.* Chicago: Covenant Press, 1973. No. 423.

"Att vakna upp ur Sömnen: Rom. 13: 11-14," *Tro och Liv* (1) 1973: 2-8.

"Dialogues with Myself: The Will," *Covenant Companion* January 1, 1973: 30-31.

"Dialogue with Myself: The Will," *Covenant Companion* January 15, 1973: 30-31.

"Dialogues with Myself: Intellect," *Covenant Companion* February 1, 1973: 30-31.

"Dialogues with Myself: Intellect," *Covenant Companion* February 15, 1973: 30-31.

"The Liberation of the Particular," *Faith At Work* 86 (1) 1973: 12,27.

"Dialogues with Myself: My Conscience," *Covenant Companion* March 1, 1973: 30-31.

"Dear Inwit," *Covenant Companion* March 15, 1973: 30-31.

"Dialogues with Significant Others: The Doctor," *Covenant Companion* April 1, 1973: 30-31.

"Dialogues: My Doctor," *Covenant Companion* April 15, 1973: 31.

"Hope and Idolatry," *Faith At Work* 86 (2) April 1973: 23.

"Dialogue with My Pastor," *Covenant Companion* May 1, 1973: 31.

"Dialogue with My Pastor," *Covenant Companion* May 15, 1973: 31.

"Dialogue with My Pastor," *Covenant Companion* June 1, 1973: 31.

"Dialogue with My Pastor (IV)," *Covenant Companion* June 15, 1973: 31.

"The 'Bad' Samaritan," *Faith At Work* 86 (3) 1973: 31.

"Dialogue with the President," *Covenant Companion* July 1, 1973: 23.

"Letter on Behalf of the President," *Covenant Companion* July 15, 1973: 23.

"Letter to Mr. John Appleseed," *Covenant Companion* August 1, 1973: 23.

"Memorandum to Myself," *Covenant Companion* August 15, 1973: 19.

"Vision and Miracle," *Faith At Work* 86 (4) 1973: 27.

"Kom till Festen: mot en friare livsstil," *Tro och Liv* (3) 1973: 116-124.

"Variations on a Theme," *Covenant Companion* September 1, 1973: 29.

"A Little Gray Bird," *Covenant Companion* September 15, 1973: 29.

"Big Game," *Covenant Companion* October 1, 1973: 31.

"Wide Load," *Covenant Companion* October 15, 1973: 27.

"Redeeming the Time," *Faith At Work* 86 (5) 1973: 24.

"Casper, the Magnificent," *Covenant Companion* November 1, 1973: 29.

"No Tomorrow," *Covenant Companion* November 15, 1973: 29.

"An Old Script," *Covenant Companion* December 1, 1973: 31.

"The Burning Star," *Covenant Companion* December 15, 1973: 29.

"The Innkeeper of Nelma," *Faith At Work* 86 (6) 1973: 30.

1974

Find Yourself in the Bible: A Guide to Relational Bible Study for Small Groups. Minneapolis: Augsburg Publishing House, 1974.

"The Deed," *Covenant Companion* January 1, 1974: 29.

"Moving Parts," *Covenant Companion* January 15, 1974: 29.

"Sterilized Culture," *Covenant Companion* February 1, 1974: 29.

"Taking Sides," *Covenant Companion* February 15, 1974: 29.

"My Experience, Your Obligation?" *Faith At Work* 87 (1) 1974: 28-29.

"Clay Birds and Polka Dots," *Covenant Companion* March 1, 1974: 29.

"The Mystery of Fred," *Covenant Companion* March 15, 1974: 29.

"The Hidden Dictator," *Faith At Work* 87 (2) 1974: 26-27.

"Approaching Utopia," *Covenant Companion* April 1, 1974: 29.

"Struggling Upward," *Covenant Companion* May 1, 1974: 29.

"Apples Keep Falling on My Head," *Covenant Companion* May 15, 1974: 29.

"You See, It Was This Way," *Covenant Companion* June 1, 1974: 29.

"Reflections on a Wash Room," *Covenant Companion* June 15, 1974: 29.

"The 'Second Life,' " *Faith At Work* 87 (4) 1974: 24-25.

"Let It Be," *Covenant Companion* July 1, 1974: 21.

"Let Freedom Ring," *Covenant Companion* July 15, 1974: 21.

"Joyful, Joyful, We Adore Thee," *Covenant Companion* August 15, 1974: 21.

"Second Sight," *Faith At Work* 87 (5) 1974: 28.

"A Kind of Witchcraft," *Covenant Companion* September 1, 1974: 21.

"Trees Die at the Top," *Covenant Companion* September 15, 1974: 29.

"Free Learning," *Faith At Work* 87 (6) 1974: 32-33.

"Brave New World," *Covenant Companion* October 1, 1974: 29.

"Guilt in Eden," *Covenant Companion* October 15, 1974: 29.

"Lonely Loneliness," *Faith At Work* 87 (7) 1974: 24-25.

"A Convert from the Tempest," *Covenant Companion* November 1, 1974: 29.

" 'Let Us Put an End to Such Tales,' " *Covenant Companion* November 15, 1974: 29.

"Assembly Line Culture," *Covenant Companion* December 1, 1974: 29.

"Lord God of the Flesh," *Covenant Companion* December 15, 1974: 29.

"The Wonderment of Healing," *Faith At Work* 87 (8) 1974: 32-33.

1975

A Family of Faith: 90 Years of Covenant History. Chicago: Covenant Press, 1975.

"Open Heart Ministry," *World Vision* v.19, January 1975: 10-11.

"The God without Ears," *Covenant Companion* January 1, 1975: 29.

"Jesus Saves," *Covenant Companion* January 15, 1975: 29.

"The Birth of a Book," *Covenant Companion* February 1, 1975: 8-9.

"The Old Beds," *Covenant Companion* February 1, 1975: 29.

"Getting Ready to Live," *Covenant Companion* February 15, 1975: 29.

"Have You Received the Holy Spirit?" Evangelical Covenant Midwinter Conference, St. Paul, Minnesota, February 5-7, 1975. [Tape]

"The Power to Be And to Bless," *Faith At Work* 88 (1) 1975: 24-25.

" 'What's in a Name,' " *Covenant Companion* March 1, 1975: 29.

"Tarnished Heroes," *Covenant Companion* March 15, 1975: 29.

"Pain of Passage," *Faith At Work* 88 (2) 1975: 30-31.

"Ho Hum Humility!" *Covenant Companion* April 1, 1975: 29.

" 'Where the Spirit Is . . . ' " *Covenant Companion* April 15, 1975: 29.

"TRADITION, TRADITION!" *Faith At Work* 88 (3) 1975: 28-29.

"Basics," *Covenant Companion* May 1, 1975: 29.

"Theological Affirmation," *Covenant Companion* May 15, 1975: 29.

"Monorail," *Covenant Companion* June 1, 1975: 29.

" 'That Last Informity of Noble Mind . . . ' " *Covenant Companion* June 15, 1975: 29.

"Is the Bible True?" *Faith At Work* 88 (4) 1975: 28-29.

"Pensive Pilgrimage," *Covenant Companion* July 15, 1975: 21.

"The Lost Leader," *Covenant Companion* August 15, 1975: 21.

" 'Filthy Lucre,' " *Faith At Work* 88 (5) 1975: 24-25.

"Twenty Years," *Covenant Companion* September 1, 1975: 21.

"On Building a Gate," *Covenant Companion* September 15, 1975: 29.

"Lord of Change," *Faith At Work* 88 (6) 1975: 26.

"Goddess with Clay Feet . . . " *Covenant Companion* October 1, 1975: 29.

"Fear Not, Little Flock," *Covenant Companion* October 15, 1975: 29.

"Point, Counter-Point," *Faith At Work* 88 (7) 1975: 28-29.

"Fear of Flying," *Covenant Companion* November 1, 1975: 29.

"The Given and the Gift," *Covenant Companion* November 15, 1975: 29.

"A Tale of Two Cities," *Covenant Companion* December 1, 1975: 29.

" 'When the Time Was Right,' " *Covenant Companion* December 15, 1975: 29.

"The Family of Grace," *Faith At Work* 88 (8) 1975: 26-27.

1976

"There Breathes throughout Our Earthly Stress," lyrics by Carl Boberg, translated by KAO, *Here We Go A-Caroling*. Chicago: Covenant Press, 1976. No. 1. [reprinted in *Covenant Companion* December 15, 1979: 12.]

"To Bethlehem We Would Hasten," lyrics by Joel Blomquist, translated by KAO, *Here We Go A-Caroling*. Chicago: Covenant Press, 1976. No. 2. [reprinted in *Covenant Companion* December 15, 1979: 13.]

"Now Shine a Thousand Candles Bright," lyrics by Nils Frykman, translated by KAO, *Here We Go A-Caroling*. Chicago: Covenant Press, 1976. No. 6.

"A Child to Us Has Been Given," lyrics by Betty Ehrenborg-Posse, translated by KAO, *Here We Go A-Caroling*. Chicago: Covenant Press, 1976. No. 14.

"To Us a Child Is Born This Day," lyrics by Martin Luther and Olaus Martini, translated by KAO, *Here We Go A-Caroling*. Chicago: Covenant Press, 1976. No. 15.

"Blowing the Cover," *Covenant Companion* January 1, 1976: 29.

"Listerine by the Throat," *Covenant Companion* January 15, 1976: 29.

" 'Lead, Kindly Light,' " *Covenant Companion* February 1, 1976: 29.

"Power of Prophecy," *Covenant Companion* February 15, 1976: 29.

"Land That I Love," *Covenant Companion* 89 (1) February 1976: 28-29.

"Hindsight," *Covenant Companion* March 1, 1976: 29.

" 'Such a Tender Ball as the Eye,' " *Covenant Companion* March 15, 1976: 29.

"The Given and the Gifts," *Faith At Work* 89 (2) 1976: 24-25.

"Kicks," *Covenant Companion* April 1, 1976: 29.

"The Child and the Man," *Covenant Companion* April 15, 1976: 29.

"Ideas for Groups," *Faith At Work* 89 (3) 1976: 19-22.

"The Cafeteria," *Faith At Work* 89 (3) 1976: 24-25.

"Family Album," *Covenant Companion* May 1, 1976: 29.

"Able to Comfort," by Nils Mjönes, translation and introduction by KAO. *Covenant Companion* May 15, 1976: 10-11.

"Good Friday, 1976, Riding Westward," *Covenant Companion* May 15, 1976: 29.

" 'Things Old and New,' " *Covenant Companion* June 1, 1976: 29.

"Confessions of a Book Lover," *Covenant Companion* June 15, 1976: 29.

"Intermittent Miracle," *Faith At Work* 89 (4) 1976: 24-26.

"A Citizen of Two Worlds," by Nils Mjönes, translated by KAO, *Faith At Work* 89 (4) 1976: 32-33.

"The Ecstasy and Agony of Books," *Covenant Companion* July 1, 1976: 21.

"Fear of Failure," *Covenant Companion* August 1, 1976: 21.

"In Celebration Of . . . " *Covenant Companion* August 15, 1976: 21.

"Cuckooland: Perils and Pratfalls of the Relational Lifestyle," *Faith At Work* 89 (5) 1976: 24-25.

"Twice-Born Hymns—a Review," *Covenant Companion* September 15, 1976: 6-7.

"Ralph Nader and the Grand Inquisitor," *Covenant Companion* September 15, 1976: 29.

"The Twin Towers," *Faith At Work* 89 (6) 1976: 24.

"Austerity," *Covenant Companion* October 1, 1976: 29.

"Cuckooland," *Covenant Companion* October 15, 1976: 12-13. [Reprint from *Faith At Work.*]

"Horses," *Covenant Companion* October 15, 1976: 29.

"The Year of the Mouse," *Covenant Companion* November 1, 1976: 29.

"Good Buddy!" *Covenant Companion* November 15, 1976: 29.

"Computer Land," *Covenant Companion* December 1, 1976: 29.

" 'No Crying He Makes,' " *Covenant Companion* December 15, 1976: 29.

"Even Greater," *Faith At Work* 89 (8) 1976: 24-25.

1977

Meet Me on the Patio: New Relational Bible Studies for Individuals and Groups. Minneapolis: Augsburg Publishing House, 1977.

"Dialogues with Myself: The Will," *Covenant Companion* January 1, 1977: 29.

"A Tale of Two Cities, Dialogue with Myself: The Will," *Covenant Companion* January 15, 1977: 29.

"Celebrating the Feast," *Covenant Companion* February 1, 1977: 29.

"History as Hope," *Covenant Companion* February 15, 1977: 29.

"Taking What Doesn't Belong to Me," *Faith At Work* 90 (1) 1977: 24-25.

"The Priestly Role," *Covenant Companion* March 1, 1977: 29.

"Memory of a Washout," *Covenant Companion* March 15, 1977: 29.

"The Free Gift Came," *Faith At Work* 90 (2) 1977: 24-25.

"Tower of Babel," *Covenant Companion* April 1, 1977: 29.

"Redress of Grievance," *Covenant Companion* April 15, 1977: 29.

"Making Mortar," *Faith At Work* 90 (3) April 1977: 24.

"The Man Gave Names to All . . . " *Covenant Companion* May 1, 1977: 29.

"A Piece of String, Part I," *Covenant Companion* May 15, 1977: 29.

"A Piece of String, Part II," *Covenant Companion* June 1, 1977: 29.

"Caring for the May Apples," *Covenant Companion* June 15, 1977: 23.

"Relics," *Covenant Companion* July 1, 1977: 23.

"Motion in Time and Space," *Covenant Companion* August 1, 1977: 23.

"Some Kind of Victory," *Covenant Companion* September 1, 1977: 23.

" 'Moider' on the Trans-Siberian Express," *Covenant Companion* September 15, 1977: 29.

"The Trans-Siberian," *Covenant Companion* October 1, 1977: 29.

"Back Home Again," *Covenant Companion* October 15, 1977: 29.

"Contrasts," *Covenant Companion* November 1, 1977: 29.

"Balance and Imbalance," *Covenant Companion* November 15, 1977: 29.

"Welcoming the Child," *Covenant Companion* December 1, 1977: 29.

" 'He Appeared Also to Me,' " *Covenant Companion* December 15, 1977: 29.

1978

"Whose'er Anywhere," by Nils Frykman, translated by KAO, *New Hymns & Translations.* Chicago: Covenant Press, 1978.

No. 12.

"Poor, but Rich Withal," by Lina Sandell, translated by KAO, *New Hymns & Translations.* Chicago: Covenant Press, 1978. No. 15.

"To Say Good-Bye," *Covenant Companion* January 1, 1978: 29.

"The Pomp of Yesterday," *Covenant Companion* January 15, 1978: 29.

"The Second Day of Christmas," *Covenant Companion* February 1, 1978: 29.

"The Book Flood," *Covenant Companion* February 15, 1978: 29.

"Winter Wonderland," *Covenant Companion* March 1, 1978: 29.

"The Emperor's Clothes," *Covenant Companion* March 15, 1978: 29.

"Contrasts on the Tube," *Covenant Companion* April 1, 1978: 29.

"Happiness Is . . . " *Covenant Companion* April 15, 1978: 29.

"The Old Order Changes . . . " *Covenant Companion* May 1, 1978: 29.

"I'm Going Fishing," *Covenant Companion* May 15, 1978: 29.

" 'Sumer Is Icumen In,' " *Covenant Companion* June 1, 1978: 29.

"The Foolish Man Built . . . " *Covenant Companion* June 15, 1978: 29.

"Selective Cream-Puffism," *Covenant Companion* July 1, 1978: 21.

"Miracle," *Covenant Companion* August 1, 1978: 21.

"On Being Sixty-Five," *Covenant Companion* September 1, 1978: 21.

"Recking Your Own Rede," *Covenant Companion* September 15, 1978: 29.

"The Singing Planet," *Covenant Companion* October 1, 1978: 29.

"Uninhabited Ruins," *Covenant Companion* October 15, 1978: 29.

"The Need of a Devil," *Covenant Companion* November 1, 1978: 29.

"Billy Graham in Scandinavia," *Covenant Companion* November 15, 1978: 29.

"Seasons of Mist and Mellow Fruitfulness," *Covenant Companion* December 1, 1978: 29.

"Hands," *Covenant Companion* December 15, 1978: 29.

"The Vulnerable Jesus," [excerpt from *When The Road Bends*], *Faith At Work* 91 (8) 1978: 2-8,32 + .

1979

When the Road Bends: A Book About the Pain and Joy of Passage. Minneapolis: Augsburg Publishing House, 1979.

Building Community. Columbia, Md.: Resources Unlimited, 1979. [Cassette, 70 min.]. With Beryl Little.

"Dream of Splendor," in *Clipper Ship and Covered Wagon: Essays from the Swedish Pioneer Historical Quarterly,* edited by H. Arnold Barton. New York: Arno Press, 1979. [See entry for January 1961.]

"The City of Love," *Covenant Companion* January 1, 1979: 29.

"Solidarity," *Covenant Companion* January 15, 1979: 29.

"Solidarity (cont.)," *Covenant Companion* February 1, 1979: 29.

"A Christmas Carol," *Covenant Companion* February 15, 1979: 29.

"Confessions of a Book Lover," *Covenant Companion* March 1, 1979: 29.

" 'England's Green and Pleasant Land,' " *Covenant Companion* March 15, 1979: 29. [Includes notice of heart attack suffered by KAO in Copenhagen.]

"The Child and the Man," *Covenant Companion* April 1, 1979: 29. [Reprinted from the April 15, 1976 *Companion*.]

"Kicks," *Covenant Companion* April 15, 1979: 29. [Reprinted from the April 1, 1976 *Companion*. Includes update on KAO's medical condition.]

"Blowing the Cover," *Covenant Companion* May 1, 1979: 29. [Reprinted from the January 1, 1976 *Companion*. Further update on KAO's condition.]

"Hindsight," *Covenant Companion* May 15, 1979: 29. [Reprinted from the March 1, 1976 *Companion*.]

"Under the Mercy," *Covenant Companion* June 1, 1979: 29.

"No-no in Paradise," *Covenant Companion* June 15, 1979: 29.

"Event and Process," *Covenant Companion* July 1, 1979: 29.

"The Beautiful Duckling," *Covenant Companion* August 1, 1979: 21.

"The Return of the King: I," *Covenant Companion* September 1, 1979: 21.

"The Return of the King: II," *Covenant Companion* September 15, 1979: 29.

"The Unheroic Hero," *Covenant Companion* October 1, 1979: 29.

"Running without a Goal," *Covenant Companion* October 15, 1979: 29.

"A Man Who Built His House," *Covenant Companion* November 1, 1979: 29.

"The Mystery," *Covenant Companion* November 15, 1979: 29.

"The Family," *Covenant Companion* December 1, 1979: 29.

"Mosses from an Old Manse," *Covenant Companion* December 15, 1979: 29.

1980

"Camelot Revisited," *Covenant Companion* January 1, 1980: 29.

" 'They Kindled a Fire . . . ' " *Covenant Companion* January 15, 1980: 29.

"The Green Locomotive," *Covenant Companion* February 1, 1980: 29.

"Good Eyes and Evil," *Covenant Companion* February 15, 1980: 29.

"Fiasco," *Covenant Companion* March 1, 1980: 29.

"Journey to the End of Time," *Covenant Companion* March 15, 1980: 29.

"Dutch Masters," *Covenant Companion* April 1, 1980: 29.

"The Little Teacher," *Covenant Companion* April 15, 1980: 29.

"The Counterpoint Questions," *Covenant Companion* May 1, 1980: 29.

"The Dream That Won't Die," *Covenant Companion* May 15, 1980: 29.

" 'A Night and a Day I Have Been in the Deep . . . ' " *Covenant Companion* June 1, 1980: 29.

"The Growing Need for Authority," *Covenant Companion* June 15, 1980: 29.

"Irreversibles," *Covenant Companion* July 1, 1980: 21.

"The Annual Meeting," *Covenant Companion* August 1, 1980: 21.

"The Superior Mousetrap," *Covenant Companion* September 1, 1980: 21.

"Rough Places Plain (Brule Lake)," *Covenant Companion* October 1, 1980: 29.

"My Body, My Friend," *Covenant Companion* October 15, 1980: 29.

"The Body as Likeness," *Covenant Companion* November 1, 1980: 29.

"The Body and Its Head," *Covenant Companion* November 15, 1980: 29.

"The Submission of the Body," *Covenant Companion* December 1, 1980: 29.

"The Body as Teacher," *Covenant Companion* December 15, 1980: 29.

1981

"Rational Theology: An Evangelistic Theology." Westerdahl Lectures, North Park Theological Seminary, 1981. [Tape]

"The Body as Power I," *Covenant Companion* January 1, 1981: 29.

"The Body as Power II," *Covenant Companion* January 15, 1981: 29.

"The Body and Denial," *Covenant Companion* February 1, 1981: 29.

"Japan Interlude: I," *Covenant Companion* February 15, 1981: 29.

"Japan Interlude: II," *Covenant Companion* March 1, 1981: 29.

"Japan Interlude: III," *Covenant Companion* March 15, 1981: 29.

"Japan Interlude: IV," *Covenant Companion* April 1, 1981: 29.

"Nemesis or Promise," *Covenant Companion* April 15, 1981: 29.

"The Body's Speech," *Covenant Companion* May 1, 1981: 29.

"The Body's Rapture," *Covenant Companion* May 15, 1981: 29.

"Sweden Interlude: I," *Covenant Companion* June 1, 1981: 29.

"Sweden Interlude: II," *Covenant Companion* June 15, 1981: 29.

"Sweden Interlude III: Miracle," *Covenant Companion* July 1, 1981: 21.

"Sweden Interlude: Foundations," *Covenant Companion* August 1, 1981: 21.

"Sweden Interlude: Foundations," *Covenant Companion* September 1, 1981: 21.

"The Man with the Axe," *Covenant Companion* October 1, 1981: 29.

"Good Night, Sweet Prince!" *Covenant Companion* October 15, 1981: 29.

"Good Night, Sweet Prince! (cont.)," *Covenant Companion* November 1, 1981: 29.

"Mugging," *Covenant Companion* November 15, 1981: 29.

"Some Days Must Be . . . Dreary," *Covenant Companion* December 1, 1981: 29.

" 'Angels and Ministers of Grace Defend Us!' " *Covenant Companion* December 15, 1981: 29.

1982

Kontinuitet och Förvandling Inom Svenska Immigrantsamfund i USA. [Continuity and Transformation in Swedish Denominations in the United States.] Uppsala, Sweden: Svenska Kyrkohistoriska Föreningen, 1982. [Summary is in English. Reprint from *Kyrkohistorisk Årsskrift 1982.*]

"Frankenstein Unmasked," *Covenant Companion* January 1, 1982: 29.

" 'In Prison You Visited Me,' " *Covenant Companion* January 15, 1982: 29.

" 'Some Things . . . Hard to Understand,' " *Covenant Companion* February 1, 1982: 29.

"Gifts and Taxes," *Covenant Companion* February 15, 1982: 29.

"Too Much Time: I," *Covenant Companion* March 1, 1982: 29.

"Too Much Time: II," *Covenant Companion* March 15, 1982: 29.

"Too Much Time: III," *Covenant Companion* April 1, 1982: 29.

"Too Much Time: IV," *Covenant Companion* April 15, 1982: 29.

"Too Much Time: V," *Covenant Companion* May 1, 1982: 29.

"Too Much Time: VI," *Covenant Companion* May 15, 1982: 29.

"Too Much Time: VII," *Covenant Companion* June 1, 1982: 29.

"Too Much Time: VIII," *Covenant Companion* June 15, 1982: 29.

"Too Much Time: IX," *Covenant Companion* July 1, 1982: 21.

"Too Much Time: X," *Covenant Companion* August 1, 1982: 21.

"Too Much Time: XI," *Covenant Companion* September 1, 1982: 21.

"Too Much Time: XII," *Covenant Companion* September 15, 1982: 29.

"Too Much Time: XIII," *Covenant Companion* October 1, 1982: 29.

"Too Much Time: XIV," *Covenant Companion* October 15, 1982: 29.

"Too Much Time: XV," *Covenant Companion* November 1, 1982: 29.

"Lay Participation in the Board of Ministry," [paper presented to the Board of Ministry, Evangelical Covenant Church,

October 1982]. Covenant Archives: Karl A. Olsson Papers.

"Forgive Us Our Debts," *Covenant Companion* November 15, 1982: 29.

"Would Paul Send Christmas Cards?" *Covenant Companion* December 1, 1982: 29.

"The Sullen Praetorians," *Covenant Companion* December 15, 1982: 29.

1983

"Visitations," *Covenant Companion* January 1, 1983: 29.

"Visitation: 2," *Covenant Companion* January 15, 1983: 29.

"Visitation: 3," *Covenant Companion* February 1, 1983: 29.

"Visitation: 4," *Covenant Companion* February 15, 1983: 29.

"The Covenant Constitution and Its History," *NARTHEX* 3 (1) February, 1983: 5-25.

"Response to Respondents," *NARTHEX* 3 (1) February, 1983: 42-46.

"Visitation: 4 (cont.)," *Covenant Companion* March 1, 1983: 29.

"Visitation: 4 (concluded)," *Covenant Companion* March 15, 1983: 29.

" 'Thy Light Has Come,' " *Covenant Companion* April 1, 1983: 29.

" 'A . . . Woman Nobly Planned,' " *Covenant Companion* April 15, 1983: 29.

" 'A . . . Woman Nobly Planned' (cont.)," *Covenant Companion* May 1, 1983: 29.

" 'A . . . Woman Nobly Planned' (conclusion)," *Covenant Companion* May 15, 1983: 29.

" 'There Were Eighty and Eight That Safely Lay'," *Covenant Companion* June 1, 1983: 29.

"Trivia," *Covenant Companion* June 15, 1983: 29.

"Pearls by the Sea," *Covenant Companion* July 1, 1983: 21.

"Mowing a Field," *Covenant Companion* August 1, 1983: 21.

"When the Graves Are Opened: I," *Covenant Companion* September 1, 1983: 21.

"When the Graves Are Opened: II," *Covenant Companion* September 15, 1983: 29.

"When the Graves Are Opened: III," *Covenant Companion* October 1, 1983: 29.

"The Baltic: a Context," *Covenant Companion* October 15, 1983: 29.

"The Baltic: Story of a Milieu," *Covenant Companion* November 1, 1983: 29.

"The Baltic: Seafarers," *Covenant Companion* November 15, 1983: 29.

"The Baltic: the Vikings," *Covenant Companion* December 1, 1983: 29.

"The Baltic: Sea Change," *Covenant Companion* December 15, 1983: 29.

1984

"Sven Lidman Som Förkunnare," *Tro och Liv* 43 (3) 1984: 2-14.

"The Baltic: The Truce of God," *Covenant Companion* January 1, 1984: 29.

"The Baltic: Christian Impact," *Covenant Companion* February 1984: 45.

"The Baltic: Domination," *Covenant Companion* March 1984: 45.

"The Baltic: Conquest and Dominance," *Covenant Companion* April 1984: 45.

"The Tragedy of the Baltic," *Covenant Companion* May 1984: 45.

"The Very Good Shepherd," *Covenant Companion* June 1984: 45.

"Nature, 'Poor Stepdame,' " *Covenant Companion* July 1984: 45.

" 'Unfading Garland,' " *Covenant Companion* August 1984: 45.

"H.C. Andersen, the Duckling Who Wanted to Be a Swan," *Covenant Companion* September 1984: 45.

" 'Full Many a Glorious Morning . . . ' " *Covenant Companion* October 1984: 45.

"The Great Danes," *Covenant Companion* November 1984: 45.

"The Kangaroo and the Ugly Duckling: I," *Covenant Companion* December 1984: 45.

1985

Into One Body . . . by the Cross. v. 1. Chicago: Covenant Press, 1985.

"The Kangaroo and the Ugly Duckling: II," *Covenant Companion* January 1985: 45.

"A Time for Meditation," *Covenant Companion* February 1985: 45.

" 'When I Was Two and Twenty . . . ' " *Covenant Companion* March 1985: 45.

" 'I'm Going to Wait Right Here for Jesus . . . ' " *Covenant Companion* April 1985: 45.

"Remember," *Covenant Companion* May 1985: 45.

"Sorrow and Joy," *Covenant Companion* June 1985: 45.

"Things That Have Gone Away," *Covenant Companion* July 1985: 45.

"The Tyranny of Taste," *Covenant Companion* August 1985: 45.

"We Are the Children," *Covenant Companion* September 1985: 45.

"Little League," *Covenant Companion* October 1985: 45.

Review of *A Precious Heritage: A Century of Mission in the Northwest 1884-1984* by Philip J. Anderson. *Swedish-American Historical Quarterly* 36 (4) October 1985: 305-308.

"Eucharist," *Covenant Companion* November 1985: 45.

"The Mystical and Corporate Nature of the Covenant Church" [Covenant Ministers' Midwinter Conference, 1985], *Covenant Quarterly* 43 (4) November 1985: 3-12.

"The Time Has Come," *Covenant Companion* December 1985: 45.

1986

Into One Body . . . by the Cross. v. 2. Chicago: Covenant Press, 1986.

"Svensk fromhet i Amerika," *Det började vid Delaware: om Svenska Hembygder i Amerika.* Karlskrona, Sweden: Axel Abrahamsons, 1986: 123-133.

"Developments in Covenant Ecclesiology, 1914-1933," *Covenant Quarterly* 44 (1) 1986: 25-35.

"MBE: 'Here's Hail to the Rest of the Road,' " *Covenant Companion* August 1986: 9.

1987

"Deserted by His Own," *Covenant Home Altar* 49 (2) April 12 (Palm Sunday), 1987.

"Suffering for Others," *Covenant Home Altar* 49 (2) April 13, 1987.

"Rejected of Men," *Covenant Home Altar* 49 (2) April 14, 1987.

"Pouring Out His Soul," *Covenant Home Altar* 49 (2) April 15, 1987.

"Broken for You," *Covenant Home Altar* 49 (2) April 16, 1987.

"Ecce Homo! (Behold The Man!)," *Covenant Home Altar* 49 (2) April 17 (Good Friday), 1987.

"Dying for the Unrighteous," *Covenant Home Altar* 49 (2) April 18, 1987.